RETAIL MARKETING AND BRANDING

RETAIL MARKETING AND BRANDING

A DEFINITIVE GUIDE TO MAXIMIZING ROI

JESKO PERREY
and
DENNIS SPILLECKE

A John Wiley and Sons, Ltd, Publication

CONTENTS

INTRODUCTION

The occasion is the weekly management meeting of a leading food retailer. The CFO's report gets the ball rolling: 'Sales are down 5 percent from the same period last year, for the third week in a row.' The CMO takes his chance: 'This clearly shows our brand is losing attractiveness. We need to ramp up our share of voice on TV!' Then all hell breaks loose. 'You keep saying that,' the northern region's commercial director yells, 'but your fancy commercials just don't sell the goods. We should run more in-store promotions. That's where people make their choices.' The southern regional manager echoes: 'Absolutely! In-store is the way to go. Why don't we also send out an additional leaflet next week? That's how we'll lure shoppers back into the store.' The CEO, who until this moment had been staring out of the window, now turns to the group. 'TV, promotions, leaflets. I've heard it all before. It's the same story week in, week out. But can any one of you tell me what we really get out of any of these things?' Silence fills the room. The CMO reaches for his coffee. The commercial directors fiddle with their BlackBerrys. The CFO keeps staring at the sales chart, as if to reverse the trend line through sheer willpower. But they all know that none of them has a real answer to the CEO's question. What a way to start the day!

Why you should read this book

Most readers will have been in similar situations at one time or another. Marketing and branding discussions that take place in the board rooms of retail companies are frequently laden with emotion. Due to the lack of hard facts and quantified impact, decisions are all too often based on gut feeling, individual experience or plain hope. But retailers are acknowledging the increasing importance of marketing and branding as key factors in the success and the sustainability of their business. Consequently, they have started to bring a more fact-based approach to their marketing efforts.

With this book, we aspire to contribute to the demystification of marketing and branding discussions. The idea emerged in conversation with executives who complain that most retail marketing books tend to be either theoretical or trivial, and usually fail to give them any meaningful guidance on how to run their business. What they were looking for, they told us, was a systematic, yet practically relevant treatment of the subject. In response we have compiled this practical guide on how to maximize the return on marketing investment in retail, based on the experience derived from hundreds of retail marketing and branding projects. We have made a point of covering both the conceptual and analytical foundations as well as their application, enriched by a wide range of retail case examples and practical hints. Unless otherwise noted, all references to the practice of individual companies are based on outside-in research.

Who this book is for

We are confident that what we say in this book will be relevant to retail executives all over the world, no matter whether their retail organization is large or small, whether it operates in the food or non-food segment, or whether it sells its goods through brick-and-mortar outlets or e-commerce shops.

Companies working with retailers as their suppliers, distribution partners or marketing service providers may want to use this book to deepen their understanding of the marketing and branding questions faced by retailers, and to adapt their proposals or services accordingly.

Also, executives from other consumer-facing industries such as FMCG, consumer electronics, energy or telecommunications will be able to derive considerable benefit from this book. Because of its sizeable marketing budgets and huge customer databases, retail is one of the most active and most sophisticated sectors when it comes to marketing and branding.

We hope academics, students and other marketing professionals will also find the book helpful to acquaint themselves with some of the latest and most advanced tools and methods retailers use to measure and manage the return on marketing investment.

How this book was created

To leverage the widest possible range of expertise and experience, we have invited the cooperation of the leading retail marketing specialists among our colleagues, both from Europe and from overseas. Yet this is anything but a run-of-the-mill editor book. We have both taken an active role in shaping the structure and the content of all chapters – in close cooperation with the respective teams of authors. As a result, this book is not a collection of loosely connected articles, but a consistent compendium. Each chapter builds on the foundations laid in the earlier parts of the book, and they all highlight different aspects of retail marketing ROI optimization. This approach will be immediately apparent, even to the most casual reader, due to the consistent look and feel of the chapters. As a result, the book presents an integrated and consistent body of knowledge on the subject.

How you should read this book

This book comprises three principal parts:

I   Building Superior Retail Brands
II   Optimizing Marketing ROI
III Ten Perspectives on Retail Marketing.

In the first part, we focus on building strong retail brands, covering topics such as segmentation-enabled target group selection, retail brand management, store brand portfolio optimization and private label management – all based on a conceptual approach to brand management that revolves around the interplay of art, science and craft.

In the second part, we discuss sizing the overall marketing budget, as well as its allocation to different formats, stores, regions and marketing instruments. In addition, we present guidelines on how to make the most of key retail marketing instruments, including digital media, POS, local media, classical media and CLM. This part concludes with our view about how to optimize the purchasing of marketing-related goods and services.

The final part is a short manifesto of our core beliefs on retail marketing and branding.

We hope you will feel free to read this book in whatever order you see fit. We would be more than happy if you choose to read this book cover to cover, but it is equally possible to go directly to a specific chapter. While later chapters build on the earlier ones, each chapter is also written to be a stand-alone treatment of its subject.

Each chapter starts with a short overview of its key topics to facilitate browsing. At the end of each chapter, you will find a list of key takeaways. We trust that you will come back to certain parts many times, and that you will use this book as a work of retail marketing reference. As this is intended to be the first volume in a series of books on related subjects, we would very much welcome your feedback. All comments, criticism and suggestions for improvements should be addressed to the authors.

ACKNOWLEDGEMENTS

We are indebted to all our fellow authors and the teams that have supported them in researching and developing each of the chapters. They all share the experience of having gone through many rounds of writing and editing during the evolution of this book. Additionally, a few individuals from McKinsey & Company's international leadership group have kindly acted as an internal sounding board, namely Peter Dahlström, Tjark Freundt and Frank Sänger. We would like to thank all of them for their commitment and patience.

We would also like to thank our external partners and the companies that have supported this effort through participating in the co-creation of knowledge, in the clearance of case examples and in granting permission to use quotes, images and other materials in the text or in the exhibits. Special thanks are due to our interview partners for sharing their views on retail marketing and branding: Pia Marthinsen Mellbye at ICA, Thomas Koch at TKM, Alastair Bruce at Google, Michael Trautmann at kempertrautmann and Daniela Mündler at Douglas.

Special thanks are due to Klaus Behrenbeck, Peter Breuer and Nicolò Galante, our colleagues at McKinsey & Company, for their commitment in seeing this project through from the initial idea to the finished book. Thank you to Anja Weissgerber, who led and coordinated this effort on behalf of McKinsey's European Consumer Industries & Retail Group, and to Tobias Karmann for tying up all the loose ends. Very special thanks to Cornelius Grupen, our Expert for Marketing Knowledge Development, for making the whole more than just the sum of its parts, and to Ivan Hutnik for his meticulous editing. In addition, we also thank our secretaries – Michaela Dülks, Claudia Schmidt and Stefanie Schmitz – for keeping us on track throughout this project.

We hope that this book not only makes good reading, but that it will also help its readers to build strong retail brands that generate superior returns on marketing investment.

Dr Jesko Perrey and Dr Dennis Spillecke
Düsseldorf, January 2011

FOREWORD

Today's shoppers go online to research locations, compare prices or read reviews before they go to a store, and as soon as they are back home, they post details about their shopping experience on Facebook and other social media platforms. Online agencies rave about viral campaigns, guerrilla marketing and 360° communication. IT specialists are peddling one-to-one marketing tools and integrated customer data warehousing solutions. Should retailers care about any of this? I firmly believe that they should – but in an environment of accelerating change, even veterans of the trade are looking for guidance: How do I combine traditional and new marketing vehicles? How can I stay on top of what my customers want? How can I reach them efficiently? Do they still look at leaflets, or should I shift local marketing funds to social media?

In my conversations with retailers over the past few years, I have sensed a growing concern about these questions. Successful retail management might once have been about 'just doing it', but that is no longer the case. Increasingly, retailers are looking for robust, yet pragmatic, ways to professionalize their marketing function and align marketing investments with business objectives. This book consolidates McKinsey & Company's know-how in the field, created and refined over many years in performance partnerships with our clients. The effort has been led by Dr Jesko Perrey and Dr Dennis Spillecke, seasoned specialists with a joint total of more than 20 years of client service in retail branding and marketing.

It is an honour and a privilege to present *Retail Marketing and Branding: A Definitive Guide to Maximizing ROI*. Although it covers some of the latest and most sophisticated approaches to the subject, it is anything but a theoretical treatise. The hands-on mentality of its authors – and the wealth of case examples – make it a practical guide for all consumer-minded retailers. This book is intended to be the first of several 'Perspectives on Retail and Consumer Industries'. I hope you will share my excitement about this book – and will be encouraged to seek out future volumes in the series.

Dr Klaus Behrenbeck

Director, McKinsey & Company, Inc.

Leader, Consumer Industries & Retail Group, Europe

Cologne, January 2011

Part I

Building Superior Retail Brands

CHAPTER 1

Jesko Perrey, Dennis Spillecke

Every brand is a promise. And like any promise, brands attract and excite us; they capture our hearts and minds; they give us a glimpse of a better life. But most importantly, brands create tangible value. They are a retailer's most powerful connection to the outside world. Brands enable retailers to form deep and lasting attachments to customers and potential employees, and even investors, that translate into higher sales, stable profits, superior capabilities and above-average stock market performance. This chapter explores the three principal elements of superior brand management – art, science and craft – and presents a wide range of case examples, illustrating how leading retailers bring these elements to bear on the management of their brands.

Branding is the secret weapon of retail marketing: it can create substantial value, but it is under-leveraged by most retailers.

Brands have many benefits, but, above all, they create value. Brands help companies achieve price premiums and they save costs due to their inherent appeal to customers. Companies with strong brands consistently outperform their peers in the stock market. According to a recent McKinsey analysis, brands with a top ranking in *Business Week*'s annual 'Best Global Brands' report have consistently outperformed traditional benchmarks like the MSCI World or the S&P 500 index over the past 10 years (Exhibit 1.1). Credit Suisse came to a similar conclusion in 2010, based on an analysis spanning a 12-year period: companies that invest at least 2 percent of sales in their brand ('brand stocks') have consistently outperformed the S&P 500.

But to what extent do brands make a difference in retail? Research has shown that the impact of retail brands on consumer decision-making is substantial; it is based on three key functions.

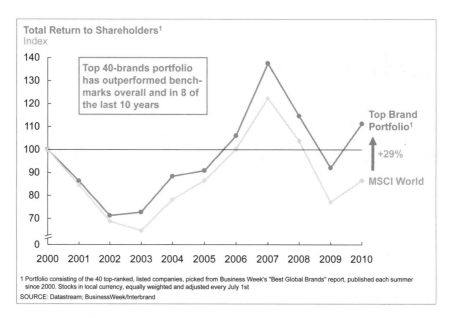

Exhibit 1.1 Strong brands outperform the market continuously.

- *Image*: retail brands help consumers express whom they are, effectively making their choice of retail brands a lifestyle statement – think of IKEA.
- *Orientation*: retail brands provide consumers with orientation. They make it easier to process information and help consumers save time – think of Amazon.
- *Risk reduction*: retail brands reduce the perceived risks involved in making a purchase. They provide consumers with a 'safe choice' – think of John Lewis.

Are leading retailers capturing the full value of these opportunities? You would think that at least some of them do. Surely, well-known global retail brands like H&M, IKEA or Tesco must be among the world's most valuable brands? Not so: H&M, the top retail brand, does not make it into the top 20 of any brand ranking of note – and all other leading retailers are even further away from true branding excellence. (Source: Interbrand Brand Marketers Report.)

There is a simple reason for this situation. For decades, retailers have not made branding their priority. Many retailers, especially those in Europe, have been focused on price until very recently, with leaflets promoting low prices being their most important marketing instrument. But by and by, retailers around the globe are now waking up to the challenge of professional brand building and management. For example, eBay, Sears and 7-Eleven have recently received EFFIE awards in recognition of the effectiveness of their advertising.

It takes three elements to build and sustain a strong brand in retail: *art, science and craft*

- The *art* is about endowing the brand with a relevant, credible and unique value proposition that is up-to-date, consistent and executed in a creative way.
- The *science* is about understanding and measuring relevant consumer needs, as well as the performance of the brand in the targeted customer segments.
- The *craft* is about managing the brand rigorously in all its individual aspects throughout the organization and across all customer touch points.

Of course, a brand can be strong without attaining perfection in all three areas. Inevitably, companies have different approaches to brand management, and their organizations have different strengths and weaknesses. Nonetheless, however well a company might master an individual element, we believe that this will be of little use to them if they do not achieve a minimum standard in the other two elements as well (Exhibit 1.2).

Exhibit 1.2 Three elements of successful brand management.

The art is about balancing creativity with consistency
to endow a brand with an emotional appeal that builds on its heritage

To succeed, retail brands must strike the right chord to make them appeal to consumers and generate demand. They need to engage consumers emotionally, yet their claims have to be credible and trustworthy. But with which brand elements should you start as a retailer? Should you focus on rational elements, like price or location, which give consumers concrete reasons to buy or at least to visit a store? Or should you prioritize emotional elements like honesty or modernity that speak to consumers' feelings? In fact, strong brands always do both, although the balance between the two varies. There are hardly any strong products or services that are not at least as good as the competition in their rational elements, and they are usually better in one or two attributes. At the same time, real brand champions, like IKEA, H&M, Nespresso or Apple, stand out because of their emotional appeal. Although the products they offer may not in all cases be superior to competitors' alternatives, it is the way they make consumers feel about themselves and their purchases that differentiates these brands from others.

But the importance of the art element should not be misread as a license to go crazy. Constant changes to a brand's positioning, target group or communication style will eventually destroy its value. In fact, consistency is an important element of artful brand propositions. In a survey among 300 marketing experts, consistency was identified as by far the most important aspect of branding, with more than one-third of respondents naming it as number one in an open-ended question. (Source: 2007 Brand Marketers Report, Interbrand.) Consistency is not to be confused with stagnation. Had it stayed true to its roots as a run-of-the-mill DIY retailer, Germany's Hornbach would never have become the premium brand it is today. In effect, consistency is about balancing relevant innovation and originality with a brand's heritage. A now legendary example is that of how Roberto Menichetti and Christopher Bailey rejuvenated the Burberry brand over a 10-year period. In 1998, Menichetti famously laid bare the company's traditional tartan lining and started using it as a prominent pattern for apparel and accessories. By turning a hidden asset into a tangible brand differentiator, his approach was original and creative, yet fully in line with the brand's heritage.

Another key prerequisite for bringing a brand's emotional appeal to life is the creativity of its communication. Some brands achieve consistent competitive advantage by means of superior creativity in their communication; they have mastered the art of placing the bait exactly where the fish will bite. Strong brands are highly effective in the use of creative campaigns that distinguish

Artful communication

Case example: Edeka

The German food retailer Edeka is a pioneer of artful brand building. In Germany, Edeka was the first retailer to take brand communication beyond rational elements like price, product range or freshness. Their 'We love food' campaign, launched in 2005, is all about atmosphere and emotion: the images featured in it include fresh food, passionate staff and happy customers (Exhibit 1.3). The distinctive idea of the company's heartfelt passion for its products was communicated with a high degree of consistency across all customer touch points.

SOURCE: Edeka website; xtremeinformation

Exhibit 1.3 Images from Edeka's 'We love food' campaign.

them from the competition, strengthen their brand image and leverage this image to generate sales.

As a joint study by McKinsey & Company and the Art Director's Club on 'Creativity in Advertising' has shown, creativity can take many different forms; see Chapter 14: 'Excellence in classical media' for details of this study. Successful creative advertising often contains a disturbing element – one that initially seems irritating, provocative or funny, whether this be in pictures or in words. One example of this phenomenon is a campaign by German DIY retailer Hornbach. In one of their TVCs, we see a shopper pouring out his heart to a store employee over the death of a beloved pet: 'I ran over my son's rabbit!' he says, before breaking into tears. The spot closes to Hornbach's brand claim: 'If you trust us with your remodelling, you can trust us with everything.'

There is more to strong brands than awareness: *the science is in measuring a brand's strengths and weaknesses across the entire purchase funnel*

Science is the second element of superior brand management. Most retail marketing managers and agencies still use brand awareness and advertising recall as the primary or even exclusive indicators of brand performance. While there is nothing wrong with these metrics in themselves, we believe they are insufficient to capture the specific strengths and weaknesses of a brand, let alone the root causes of its performance. In some cases, the focus on awareness and recall may even create the illusion of a healthy brand, when in fact the brand is in trouble. Retailers should expand their brand management toolbox and then use the extended toolkit comprehensively in their brand management decisions.

The hazards of the traditional approach are many. While a given brand may, for example, score highly on both awareness and advertising recall, its target audience may know next to nothing about the specific benefits provided by the brand. And how can you be sure the promoted benefits are even relevant to the target group? To tell a well-known brand from a really strong brand, you need a sense of whether consumers know what the brand stands for in terms of products or services, and whether they favour the brand over its competitors in their purchase considerations. In other words, strong brands perform well along the entire purchase funnel from awareness and consideration to purchase, repurchase and loyalty. For details on the concept of the purchase funnel and its stages, please see Chapter 3: 'A Guide to Excellence in Retail Brand Management'.

This is not to say that all strong brands perform equally well at each and every stage of the purchase funnel; most brands reveal slight weaknesses at one stage or another. Whatever the case, the accurate measurement of a brand's relative strengths and weaknesses in the target group's purchase funnel is the starting point for fact-based brand management.

Rigorous retail brand managers look beneath the surface of awareness and advertising recall. They explore the strengths and weaknesses of their brands across all stages of the purchase funnel and each customer's lifecycle. They take detailed measurements and constantly hone their measurement techniques.

The craft is about bringing the essence of the brand to life *at all touch points*

It is one thing to put the brand positioning on paper, but it is quite another to make it a real presence in consumers' lives: in TV commercials, print ads, leaflets, newsletters, store displays, loyalty programmes and personal interactions. Retailers with strong brands go to great pains to ensure superior and consistent consumer experience of the brand's proposition at all touch points. (See Exhibit 1.4 for an overview of in-store touch points.) For example, imagine 'freshness' is one of the differentiating attributes in your brand positioning. While it may seem obvious what this means for touch point 5 ('products offered'), it is a lot less obvious how freshness could be brought to bear on the store's exterior or at the checkout.

In terms of holistic activation of the brand positioning at all touch points, many would agree that Apple sets the standard. The company does a fantastic job when it comes to translating their brand values of stylish design, creativity and uniqueness into products like the iPod, the iPhone or the iPad, as well as into a unique experience at its more than 300 Apple stores worldwide, many of which have won architectural awards.

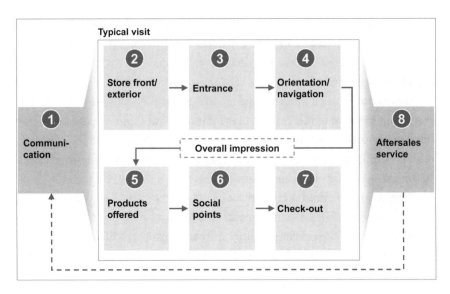

Exhibit 1.4 Overview of customer touch points in retail.

Excellent execution is not necessarily limited to tangible touch points like store design. For Aldi, the discount retailer, price is key. Consumer perception of the company as a provider of good value for money has made the Aldi brand strong and low prices are the source of Aldi's competitive advantage (its private label products nevertheless provide A-brand quality). Right from the start, Aldi stressed that every article it sold was cheaper than the equivalent found elsewhere. Based on this premise, it has turned simplicity of execution into a guiding principle, from its no-frills stores to its narrow assortment of around 750 products. Logistics cost plays a major role when establishing a new outlet: the store must be accessible to articulated trucks, and the aisles must be wide enough to manoeuvre pallets. Aldi's stores are usually located either on side streets near high-traffic areas, or on the edge of town where there are good parking facilities and low rental costs. Its comparatively narrow assortment of goods ensures simplicity in buying and handling, and its scale gives it massive bargaining power in negotiations with suppliers. Aldi also keeps labour costs down by reducing management to an absolute minimum. For example, the company's central functions have a very low headcount.

More than okay coffee

Case study: Starbucks

Protecting a brand's heritage is a top management job. When Howard Schultz, who had earlier stepped down as the CEO of Starbucks, decided he had seen enough of what he called 'the commoditization of the Starbucks experience', he took decisive action. In a memo to the company's leadership group, he criticized a series of decisions which, though they might have seemed right on their own merit, when taken together diluted the Starbucks' brand. For example, the introduction of automatic coffee machines increased the speed of service and efficiency but destroyed much of the romance and theatre afforded by the old machines. Moreover, the height of the new machines blocked the customer's line of sight, making eye contact with the barista nearly impossible. Similarly, while the introduction of flavour-locked packaging clearly improved the quality of the fresh-roasted bagged coffee, it also meant that the smell of coffee that had previously filled the premises was gone. Schultz considered the coffee aroma one of the brand's most powerful non-verbal signals. As a result of these changes, the stores lost their former soul, the warm feeling of a neighbourhood store, and instead began to seem like chain stores. To make things worse, the increasing number of merchandising articles, such as music CDs, took Starbucks even further away from its heritage as a coffee shop. 'In fact, I am not sure people today even know we are roasting coffee. You certainly can't get the message from being in our stores,' Schultz wrote.

Less than 12 months later, Schultz returned as CEO to help the company refocus on the original Starbucks experience. One of his first decisions was to stop selling hot-breakfast sandwiches. These sandwiches accounted for revenues of around USD 500 million for the company, but they made the stores smell like cheese factories and the baristas feel as if they were working in a fast-food store. 'The decision and the courage it takes to remove something when there's pressure on the business – like the sandwiches – is emblematic that we're going to build for the long term and get back to the roots and the core of our heritage, which is the leading roaster of specialty coffee in the world.' Starbucks then ordered all-new espresso machines from Thermoplan, a relative newcomer in the category long-dominated by traditional Italian manufacturers. Thermoplan's USP was that the coffee is ground individually for each cup of espresso. What is more, the new machines are much lower than the earlier automated machines, making eye contact between the barista and customer possible once more. Schultz says the new machines were meant to bring back some of the old charm: 'Once again, it will be all about the coffee.'

James Alling, responsible for the company's overseas business as President of Starbucks International, sums up the company's ongoing brand management challenge as: 'There's always going to be someone selling okay coffee at a low price. It's our job to make sure Starbucks is more than okay coffee.' (Source: Roland Lindner, 'Die neue Bescheidenheit von Starbucks', 22 March 2008, No. 69, p.20; interview with James Alling, President of Starbucks International, 'Wir dachten, die Kunden kommen von selbst', *Frankfurter Allgemeine Zeitung*, 21 March 2008, www.faz.net/.)

Much has happened since the early days of the return of Howard Schultz. For one thing, many Starbucks outlets have added Panini sandwiches to their menu again. But there is no denying that the focus on core competencies and brand heritage triggered by Schultz's memo played an important part in the company's ultimate recovery.

Last, but not least, excellent craftsmanship in brand management also demands sufficient top-management attention and leadership. The CEO or other chief caretaker of a brand should live and breathe its positioning in order to be able to manage the day-to-day trade-offs between generating additional revenue and protecting the brand heritage. While it may be tempting, for example, to engage in a short-term price war with a brand's closest competitor, it could well damage the brand's reputation as a provider of reliable quality in the longer term. Decisions such as these illustrate that brand management is a top management issue; it cannot safely be delegated to product managers, external agencies or any other third party. Steve Jobs, for instance, makes it a point to approve every new product design and every global advertising campaign personally, thus making sure the brand's value proposition is reflected in every aspect of Apple's business.

As illustrated by such examples, many retailers excel at one of the elements of superior brand management: the art, science or craft. But only a chosen few master all three elements in equal measure. We conclude this chapter by taking a close look at IKEA, arguably one of the world's most successful retailers. In the next chapter we look at the specific success factors of retail brand management in more detail, based on McKinsey & Company's BrandMatics approach.

Best practice example

IKEA: combining art, science and craft

IKEA, the largest furniture retailing chain in the world, is a fine example of how art, science and craft work together to create and sustain a superior brand. As of 2009, IKEA had more than 300 stores in 37 countries, generating revenues of EUR 21.5 billion (Exhibit 1.5). Wherever you shop,

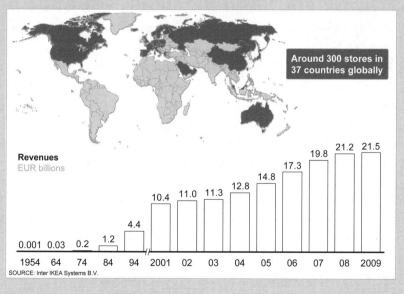

Exhibit 1.5 IKEA's path to a global brand.

IKEA stands for furniture and home accessories that combine function and design at affordable prices. We will look at each of the three elements in more detail to find out how IKEA does it.

The art: creative communication creates emotional appeal. Many of IKEA's campaigns have presented ingenious decoration or storage solutions achieved with the help of their products. But artful communication is not only about original messages. It can also be about clever media selection: for example, the company's recent store opening in Malmö, Sweden, was supported by intensive use of social media. They created a Facebook profile for the store's manager and uploaded pictures of the store's showrooms. By tagging products featured in these pictures, Facebook members could enter a prize draw for these products. The campaign created enormous excitement: users kept asking for more pictures and shared them with thousands of people via newsfeeds and links. (Source: Most Contagious Report 2009; also see Chapter 15: 'Digital marketing excellence' for further details.)

In Tokyo, the company built fourteen small 'IKEA 4.5 museums'. In an area the size of just four-and-a-half *tatami* mats (around 7.5 meters square, slightly smaller than the standard room size in Tokyo) the retailer showcased how to make the most of small rooms using its furniture. The campaign led to a new record in store visitors and was awarded a Cannes Golden Lion in 2007. (Source: Hajo Riesenbeck, Jesko Perrey, *Power Brands: Measuring, Making and Managing Brand Success*, p. 44, Wiley, 2008.)

IKEA's most important tool for building relationships with its customers, apart from the stores themselves, is its catalogue. Almost 200 million copies are printed worldwide, and more recently it has introduced a unique concept of a personalized catalogue. Customers have their photos taken at one of the stores, and a few days later they can pick up a copy of the catalogue featuring pictures of themselves, rather than those of a professional model, in the catalogue's living room illustrations. This not only brings customers back into their stores but creates a deep personal connection with the brand. The personalized catalogue is yet another example of how the company's communication conveys the impression that the brand has a lot more to offer than just decently priced pine furniture.

The science: systematic consumer research ensures fact-based brand management. IKEA engages in extensive market research to ensure the brand meets consumers' needs at key touch points, such as the product and store experiences. The retailer explores what it calls the 'three moments of truth' in its research: the planning of the shopping trip, the core brand experience at one of the IKEA stores and the product experience once back home. By using a wide range of observational techniques, the retailer aspires to generate insights that will enable it to develop inventive interior decoration solutions that solve customer's real-life problems, rather than merely providing them with items of furniture.

Consumer feedback management is another area in which IKEA adheres to strict and systematic standards to ensure that it is provided with continuous input on the quality of its products, stores and services. Shopper insights derived from transaction data and the 'IKEA family' loyalty card are pooled and leveraged systematically. Partly as a result of the targeted offers it produces based on these insights, the retailer generates more than half of its total revenues through non-furniture sales, including small design items and snacks.

Even when their apartments are fully equipped, shoppers can be lured back for smaller, more decorative, items, or for the sheer store experience. Says former CEO Anders Dahlvig: 'We are trying to become like Disneyland'.

The craft: consistent global brand promise, carefully adapted to local needs. At IKEA, brand management is all about consistency. The store is largely standardized wherever it is located around the world. The same is true for the product line-up. Says product developer Tomas Lundin: 'A product must do well in all countries to be successful'. The catalogue, however, can be adapted more easily and cost-effectively, presenting the company to the world at large as one that thinks globally and acts locally. Although the country editions of the catalogue are all produced in Sweden, they reflect local peculiarities: television sets in the American edition are bigger than elsewhere, while the Chinese edition features kitchen supplies labelled in *kaishu* characters.

IKEA sums up its brand promise as: 'Trends come and go, but combining a low price with good design and function never goes out of style'.

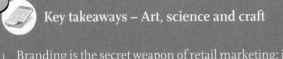

Key takeaways – Art, science and craft

1 Branding is the secret weapon of retail marketing: it can create substantial value, but it is underleveraged by most retailers.
2 It takes three elements to build and sustain a strong brand in retail: art, science and craft.
3 The art is about balancing creativity with consistency to endow a brand with an emotional appeal that builds on its heritage.
4 There is more to strong brands than awareness: the science is about measuring a brand's strengths and weaknesses across the entire purchasing funnel.
5 The craft is about bringing the essence of the brand to life at all touch points.

CHAPTER 2

SEGMENTATION

Reinhold Barchet, Georges Desvaux, Tobias Karmann

Market segmentations are the maps you need to navigate the world of marketing. But as anyone with even a passing interest in cartography knows, there are many ways to describe the complexity of three-dimensional reality in a two-dimensional representation – and every projection is compromised in some way or another. While segmentation is well understood and widely used in consumer goods companies, the ins and outs of retail can easily turn segmentation into an expedition into the wilderness. For one thing, retail as a business is a lot less homogeneous than FMCG across regions and countries. What is more, with its continual, fast cycle of testing and learning, the pace of change in retail marketing is much more rapid than in the management of international consumer brands.

Additionally, the questions that segmentations need to answer differ greatly between retailers, or even between different categories. For example, grocery retail is all about location. In high-involvement, low-frequency categories such as fashion or electronics, however, the key is the range and type of brands and products featured in a specific format.

Yet we believe that a robust consumer segmentation is as advantageous to a retailer as it is to a consumer goods company. While the objectives and uses may be slightly different, the strategic relevance is the same. In this chapter, we will focus on what it takes to make segmentation matter in retail: solid strategy, top management attention, market research expertise, superior statistical skills – and sound judgment.

Segmentation is just as important to retailers as it is to consumer goods companies – *but for different reasons and in different ways*

Consumer goods companies use segmentations to understand variations in consumer needs, brand image, product preference or usage occasions as the basis for targeted brand management, product development and distribution strategy. For retailers, in contrast, market segmentation is a key source of information for making more informed decisions on store formats, assortment strategy, featured brands and CRM activities – all of which are ultimate profit drivers. By association, this makes segmentation a major factor to improve a retailer's return on marketing investment.

The example of a US-based grocery chain can show us what segmentation can do for a retailer. At the start of the segmentation effort, it was the marketing department's firm belief that shopper needs were similar within a given region, but differed greatly across regions. Based on this assumption, the company had one type of store in region 1 and another type of store in region 2. Retail is a location game, after all, isn't it? Yet the segmentation proved this assumption to be very wide of the mark. It turned out that there was considerable heterogeneity at the region level, but that there were a few distinct types of shopper, occurring in similar proportions across all regions. Why care? Because, in this case, the needs of these different types, or segments, were the direct drivers of both store and brand choice. This link becomes more obvious once you take a closer look at some of the segments the grocery retailer identified (Exhibit 2.1).

- The 'cost-conscious homemaker' has a love of food, but a tight budget, and is looking for a broad but affordable assortment. For practical reasons, these customers have a clear preference for one-stop shopping at a large store.
- The 'daily-routine shopper' is driven primarily by convenience, both regarding products and store locations. These customers typically look for pre-cooked meals in a neighbourhood or downtown store.
- The 'highly involved gourmet' has little or no price sensitivity, a strict preference for the best unprocessed ingredients and the willingness to shop at multiple stores to get exactly the right products.

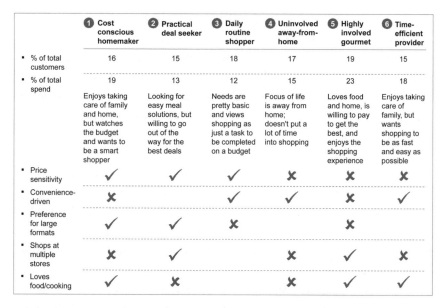

	① Cost conscious homemaker	② Practical deal seeker	③ Daily routine shopper	④ Uninvolved away-from-home	⑤ Highly involved gourmet	⑥ Time-efficient provider
• % of total customers	16	15	18	17	19	15
• % of total spend	19	13	12	15	23	18
	Enjoys taking care of family and home, but watches the budget and wants to be a smart shopper	Looking for easy meal solutions, but willing to go out of the way for the best deals	Needs are pretty basic and views shopping as just a task to be completed on a budget	Focus of life is away from home; doesn't put a lot of time into shopping	Loves food and home, is willing to pay to get the best, and enjoys the shopping experience	Enjoys taking care of family, but wants shopping to be as fast and easy as possible
• Price sensitivity	✓	✓	✓	✗	✗	✗
• Convenience-driven	✗		✓	✓	✗	✓
• Preference for large formats	✓	✓	✗		✗	
• Shops at multiple stores	✗	✓		✗	✓	✗
• Loves food/cooking	✓	✗		✗	✓	✓

Exhibit 2.1 US grocery retail segmentation example.

In an ideal world of one-to-one retail, you would build a different kind of store for each of these types. In reality, the company used these insights to prioritize their budget allocation to different store formats and assortment categories. Marketing investments were tied directly to the size and attractiveness of the various segments, resulting in significantly higher marketing ROI once the changes took effect.

Segmentation is a strategic topic and deserves top management attention: *if the CEO doesn't care, nobody will*

Segmentation matters. When budgets are tight, a new retail segmentation can be a great way both to prioritize investments and enhance the fact base for marketing decisions. But how do you build a segmentation that stands the test of time and becomes the ongoing basis for marketing decisions? In a survey conducted by the Economist Intelligence Unit among 200 senior executives in 2005, every second company said they used market segmentation, or had at least launched a segmentation project. Quite a few retailers develop multiple segmentations to fit the requirements of different store formats, vendors or countries. But whether you opt for a 'one segmentation fits all' approach or believe 'the more the merrier', experience shows that the vast majority of segmentations are one-off efforts, filed away for good once the project is wrapped up. What a waste!

So what can you do to increase the segmentation's longevity? The answer is simple: before you start building a segmentation, decide what you want it for. As the US grocery retailer example shows, segmentation findings can change the fundamental assumptions behind a business strategy. Superior understanding of shopper needs can be a substantial source of potential competitive advantage, and as such it deserves the undivided attention of a retailer's most senior executives.

There are many potential purposes for a segmentation. For a global multi-category retailer, a segmentation might be required to track down the last unclaimed consumer niches or to identify new types of shopping behaviour emerging from changing consumer lifestyles and trends. By contrast, a segmentation for a newcomer to a specific category would typically fulfil a much broader purpose, e.g. to generate the fact base to define and profile the company's primary target group.

Either way, the segmentation will only be truly useful in informing the way a retailer does business if it reflects the top management agenda. No matter how inventive the segmentation approach or how original the segment names, if the segmentation doesn't help answer the questions on the CEO's mind, it will only ever be a theoretical weapon. But senior attention is critical for more mundane reasons as well: only top management can ensure the involvement of all the executives from functions that will be affected by the outcome of the segmentation. Depending on the exact purpose and nature of the segmentation, it can impact commercial strategy, marketing, supply chain and vendor management, store management and the merchandising department. All the relevant stakeholders will need to have a say in the process if they are to embrace the results of the segmentation.

In many of the segmentation efforts we have seen, companies and their service providers spend a lot of time fine-tuning their arsenal of statistical methods and clustering techniques. There is nothing wrong with the aspiration of applying first-rate research and analysis methodology, of course. However, this all too easily puts the cart before the horse, as the entire effort will go to waste unless senior stakeholders fully buy into the strategic priorities and the future use of the segmentation at the outset. To ensure its strategic relevance, the retailer will want to align the criteria used in the segmentation with the targets of their most important long-term business objectives – such as revenue potential or profitability.

Defining the relevant market

One of the most important issues in any segmentation – one that deserves top management attention – is the definition of the relevant market and study sample. For example, if you are looking for growth, the market definition should be relatively broad, perhaps including other retailers that you would not normally consider direct competitors because of their assortment or price position. Also, you will want to include consumers who are not currently your customers. But if profitability is your primary worry, the market definition should be narrower, and more granular, to ensure that you end up with the required level of detail; for example, data on customer lifetime value. In this case, it may be sufficient to limit the sample to current customers – an easy way to save time and money. But watch out: you might need to understand consumers other than those who actually do the shopping in order to improve your business. As any parent can tell you, at least when it comes to candy bars or cereals, their choice of product and brand is often driven by their children's preferences – and this will not show up in any standard shopper survey. Even strict vegetarians might well pick up steaks and sausages for their carnivore family! Focus groups and store exit-interviews are quick ways to help you avoid such pitfalls.

Consumer needs are at the root of shopper behaviour
and should be the basis of a strategic retail segmentation

Top management need to agree on the objectives of a segmentation and what use it will be put to – but any such decision is unlikely to be unanimous. It is quite likely that the different functional departments will have different and potentially conflicting views about the questions the segmentation should answer. For instance, the commercial director might wish to cluster shoppers based on their turnover potential, and generate insights about how to address the most promising ones. For this purpose, factors like disposable income and demographic data would be relevant segmentation variables. In contrast, a regional store manager will probably be more interested in shoppers' brand preferences and other purchase drivers as a basis for streamlining the in-store category mix and brand selection. But since brand preference and demographics do not usually correlate, a single segmentation cannot answer both sets of questions at the same time with the same level of granularity and precision.

If there wer actually a good correlation between demographic data and behaviour, then a demographic segmentation would be the natural first choice; demographic data is easily available and facilitates the targeting of segment members. However, this is not the case. Take two British subjects: both male, both born in 1948, both in their second marriage, both affluent and from well-known families. The first is Charles, Prince of Wales; the other is Ozzy Osbourne, Prince of Darkness. From their outfits and hairstyles alone it is clear that their purchasing behaviour is probably very different, despite the demographic similarities!

So if demographic data doesn't do the trick, which variables or lenses should a strategic retail segmentation be based on? McKinsey has carried out segmentations in many different countries and sectors; our experience confirms that the best course is to turn to the deepest level of shopper motivation, to the 'why?' that drives their preferences and actions. To determine why a purchase is made, it doesn't help to look at the identity of the shopper. Rather, retailers will want to explore the shopper's needs (Exhibit 2.2). A segment defined based on needs (e.g. 'health-conscious cocooner') may be harder to track and target than a simple demographic segment (e.g. 'single female aged 40–50'), but to succeed in the marketplace, retailers have to understand what shoppers want,

Lenses	Who	What	When/where	Worth	Why
Variables	Consumer	Category/behavior	Occasion (time, location)	Value	Needs
Examples	• Demographic (e.g., age, gender) • Socio graphic (e.g., income, education) • Life stage (e.g., marital status, occupation) • Region • Firmographic (SoHo, SMB, large enterprise) • Key accounts, small accounts • Internationality • Decision maker (single, group) • Scale potential (share of purchasing volume)	• Main product category (e.g., food, electronics, beauty, apparel) • Sub-category (e.g., LCD TVs, hair care) • Repurchase rate • Price level • Brand loyalty • Single/ multi- category purchase	• Buying occasion (gifts, before holidays) • Weekend • Time of day/ time of year • Planned vs. impulse • Store-location (e.g., mall, train station) • Channel pref./mix • Store loyalty • Stock renewal frequency • Shopping type (planned vs. spontaneous, alone or with whom, specific product, leisure)	• Turnover • Profitability • Lifetime value • Cost to serve • Single/multi-supplier • Purchases per year (number, value)	• Attitudes (e.g., price conscious, convenience seekers, variety seekers, pure luxury, high quality, individual style) • Buying factors (mainly product focus) • Passions (e.g., media consumption, sports, literature) • Emotions

Exhibit 2.2 Overview of segmentation lenses.

not who they are. Since the vast majority of purchase decisions are taken in the store, it is far more important to understand category needs. This understanding enables the retailer to create the right shopping experience – including, but not limited to, the product range, brand choice, price points, store layout, look-and-feel and customer service.

To make the segmentation even more useful, it is advisable to introduce a second dimension to these needs that examines their context – thereby, in effect, creating a segmentation matrix. A person's needs differ, depending on the situation they are in. To account for this, the default secondary segmentation dimension is 'occasion' or 'state'. For example, in the American apparel market, the needs of jeans buyers are shaped predominantly by whether the pair of jeans will be worn at work, on weekends at home, to go out at night or for outdoor activities. The usage situation determines what people are looking for in terms of style, cut, material and price point (Exhibit 2.3). In order to create a fact base that reflects these variations, the segmentation should include both needs and states. Only by producing such a matrix is it possible to identify the most attractive target segments and create the right product mix for different store formats to satisfy these segments.

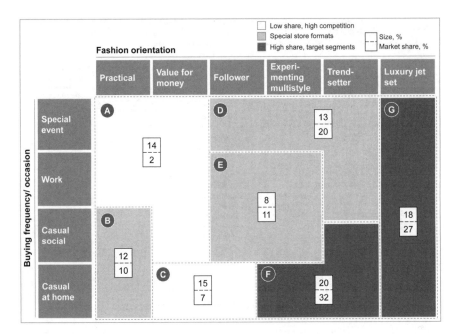

Exhibit 2.3 Exhibit of a needs-based matrix in apparel.

In the US grocery example mentioned earlier, the basic needs segmentation was greatly enhanced by adding states as a second dimension. It turns out that the differences in shopping behaviour between the needs segments were rather small, but once the frequency of shopping trips and the average basket size was added into the mix, the results became much more meaningful. Once it is known how often a member of a specific segment comes to the store, on which occasions they shop and how much they are willing to spend, it becomes easier to develop targeted propositions for such individuals.

Some retailers even rethink their format strategy based on the insights generated from a two-dimensional segmentation matrix. Says Mike Ullman, Chairman and CEO of JC Penney: 'We are learning off-mall stores can be very productive in big mid-week presence. It's closer to people's homes. It's not a mall trip. It's easier to drive to the door. It has a certain presence in the middle of the week, whereas malls perform in key holidays.' As a consequence of

Segmentation methodology

This chapter is not intended as a discussion of the statistical methods (such as hierarchical clustering or latent class) or the alternative software packages (e.g. SPSS or SAS) that are used to derive segments from a given research sample or data set. For these more technical questions, please turn to the academic literature in the field. Established sources include:

- Bonoma, T. V. and Benson P. S., *Evaluating Market Segmentation Approaches*, Industrial Marketing Management 13 (1984): pp. 257–68.
- Bonoma, T. V. and Benson P. S., *How to Segment Industrial Markets*, Harvard Business Review, March 2009.
- Perrey, J. and Ansgar H., 'Nutzenorientierte Kundensegmentierung: Eine Zwischenbilanz nach 35 Jahren,' Thexis 20, no. 4 (2004): pp. 8–11.
- Perrey, J. and Meyer T., *'Wachstum durch Wissen,'* in *Mega-Macht Marke*, 3. *Auflage*, Redline, Heidelberg (2011).
- Benson, P. S. and Sviokla, J. J., *Seeking Customers*, Harvard Business Review Books, 1993.

While superior technical and statistical skills are indispensable for successful segmentation solutions, retailers do not necessarily need to possess these capabilities in-house. Specialized service providers such as market research agencies and consumer insight consultancies offer anything from selective support to integrated full-service solutions.

these insights, JC Penney is concentrating most of its store growth in off-mall locations. In 2008, Ullman reported they were 'performing better than on-mall stores in terms of general transaction levels'. (Source: Andria Cheng, 'JC Penney scales back growth plans; Weak economy muddies earnings outlook', *MarketWatch*, 16 April 2008.)

There should be a central strategic segmentation: *any secondary segmentation should be aligned with it*

While separate segmentations for each store format, vendor or country can lead to levels of complexity that are hard to manage and communicate, this does not mean that there should only ever be one single segmentation. Additional secondary segmentations can provide additional insight in certain circumstances. Such segmentations might be required for tactical reasons, for example, for the addition of a specific function, such as CLM, or for a specific purpose, such as the launch of a new store format or entry into a new region or territory. The more clearly defined the purpose of such secondary segmentations, the better. For further detail on operational segmentations, see Chapter 16: 'Boosting customer value through CLM'.

Any additional or secondary segmentations need to be aligned with the strategic segmentation in order to leverage the existing knowledge and ensure the consistency with the retailer's marketing approach. The most common reason for an additional segmentation is to add in a new market in a specific country or region. It is well known that market characteristics differ greatly between countries. In the case of personal care retail, for example, 'a good choice of self-tanning products' is very important in most Western markets, while consumers elsewhere in the world often look for 'mild, but effective whitening products'. While this difference may be easy to accommodate in a two-dimensional segmentation based on needs and skin types, things get trickier if the needs vary more fundamentally. In India, for example, many shoppers are on such a tight budget that they can only afford mini-packs of most beauty products. This situation might require an alternative second axis, such as 'category budget', to derive the appropriate segment marketing approach. However, in order to maintain the link with the central strategic segmentation, it is important to keep the primary axis – usually that of category needs – stable across all markets. Similar rules apply to any secondary segmentations for specific functions.

If a subsidiary or third-party service provider has made its own segmentation, this can sometimes be turned to advantage for enriching and enhancing the retail company's central strategic segmentation. For example, the local media agency might hold valuable information on shoppers' media usage. If this can be matched to the existing needs segments, then the data might be used to optimize the relevant reach – and ROI – of the media mix in the retailer's advertising budget. However, it is likely that the local agency will not have used the same needs profiles as the retailer; to make the segmentation data compatible, the retailer will need to introduce a needs proxy to bridge the gap between the two sources. For instance, in categories driven by the consumers' stage of life, such as furniture or DIY, a reliable proxy could be a combination of age, marital status and number of children. For example, if a single female, aged 27, has just had her first child, there's a fair chance she's in the market for an affordable cot.

To get the most out of a segmentation: *keep it simple, bring it to life and spread the word*

Many retailers who carry out a segmentation fail to leverage it fully. To get the most out of a segmentation requires making it both tangible and memorable, and then promoting it through an internal marketing campaign. In our experience, a segmentation really starts to work once stakeholders from all parts of a retailer's organization are so convinced of its value that they start acting in sync to deliver their brand's value proposition.

The first rule for ensuring that the segmentation is both practical and memorable is to keep the number of segments as low as practicable – without sacrificing essential granularity and statistical differentiation. As a rule of thumb, the segmentation should have no more than ten segments. Any more than this, then all those using it will have difficulty in remembering and communicating the distinctive characteristics of the different segments. It also becomes a very complex task to serve each segment with a differentiated value proposition and tailored marketing activities.

The second rule is to make the segmentation both tangible and memorable: this will bring it to life for those who use it on a daily basis. For example, calling a segment 'Harry Handshake' is much more memorable than referring to it as 'Pragmatic male deal-seeker', especially if it comes with a full and vivid description of Harry Handshake's characteristics. For instance, the segment portrait of a key target segment could be displayed as a Western-style 'Wanted' poster.

The internal communication effort should seek ways to engage the staff in a truly memorable manner. This could include active learning tools: for instance, a self-typing tool based on short questions that enables employees to find out which segment they belong to. Some companies go much further in certain cases, even hiring actors to play out the defining traits of key segments during internal training sessions.

But even if your segments are tangible, memorable and low in number, their internal communication is often still a major project. You will need to show each member of your staff how the segmentation will change daily operations – and do so graphically, preferably in clear and simple language. This is no easy task, given the size of many modern retail organizations. But it is a task that cannot be avoided: the real value of a segmentation is only fully realized when all front-line staff thoroughly understand it.

Finally, like most management tools, a segmentation needs constant care if it is to prosper and remain useful in the longer term. It therefore pays to set up a small task force to monitor the ongoing validity of the segmentation solution, enrich the segments with additional information as new data becomes available and point out new uses for the segmentation. This team, or its steering committee, should include representatives of all management functions affected by the segmentation. Ideally, it should also involve key contacts from the most important service providers (e.g. creative agencies, media agencies and POS specialists), at least as corresponding members. Service providers will not only be able to contribute to the richness of a segmentation, but will also help reach the segments effectively and efficiently. Some retailers take this approach even further and collaborate with their top vendors in developing segment-specific products or packaging. Again, a segmentation is like a map: the more you unfold it, the more you see.

Key takeaways – Segmentation

1 Segmentation is just as important to retailers as it is to consumer goods companies – but for different reasons and in different ways.

2 Segmentation is a strategic topic and deserves top management attention: if the CEO doesn't care, nobody will.

3 Consumer needs are at the root of shopper behaviour and should be the basis of a strategic retail segmentation.

4 There should be a central strategic segmentation: any secondary segmentation should be aligned with it.

5 To get the most out of a segmentation, keep it simple, bring it to life and spread the word.

CHAPTER 3

Marco Mazzù, Thomas Meyer, Anja Weissgerber

Traditionally, branding has not been a top-priority for most retail CEOs. But the times, they are a-changing, and leading retailers are starting to discover their brands as a potential source of competitive advantage. Typically, this leads them to ask two kinds of question:

- How do consumers perceive our stores and our brand?
- How can we use brand management to improve our business performance?

BrandMatics, a comprehensive brand management approach developed by McKinsey & Company, provides the answers to these questions. The approach has been successfully applied in retail, as well as in other industries. In this chapter we will walk you through the most important BrandMatics concepts and analyses, including the brand diamond and the brand funnel. We will also look at how several best-practice retailers have mastered the art of consistent end-to-end brand delivery.

The brand diamond helps retailers map the attributes of their brand *in a structured and comprehensive way*

In the consumer's mind, a retailer's brand is the focal point of a wide range of perceptions about the retailer. To get to the bottom of your brand image and create a fact base for targeted improvements, you need a robust understanding of how and why the brand influences your customers. The relation between brand perception and consumer behaviour has been thoroughly researched by practitioners as well as academics. Building on this research, McKinsey & Company has developed its own framework for mapping brand image in a systematic way: the McKinsey brand diamond. This tool has been used widely as the starting point for comprehensive brand transformation efforts. The brand diamond uses four dimensions to structure brand associations (Exhibit 3.1).

The **tangible attributes** are the characteristics of the brand that are perceived by looking, listening, touching, smelling or tasting. In a retail context, these physical assets are often sub-divided into four categories:

- Store and location, e.g. the number of outlets, the layout of a store, the in-store merchandising or the availability of customer parking.
- Price and promotions, e.g. the overall price level or the type and number of promotions and discounts.
- Assortment, e.g. the total number of SKUs in a store, the range in a given category or the relative share of branded and private label products.

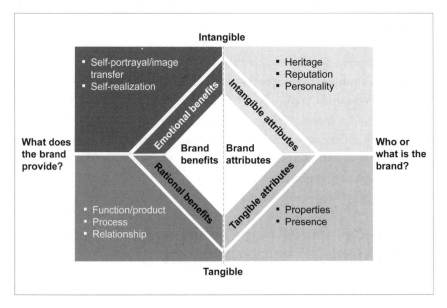

Exhibit 3.1 The brand diamond.

- service, e.g. store opening hours, number of staff, return policies or customer reward programmes.

The **intangible attributes** are the characteristics that collectively make up the identity of the retail brand, e.g. its origin, reputation or personality. Examples include:

- The Body Shop is perceived as a 'socially responsible brand'.
- Harrods is considered to be a retailer 'with a long tradition'.
- IKEA is strongly associated with its origin – 'being Swedish'.

In some cases, intangible attributes may be associated with tangible attributes. In the case of IKEA, for example, the colours blue and yellow support the image of being Swedish because they are also the colours of the Swedish national flag.

The **rational benefits** are the reasons to buy, derived from a brand's tangible attributes.

- Price-related benefits, e.g. buying at a discounter like Aldi helps you save money.
- Product-related benefits, e.g. shopping at Whole Foods helps you to stay healthy. Similarly, the products of a fashion retailer like Abercrombie & Fitch will give you a young and trendy look.
- Convenience, e.g. Tesco Express helps satisfy all your basic shopping needs in one convenient location.
- In-store experience, e.g. a visit to Harrods department store in London, the Apple flagship store in New York or Globetrotter's outdoor store in Cologne all offer unique shopping experiences.
- Service experience, e.g. Nespresso will pick up a defective coffee machine from your home and provide you with a substitute machine during the time it is being repaired.

The **emotional benefits** are the elements of a brand that help consumers express or reinforce the image they have of themselves. In our experience, many retailers have a tendency to overlook the importance of emotional benefits and focus mostly on rational buying factors, though there are some prominent exceptions.

- Customers of Prada or Louis Vuitton rarely buy the products purely because of the tangible attributes ('hand-sewn', 'finest leather') they provide. Recent McKinsey research shows that most luxury brands capitalize on a combination of their emotional appeal and their long-lasting products. In effect, shopping at luxury stores and being seen with luxury items is, in fact, a lifestyle statement.
- Similarly, for pre-teen girls, shopping at American Girl Place is as much a form of self-realization as it is a commercial transaction. Or think of the music lover frantically downloading songs on iTunes and leaving his stereo playing even when he is not at home – creating a soundtrack to his life.
- Although a self-proclaimed provider of 'casual luxury', Abercrombie & Fitch has not become the cult classic it is today solely because of its high quality T-shirts. Rather, it aspires to create a whole world for shoppers to live in. Says CEO Mike Jeffries: 'You buy into the emotional experience.' (Source: Stacy Perman/Reynoldsburg, 'Abercrombie's Beefcake Brigade', *Time Magazine*, 14 February 2000).

The most important function of the brand diamond is that it acts as a template to prepare and structure market research. To derive an accurate description of the image of the brand, including its strengths and weaknesses, it is imperative to capture all the aspects that define it (the 'brand attributes'). Any other statements that also have an influence on consumer behaviour should be included as well, even if they are not currently part of the retailer's brand identity (the 'market drivers').

The brand diamond is highly effective in structuring the discussion and research about retailers' brands, ensuring that no aspect is overlooked. Typically, following from a brand workshop or a focus group session preceding in-depth quantitative market research, you will emerge with an extensive list of statements. We recommend that you narrow down the list to no more than 20–50 statements for quantitative research purposes. Determining the

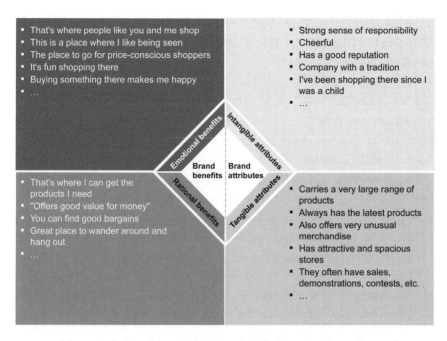

Exhibit 3.2 The brand diamond – examples of relevant attributes for retail.

actual number requires making a trade-off between the cost and reliability of the market research on the one hand (the fewer, the better), and the depth of insights generated on the other hand (the more, the merrier). See Exhibit 3.2 for sample statements that have proved useful in the retail context.

Based on the resulting shortlist of attributes and benefits, you should conduct quantitative consumer research that includes your own as well your key competitors' customers. This will create an accurate map of the relative strengths and weaknesses of all the companies in the market. When defining the research sample, bear in mind that there can be significant regional differences, especially in retail. The regions chosen for the research should be representative of your business as a whole. The research sample will also need to be large enough to allow for reliable observations at the intersection of customer groups and regions. Market research agencies and analytical specialists will be able to help determine the exact number of observations required to ensure statistically reliable results.

The brand purchase funnel helps retailers benchmark the performance of their brand *across the consumer decision journey*

The brand diamond reveals how well a brand is perceived by consumers relative to competitor brands. This information can form the basis for a comprehensive brand transformation effort, but in order to identify the opportunities for refinement to the brand image, one further step is required – taking stock of the brand's performance at each stage of the consumer's decision journey. The tool used for this purpose is the brand purchase funnel (or brand funnel, for short). The brand funnel is based on, but by no means limited to, the AIDA model (attention, interest, desire, action). The brand funnel tells you what percentage of the relevant target group fulfil each of the following criteria:

- ... is aware of the retail brand?
- ... lives near a store and considers purchasing there?
- ... has made a purchase there in the last months?
- ... uses the store frequently?
- ... are loyal customers making almost all purchases there?

Adjusting brand funnel research for store network effects

As the retail industry is a highly local business, you need to take special precautions to ensure that the purchase funnel is comparable across competing retailers. This can either be done by limiting the research sample to those who have stores of all the relevant competitors in their neighbourhood, or by including a filter or funnel step such as '... lives near a store' or '... has a store available in their area' explicitly (see Exhibit 3.3). Without this kind of adjustment, the brands of retailers with an extensive store network will appear to be disproportionately strong.

Exhibit 3.3 presents an example of the brand funnel as applied to a retailer's brand. Note that almost any stage of the funnel can be further subdivided in order to increase the granularity of insight. For example, providers of products

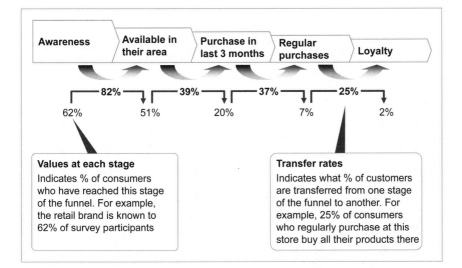

Exhibit 3.3 The brand funnel in retail.

with high ticket prices and low purchase frequency, like automobiles or real estate, will be looking for additional detail in the pre-purchase phases, for instance, regarding how specific brands enter or exit the consumer's consideration set. In contrast, retailers will typically wish to increase the resolution of the later funnel stages to reflect the fact that 'repurchase', 'favourite retail brand' or 'long-term loyalty' are often make-or-break factors for retailers.

The values at each stage of the funnel indicate the percentage of customers in the sample who have reached this stage. For example, the brand featured in Exhibit 3.3 is known to 62 percent of the survey's participants. The transfer rates from one funnel step to the next indicate what percentage of customers has completed the transfer. In Exhibit 3.3, 25 percent of those who regularly purchase at one of the brand's stores also say that they are loyal to the brand.

Exhibit 3.4 provides a real-life example of brand funnel research comparing multiple brands, in this case in the Italian grocery market in 2006 and 2004/2005. This shows, for example, that in this market Coop has the highest percentage of loyal customers and very good overall transfer rates. It is the market leader in terms of the transfer from 'available in their area' to 'purchased

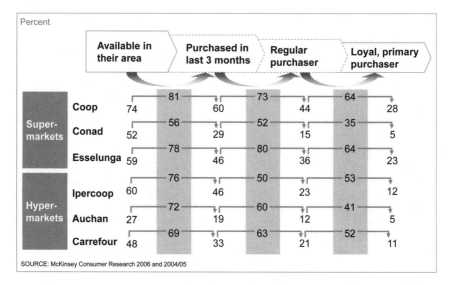

Exhibit 3.4 The brand funnel – example from Italian grocery market (percentage of respondents).

in the last three months', as well as from 'regular purchaser' to 'loyal, primary purchaser'. There is some improvement potential, however, regarding the transfer from occasional to regular purchase; in this regard, Esselunga shows the highest transfer rate. In contrast, Auchan shows good transfer rates along the brand funnel, all the way to the stage of 'regular purchaser', but has potential for improvement in loyalty creation.

Factoring in the consumer's average basket size and purchase frequency will enable the retailer to estimate the sales uplift that would result from increasing the transfer rate from one funnel stage to the next. The result of this calculation is often referred to as the 'customer conversion value'. But understanding the root causes of a given gap in the funnel is even more important than the size of the prize that can be claimed by closing it. In the Italian grocery example from 2006, for instance, Auchan would want to know what it could do to improve their below-average transfer rate from 'regular purchaser' to 'loyal, primary purchaser'.

BrandMatics is a comprehensive brand management approach *for assessing and improving brand performance across all stages of the brand funnel*

BrandMatics is a comprehensive brand management approach. It goes beyond the diagnostic insights provided by the brand diamond and brand funnel research to enable retailers to identify the specific attributes they need to address in their marketing mix in order to improve their performance in the purchase funnel.

Typically, the first step in tailoring the BrandMatics toolkit to the retailer's target groups is to conduct a market segmentation. This enables the retailer to identify its principal audience and to define these based on the criteria of attractiveness and accessibility; see Chapter 2: 'Segmentation' for further details.

BrandMatics is a five-step process (Exhibit 3.5):

- *Conduct market segmentation*: use consumer segmentation to determine your target audience and pre-select segments for the funnel analysis.
- *Identify brand drivers*: analyze how the attributes and benefits identified by the brand diamond drive consumers through the funnel.

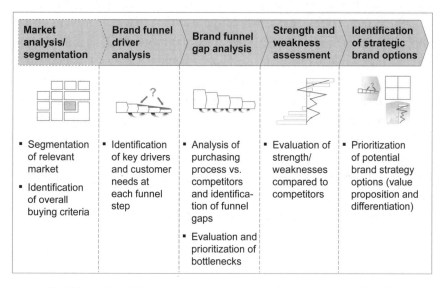

Market analysis/ segmentation	Brand funnel driver analysis	Brand funnel gap analysis	Strength and weakness assessment	Identification of strategic brand options
• Segmentation of relevant market • Identification of overall buying criteria	• Identification of key drivers and customer needs at each funnel step	• Analysis of purchasing process vs. competitors and identification of funnel gaps • Evaluation and prioritization of bottlenecks	• Evaluation of strength/ weaknesses compared to competitors	• Prioritization of potential brand strategy options (value proposition and differentiation)

Exhibit 3.5 BrandMatics – a step-by-step approach to manage your brand.

- *Identify brand funnel gaps*: compare the transfer rates of the brand with those of key competitors to identify bottlenecks.
- *Analyze strengths and weaknesses*: identify the relative strengths and weaknesses of the brand in terms of the most important brand drivers.
- *Derive a matrix of options*: combine the insights from the first four steps to derive a set of strategic options to improve the performance of the brand.

The brand driver analysis helps determine the root causes of consumer behaviour for each step of the brand purchase funnel.

Let us return to Auchan's hypothetical question in 2006: what do we need to do to improve our brand's performance on the transfer to brand loyalty? Conceptually, brand drivers are the brand items (attributes or benefits) that have the greatest influence on consumer purchasing behaviour, so to answer this question Auchan first needs to understand what turns its regular customers into loyal ones.

There are many approaches to analyzing the behavioural relevance of brand items. A simple and popular method is to ask consumers what they value in a retail brand, or to carry out a direct survey of the criteria they use to make their purchases. But the results of these approaches can be misleading as respondents have a tendency to say they want it all: low prices, top quality, end-to-end convenience. But offers that satisfy all these criteria in equal measure simply don't exist. What is more, stated importance often doesn't reflect actual importance. For example, while many car buyers say they make their choice based on safety and fuel economy, the evidence generated by more sophisticated research shows that brand image and design are actually more important to their purchasing behaviour. To adjust for these factors – the lack of differentiation and the mismatch of stated and actual importance – we recommend that the brand drivers should be derived using statistical analysis rather than by relying upon survey results. To do this, you look at the perceived strengths of the brand or product a given consumer has actually purchased.

It is imperative to conduct driver analysis for each funnel stage and for each consumer segment. Brand drivers do not possess the same relevance at all stages of the purchasing funnel, nor do the same drivers apply consistently to

Exhibit 3.6 Brand drivers – deriving levers for sales increase – disguised example.

all types of customer. Price, for example, is usually very important in transferring shoppers from consideration to purchase, but, in order to create loyalty, other drivers, such as service quality, become more important.

The disguised example in Exhibit 3.6 shows the key purchase drivers, ranked according to their behavioural relevance. It is immediately obvious from this that the relative importance of the drivers is not the same at all stages of the brand funnel. For example, in order to turn someone who is merely aware of the brand into a first-time buyer, store location is the most important factor, whereas price is more important in driving purchase frequency. Finally, loyalty is driven by good customer service and trustworthy advice.

Once the brand drivers have been determined, the next step is to carry out an analysis of the strengths and weaknesses of the brand. To this end, you compare the performance of your brand on the key brand drivers to the market average and the performance of the most important competitors. For each funnel step, this comparison shows in which areas your brand has been able to establish a strong and differentiated positioning versus competitor brands.

An alternative approach is to benchmark the top drivers across the entire brand funnel, rather than for each stage individually. In this context, brand drivers are sometimes also referred to as market drivers.

The resulting matrix of options can be used to close performance gaps, to differentiate the brand and to define the brand promise.

In the next stage of the BrandMatics approach, the results of the brand driver analysis are combined with those from the strengths and weaknesses benchmarking to form a matrix; this provides the retailer with a variety of options that can be used to improve its brand's performance in the purchase funnel by deriving concrete measures for brand building and brand management:

- *Close the gaps in critical areas*: if the retailer's brand shows weaknesses on highly relevant market drivers, correcting these is the natural starting point for making improvements to the brand's image and performance.
- *Expand competitive differentiation for the top drivers*: if your brand is very strong on items with high behavioural relevance, these strengths should be maintained or further expanded as key differentiators for the brand.
- *Reserve the right to play in less critical areas*: areas that have low behavioural relevance do not deserve action if they show satisfactory levels of performance; however, see the advice in the 'Identifying the hygiene factors' box below. These areas only need be addressed if there is evidence of major weakness.

As with the brand driver analysis and competitive benchmarking, a matrix of options can be generated for each step of the purchase funnel. However, most retailers choose to focus their attention on the stage that shows the greatest performance improvement potential for their brand. Where more than one stage is highlighted, a matrix of options across the entire brand funnel can be useful in prioritizing the actions that need to be taken. Exhibit 3.7 is an example of such a matrix: the vertical axis shows the importance of the brand drivers for consumer behaviour and the horizontal axis shows how consumers perceive the brand in question.

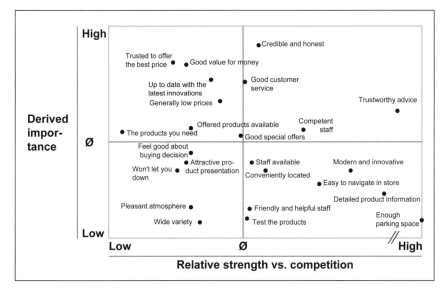

Exhibit 3.7 Matrix of options – disguised example.

Identifying the hygiene factors

Not all the attributes and benefits that emerge as highly important from the brand driver analysis will necessarily have the potential to be brand differentiators. For example, though possessing sufficient parking space might be a 'must have', it is unlikely to be a decisive factor in differentiating one brand from another. Such attributes are often referred to as 'hygiene factors'. They can easily be identified: they achieve high scores in the strength and weakness profiles of all players, but low scores for overall behavioural importance.

But brand building is more than just identifying individual brand elements for targeted improvements. It also requires strategic direction setting, ideally in the form of a synthesis of what the brand is about in plain and simple terms.

The brand promise captures the essence of a brand completely, yet concisely, *synthesizing it in plain and simple terms*

The brand promise describes both the essence of the retail brand and its differentiation from the brands of other retailers. The promise should take into account the brand's performance as well as more general strategic considerations. Summarizing the brand promise in a concise yet complete manner is one of the most challenging tasks of branding.

A certain retailer, for instance, defined its brand promise using 15 brand values, including 'inspiration', 'ingenuity', 'fun', 'self-confidence', 'honesty', 'trust' and 'good value for money'. In short, nothing was left out. The trouble with this brand promise is that it could apply to any number of retailers, from Prada to H&M. It may be complete, but it is anything but concise.

Checklist for brand promise definition

- *Distinctiveness*: concentrate on the unique and distinctive brand elements; include only those elements that differentiate your brand from others.
- *Relevance*: use the brand driver analysis to identify the root causes of consumer behaviour. If your customers don't care, neither should you.
- *Credibility*: ensure that the brand promise is credible and fully reflects your brand's perceived strengths.
- *Consistency*: build on the heritage of the brand and do not stray too far from its historical brand promise.
- *Feasibility*: only include those elements your organization can deliver on. Make sure you have the resources and capabilities for keeping the promise over an extended period of time.
- *Honesty*: Don't fool your customers, or yourself, especially when it comes to price. Not every retail brand can, or should, be a price leader.

Besides the checklist presented here, another helpful tool in defining the brand promise is the retail pentagon. This summarizes and simplifies a brand's rational benefits in five areas: price, assortment, in-store experience, service and quality. The core idea of the retail pentagon is that any retailer should be really distinctive in at least one of the five areas – and no retailer can be distinctive in more than two areas. Exhibit 3.8 presents an example of the pentagon for Lowe's. It shows that Lowe's focuses on assortment and in-store experience in its value proposition. The company is especially known for its wide, innovative and exclusive assortment that goes beyond what you would normally expect at a DIY store. Its wide assortment and attractive in-store layout turns each store visit into a fun experience. As a result, Lowe's is more attractive than many of its competitors to female shoppers, for example.

Here are some examples of clearly defined and well-differentiated retail brand promises.

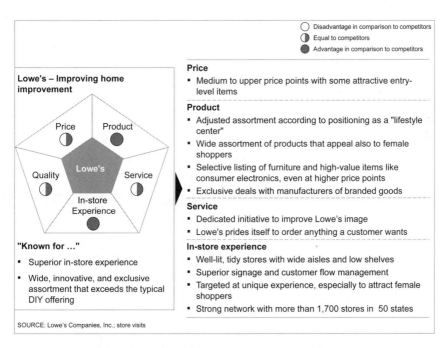

Exhibit 3.8 Applying the retail pentagon – example Lowe's.

- Edeka: 'We love food' – focus on quality, trust and commitment.
- Mercadona: 'Your trusted supermarket' – focus on regional products to ensure superior quality and freshness.
- 7-Eleven: 'Fast, convenient. 7-Eleven. Oh thank Heaven.' – focus on convenience.

Branding is more than advertising: *the brand promise needs to be delivered consistently at all customer touch points, from ATL to after-sales service*

A creative advertising campaign, a great website or an inspiring store visit may trigger a positive association, but a strong and lasting brand image only comes with multiple positive interactions over a longer period of time. Consistent brand delivery requires particular attention to retail, as retailers typically have hundreds of stores and thousands of employees. After all, nothing hurts the brand more than a broken promise.

To ensure the brand promise is delivered consistently at all touch points from newspaper advertising and internet banners to the stores and after-sales service, you have to address three challenges:

- create a brand mindset for all employees
- translate the brand promise into concrete actions
- set up the organization necessary to institutionalize the brand promise.

Creating the brand mindset necessary to keep the brand promise is a four-step process (Exhibit 3.9).

- The first step is to *inform*: all employees need to know about the brand promise. This can be done by means of a CEO presentation, a corporate information day or a feature in the corporate magazine.
- The second step is to *get buy-in*: the employees need to believe the brand promise and start explaining it to each other. Relevant formats for achieving this include workshops, internal trainings and interactive discussions. An effective tool through which to engage employees is to develop a 'brand

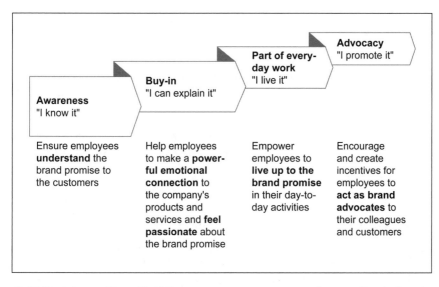

Awareness
"I know it"

Buy-in
"I can explain it"

Part of every-day work
"I live it"

Advocacy
"I promote it"

Ensure employees **understand** the brand promise to the customers

Help employees to make a **powerful emotional connection** to the company's products and services and **feel passionate** about the brand promise

Empower employees to **live up to the brand promise** in their day-to-day activities

Encourage and create incentives for employees to **act as brand advocates** to their colleagues and customers

Exhibit 3.9 Internal brand-building programmes empower employees to live the brand.

book' – a document that summarizes the brand promise which can be shared widely across the organization and provides a common language.

- The third step is to *live up to the brand promise*: this means ensuring that the new brand becomes a living reality. To achieve this, executives should go beyond merely explaining the new promise and start acting as role models. Also, they should provide front-line staff with the tools, coaching opportunities and materials they need to become brand ambassadors themselves.
- The fourth step is to *promote the brand promise*: this is the job of all employees and will, therefore, take some time to achieve. The company's processes, such as its incentive schemes, will need to be aligned with its brand promise. If the promotion of the brand promise is to be fully successful, it will require stability: once a new brand promise has been defined, stick to it.

Leading retail brands infuse their brand promise with fresh energy on a regular basis – be it in training, CEO speeches or letters to the employees. A new brand promise also has implications for HR processes, specifically for employer branding, recruiting and people development – in short, for a company's overall value proposition for current and future employees. However, according to a McKinsey survey, 60 percent of brand transformation efforts are considered failures, often because they lack senior commitment. CEO sponsorship for something that is meant to affect every part of the retail business system is absolutely essential. It is also vital that the CEO and the management team live up to the brand promise by becoming brand role models for the company.

We will now examine three best-practice examples to provide a sense of what it takes to translate a brand promise into concrete actions in the various marketing mix elements.

Keeping it simple: end-to-end minimalism at Muji

Muji provides an outstanding example of end-to-end brand delivery. The Japanese company, which manufactures and distributes stationery, household goods, clothing and small items of furniture, offers a brand promise of sleek minimalism. Somewhat paradoxically, the company has made 'no brand' its brand philosophy: the brand name, derived from the Japanese term 'Mu jirushi', translates as 'no logo'.

Its brand promise has been implemented so rigidly that it is widely considered a role model for brand delivery. Tadao Ando, the celebrated Japanese architect, sums up the company's philosophy as follows: 'Muji's succinct design reveals a Japanese aesthetic that values sustaining simplicity by completely discarding all worthless decoration'. (Source: Bianca Beuttel, 'Muji – markenlose Qualitätsprodukte', Hochschule für Gestaltung, Offenbach am Main, February 2004.) Nearly all its products are white or colourless and made of natural materials like unprepared wood and matte aluminium. Likewise, the retailer's shopping bags are made of plain and recycled paper, showing just the company logo. In order to ensure that it its brand delivery is totally consistent, Muji operates all of its 339 outlets itself (as of February 2010). Muji's consistent delivery of its minimalistic brand promise is attracting a growing fan base: sales have grown by 16 percent between 2006 and 2010.

What a girl wants: end-to-end enchantment at American Girl

American Girl's brand promise is 'celebrating girls and all they can be'. The company aspires to provide products and experiences that help girls to enjoy their childhood and to have fun, providing them with enchanting toys, clothes and games. Their product assortment is anchored by the company's range of 'right for you' dolls: little girls are encouraged to create their own doll. They can choose from a very wide range of variations of doll that exhibit different combinations of features such as skin tone, facial expression, eye colour, hair colour and hair style, enabling them to 'create' the doll that is just right for them. American Girl offers the same range of clothing for its dolls as it does for its child shoppers, thereby helping them look even more alike.

The stores, labelled American Girl Place, also support the company's brand promise by providing a fun and enchanting environment in which the girls can play. For example, there is a hair salon where the dolls can get a new hairstyle, a photo studio where girls can have their photo taken with their doll, and a bistro where the girls, their friends and their dolls can enjoy good food. The company even carries over its brand promise into publishing. Their magazine, which features stories, advice and games, reaches more than 600,000 children in the US. With each new issue, more than 5000 of them write letters to the magazine. In addition, the company produces a series of books that provide advice to girls, helping them grow up.

American Girl's consistent brand delivery is amply rewarded. In total, it has sold 132 million of its books, its home page gets more than 50 million visits a year and it has sold almost 20 million dolls thus far.

Nature's way is my way: end-to-end relaxation at Anthropologie

Anthropologie, part of URBN Inc., offers women's wear, accessories and furniture. The retailer focuses on affluent women aged 30–40. The common denominator of its marketing mix is a natural, inspiring and somewhat alternative look. The company aspires to give women a 'quality break' from their hectic everyday lives. In line with this promise, their stores do not feel like stores at all; rather, they are designed to give the feel of a living room. Clothes are featured in a comfortable environment, without heavy sell. Shoppers are explicitly welcomed to sit down and read a book or to take a closer look at some of the accessories. All products have a very natural appeal. They use fresh, organic colours combined with simple but creative design.

Key takeaways – Excellence in retail brand management

1 The brand diamond helps retailers to map the attributes of their brand in a structured and comprehensive way.
2 The brand purchase funnel helps retailers benchmark the performance of their brand across the consumer decision journey.
3 The brand driver analysis determines the root causes of consumer behaviour for each step of the brand purchase funnel.
4 The resulting matrix of options can be used to close performance gaps, to differentiate the brand and to define the brand promise.
5 The brand promise captures the essence of a brand completely, yet concisely, and synthesizes it in plain and simple terms.
6 Branding is more than advertising: the brand promise needs to be delivered consistently at all customer touch points, from ATL to after-sales service.

CHAPTER 4

STORE BRAND PORTFOLIO MANAGEMENT

Jean-Baptiste Coumau, Lars Köster, Kai Vollhardt

In the early days, being a retailer meant opening a store – a single store. Some of the pioneers carry the location of their original premises in their store or product brands to this day – think of Smythson of Bond Street, Hermès 24 Faubourg or Saks Fifth Avenue. The next phase was characterized by physical expansion: the setting up of new outlets, usually under a single brand. The retailer's brand became the promise of reliable quality, value and service, regardless of which outlet the customer bought from.

In our day, leading retail groups are juggling a multitude of networks, formats and store brands. In part, this is driven by retailers' aspirations to differentiate their value proposition according to the needs of different customer groups and purchase occasions. In part, it is a side effect of consolidation through mergers and acquisitions. The result is that retailers are left with a portfolio management challenge: does the differentiation afforded by multiple brands or formats outweigh the synergies of a mono-brand strategy? Does it pay to launch an entirely new brand for a given country or target group, or should we try to refine the positioning of an existing brand or product? This chapter outlines the BrandMatics Advanced approach, an integrated methodology that creates a robust fact base for retailers' brand portfolio decisions.

Increasingly, retailers are operating multiple formats and brands under one roof *to address a wide range of consumer needs and purchasing occasions*

To address the increasing fragmentation of consumer markets and needs, retail companies have created an ever-wider array of retail format and brands. The purpose of these new formats and brands is usually to offer more targeted propositions for specific customer groups or purchasing occasions. Take Media-Saturn, the leading European consumer electronics retail company, for example. Stores operated under the Saturn brand are usually found at premium downtown locations; the assortment is focused on technical innovation. In contrast, Media Markt stores are typically located in suburban areas. The Media Markt brand promise is anchored by its 'lowest price guarantee'. The different brands allow for highly targeted propositions that serve different consumer needs.

While Media-Saturn has chosen to run two distinct brands in similar retail formats, Tesco has taken a slightly different approach. It has six different store formats, differentiated by their size and the range of products sold, but all are branded as variants of the Tesco umbrella brand; examples include Tesco Extra (hypermarkets), Tesco Superstores (large supermarkets) and Tesco Express (convenience stores; see Chapter 3). Ahold, an international retailer that is present in both the United States and Europe, has differentiated its branding by geography. Their US hypermarkets are operated under the Giant brand, while its outlets in the Netherlands and Sweden are branded as Albert Heijn and ICA respectively. The reason Ahold operates different brands in different countries is rooted in its history of non-organic growth: while the Netherlands represent the company's home turf, the US business was acquired and ICA is part of a joint venture. In Sweden, ICA itself runs an umbrella strategy not unlike that of Tesco, with sub-brands including ICA Maxi, ICA Kvantum and ICA Supermarket.

Inditex, to take a fashion example, also operates a sizeable portfolio of brands, partly created through mergers and acquisitions. The Spanish group runs more than 4000 stores worldwide under several brands. The number of store brands in the group has increased significantly during recent years; it now includes Zara, Bershka, Massimo Dutti, Pull and Bear, Oysho, Zara Home, Stradivarius and Uterqüe.

In all such cases, the increasing proliferation of formats and brands brings about entirely new management challenges for retail companies. How does an additional brand or format affect the others in the portfolio? What is the real cost of introducing a new brand? How does the management of a wide range of formats or brands differ from a mono-brand approach? Are we losing efficiency if we scatter our marketing funds and resources over multiple brands?

These concerns have led to a drop in enthusiasm for adding new retail brands in the recent past. More and more retailers have gone from a multi-brand strategy (several individual brands) to an umbrella brand (multiple, yet related, brands under the same roof) or a mono-brand strategy (single brand), and are often housing multiple formats under one brand. The umbrella and mono-brand strategies are clearly superior to a multi-brand portfolio in terms of efficiency, for example in terms of advertising expense and image transfer. The downside is that they provide less flexibility and differentiation for addressing the needs of different customer segments. Carrefour is, perhaps, the most prominent example of brand consolidation in retail. In 1999, Carrefour merged with Promodès and added the Champion brand to its portfolio. This situation remained unchanged until 2007, when Carrefour rebranded 6 of the Champion stores in Brittany as Carrefour for test purposes. The test was successful and, as a result, Carrefour decided to rebrand the entire network of more than 1000 Champion stores as Carrefour over the course of the next two years. (Sources: *Financial Times*, 13 March 2009; *Ouest France*, 27 September 2008.) Edeka has taken their umbrella brand to all formats except discount and specialty retail, but allows for a certain differentiation by adding subtitles for different formats, e.g. 'Edeka nah & gut' (close and good) or 'Edeka Center' (E-Center).

But how do you determine what is right for your company? What are the criteria you should use to define the optimal store brand portfolio? Which brands have the highest potential to serve the different customer segments successfully? The challenge for retailers is to increase profitable penetration without creating more management complexity and inter-brand cannibalization than is absolutely necessary.

BrandMatics Advanced *allows retailers to assess the real economic impact of brand portfolio management decisions*

To address these questions, McKinsey has developed a systematic portfolio management approach that enables retailers to derive and manage multi-brand strategies: BrandMatics Advanced. It enables the assessment and evaluation of brand consolidation, new brand introduction or the acquisition and integration of new retail brands or formats. BrandMatics Advanced is based on the three golden rules of brand portfolio management:

- *Take a full P&L perspective*: assess the top-line impact as well as the marketing and format cost implications (see an example of this in Exhibit 4.1).
- *Don't neglect interdependencies*: assess spill-over effects on other brands and the potential risks of any changes being considered.
- *Make a discernible difference*: translate the new portfolio strategy into action and make it work.

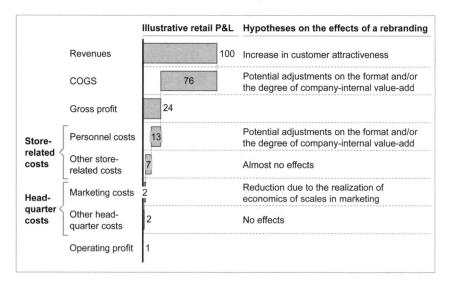

Exhibit 4.1 P&L effects of store brand portfolio management – an example.

Use the brand space map to derive different portfolio scenarios, *then evaluate them with the help of customer conversion value modelling*

For the retailer to be able to assess the sales impact of any changes to its brand portfolio, it needs to simulate potential customer migration between brands. In retail, this is more complex than in other industries because of local differences. To ensure a robust simulation of top-line impact, McKinsey has devised a three-step process.

Step 1: Situation analysis: which positions in the brand space are covered by the different retail brands?

Only a thorough analysis of the relative positions of the retailer's own brands and those of its competitors can reveal any weaknesses in its portfolio, as well as any opportunities for further growth. The tool of choice for this purpose is a two-dimensional map that locates the brands according to their specific positioning in the market (see Exhibit 4.2).

The brand position map is derived from the brand's drivers (see Chapter 3 for details). The closer a brand is to a given arrow head at the border of the map, the stronger is its performance in terms of that respective driver. Exhibit 4.2 shows, for example, that Discounter B is perceived as the price leader. It also shows that the different retail formats stake clear positions in the brand space (e.g. discounters versus supermarkets). While discounters show a good performance regarding 'low prices' and 'promotions', supermarkets are perceived as strong in terms of the level of service offered. In other words, customers have a clear and distinct perception of how the value proposition differs across the different retail formats, and this perception is directly linked to the individual brand drivers. In this example, this means it might be difficult to use the same brand across multiple formats. Consumers may be confused or even put off by a retailer that tries to carry over its discount brand into its supermarket format.

Once all your brands are plotted on the brand space, both the unclaimed areas (the 'white spots') and the over-served segments (the 'consolidation opportunities') become immediately apparent.

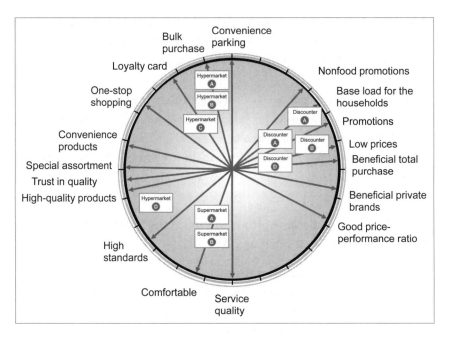

Exhibit 4.2 Two-dimensional map of brand positions.

Creating such a brand map is a relatively straightforward exercise. The research typically takes about a month; for robust results, you should aim to get at least 100 respondents per brand. The overall cost will be of the magnitude of EUR 25,000, depending on the design of the market research and the market research agency you work with.

Step 2: Scenario development: what scenarios are possible?

Is it possible to reposition individual brands to gain more customers? Are there any brands in the portfolio that should be eliminated or consolidated with another brand? Are there any white spaces that call for the launch of a new format or brand? The brand space map is the reference point for answering these questions. For example, if you consider launching a new retail concept under a new brand, this should be plotted into the brand space alongside the existing brands. Likewise, if you consider repositioning an existing format or brand, then to see how this fits into the retail landscape is simply a matter of moving its present position on the brand map to its target positioning.

Until 2006, the store brand portfolio of the Rewe Group consisted of several store brands all focused on the same format (large supermarkets): e.g. miniMal, HL, Otto Mess, Stüssgen and Petz. (Sources: Nina Trentmann, 'Eine Marke für den Markt', *Die Welt*, 22 June 2007; 'Rewe: on the attack', *Datamonitor News*, 25 January 2007; Susan Hasse, 'Immenser Kraftakt', *Lebensmittelzeitung*, 29 September 2006.) Some of these brands were just regional brands (e.g. Otto Mess and Stüssgen), while other brands were national brands (e.g. miniMal and HL). Rewe could have kept all the individual brands extant so as to achieve maximum penetration in the large supermarket format (a multi-brand strategy). Alternatively, the group could have consolidated all its large supermarkets under the same brand (a mono-brand strategy). Inditex found itself in a similar situation as it also had multiple brands, though in fashion retail rather than grocery. We will follow what these companies did and how they fared in the following section.

Step 3: Scenario evaluation: what is the business impact of the different scenarios?

In order to assess the business impact of various re-positioning scenarios and other portfolio moves, you have to simulate future customer migration. Since every change in positioning alters the balance of strengths and weaknesses of a brand, it will also change its attractiveness to specific customer groups. The brand purchase funnel can be used to determine how this change in attractiveness will affect customer decisions, producing a reliable estimate of how many people will buy from the new or adapted format or brand. This approach is often referred to as customer conversion value modelling (see Chapter 3 for details).

Any change that is made to a given retail format or brand also has implications for other brands in the same market. To account for these feedback effects, you will also need to estimate internal migration ('cannibalization') as well as external migration ('participation') in order to derive the net impact. In other words, you will need to get a sense of how many customers will switch brands as a result of your repositioning scenarios, both within your own portfolio and across retail companies (Exhibit 4.3).

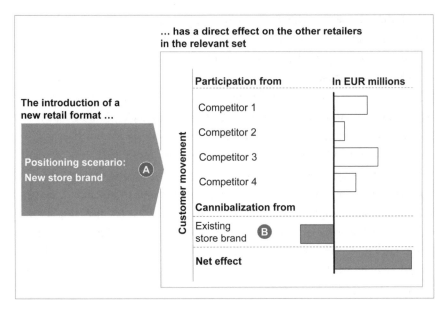

Exhibit 4.3 Brand switcher analysis to determine net scenario impact.

Returning to the examples of Rewe and Inditex: the two companies opted for different strategies. While Inditex still runs a multi-brand store portfolio strategy, the Rewe Group rebranded most of its large supermarket stores, including miniMal and HL, as Rewe. The benefits to Rewe are clear: the rebranding of its stores not only strengthened Rewe's brand image but also helped improve and expand its private label range. Rewe's own brand took the place of a wide range of private labels, such as Erlenhof and Salto, thereby generating additional economies of scale. (Source: Christian Lattmann, 'Handelsmarken zahlen auf die Händlermarke ein', *Lebensmittelzeitung*, 30 May 2008.)

To assess the full impact of a portfolio move,
estimate the one-time rebranding cost, changes in continuous marketing cost, and potential risks and synergies

To get from the top-line to the bottom-line impact of a given scenario, you need to estimate its cost effects. Typically, the one-time cost involved in (re-)

launch, re-positioning or re-branding efforts is the biggest single position – but changes in marketing costs, especially advertising spend, should by no means be neglected.

The **rebranding cost** includes all the expenses necessary to rebrand outlets or offices, administrative buildings, in-store merchandising, letterheads and other materials; this has a negative impact on the cost base of the company. Proven sources for estimating this effect include expert interviews and case studies of previous rebranding efforts. Rewe, for example, set aside some EUR 60 million in 2006 to bring all the group's 2600 stores under the Rewe brand. (Source: Susan Hasse, 'Immenser Kraftakt', *Lebensmittelzeitung*, 29 September 2006)

The **impact on advertising expenditure** depends on the required brand investment and potential advertising synergies. In general, fewer brands mean higher advertising spend synergies, for instance, because of standardized communication processes, lower creative agency fees and higher volume discounts for specific marketing vehicles, such as leaflets. Key sources for estimating the changes in advertising cost include expert interviews, internal cost data or competitors' ad spend, as observed by tracking agencies.

As well as calculating the expected costs of brand portfolio moves, you will also want to anticipate the potential risks involved. This is particularly important in the case of brand consolidation. Often brand consolidation is carried out in order to bring the stores of a 'weaker' or smaller brand or format under the umbrella of a 'stronger' or bigger brand or format – as in the case of Carrefour's integration of Champion in France or Rewe's re-branding of miniMal stores as Rewe stores. In such cases, retailers should be wary of potential negative spill-over effects. Adding less attractive store locations, or stores of inferior look and feel, that previously belonged to the discontinued brand can weaken the overall perception of the stronger brand. This effect needs to be reflected in the top-line assessment. In general, mono-brand and umbrella brand strategies are also more vulnerable to scandals or other reputation-related issues than multi-brand strategies. If one brand is severely damaged, multi-brand players can offset the negative effects with their other brands to some extent. A mono-brand player, however, will feel the downside across its entire network.

Of course, brand consolidation also affords substantial synergies. Leveraging a single, strong brand across multiple formats makes for more efficient communication and less organizational complexity. What is more, the positive perceptions associated with a strong brand can often be carried over to stores previously operated under other, less prominent, brands. Retailers contemplating brand consolidation will want to consider the potential risks as well as the expected synergies carefully before they go ahead with any re-branding efforts.

Putting brand positioning into action

Once you have selected a specific scenario for implementation, the next step is to make the changes work. Each brand, be it repositioned, consolidated or launched from scratch, should have its own, distinct profile and value proposition. Imagine, for example, that you have decided to reposition a specific retail brand to increase its service orientation and, ultimately, attract additional customers. How do you bring the service aspiration to bear on daily operations? In a given case, the analysis of the influencing factors of 'good service' revealed that the guarantee period granted to customers was one of the key drivers of service perception. But how long is long enough? A deep dive showed that prolonging the guarantee period from six months to one year increased customer satisfaction by 20 percent, while prolonging it from three to five years only added an extra 9 percent. Conducting similar calculations across all key touch points can help retailers to determine the concrete operational changes that will generate the greatest value for a new or repositioned brand. For details on brand promise and brand delivery, please see Chapter 3.

BrandMatics Advanced can be used not only to manage existing store brand portfolios but also to analyze and optimize the portfolio of branded goods and private label products it features in a given format. The next chapter (Chapter 5) will explore the changing role of private labels in retailers' assortments in more detail, paying particular attention to late-generation private labels which, increasingly, are evolving into brands in their own right. The more private label items compete directly with manufacturer brands, the more you will have to depend on sophisticated portfolio management approaches for determining the optimal mix of products in your stores.

Key takeaways – Store brand portfolio management

1 Increasingly, retailers are operating multiple formats and brands under one roof to address a wide range of consumer needs and purchasing occasions.

2 BrandMatics Advanced allows retailers to assess the real economic impact of brand portfolio management decisions.

3 Use the brand space map to derive different portfolio scenarios, then evaluate them with the help of customer conversion-value modelling.

4 To assess the full impact of a portfolio move, estimate the one-time rebranding cost, changes in continuous marketing cost, and potential risks and synergies.

CHAPTER 5

Gabriele Bavagnoli, Liv Forhaug, Lars Köster, Carina Schumacher

Private labels used to be positioned at the bottom of both the shelf and the price range, often as quick fixes to accommodate dips in consumer spending during periods of recession. Those days are gone. Private label brands are here to stay, and they have conquered new territories beyond low frills. The latest generation of private labels is, in fact, venturing into premium segments as well as consumer niches. While this promises higher returns and greater opportunity for differentiation, it also means that retailers find themselves competing head-on with brand name manufacturers. To tackle this twofold challenge, this chapter presents a simple, yet systematic framework that helps retailers to answer three basic questions.

- What is the most promising private label branding strategy?
- Which categories have the highest potential?
- Which capabilities do retailers need to deliver on their private label strategy?

Private labels are here to stay: *their share is growing across countries, sales channels and product categories*

The share of private labels, or PL, is growing in most major European markets and in the US. With a PL share of more than 42 percent, the UK has the most developed PL market in Europe, followed by Germany with just below

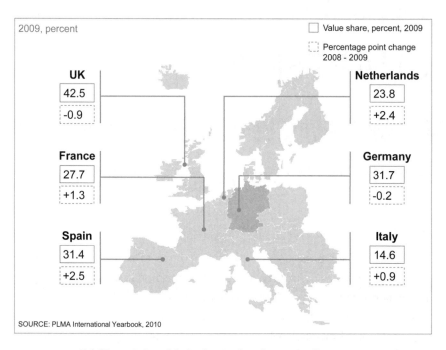

Exhibit 5.1 Private label value market shares (2008, percent).

32 percent (Exhibit 5.1). Both countries have seen spectacular PL growth in previous years (e.g. +4.3 pp in the UK between 2007 and 2008); their PL share is now effectively stagnating at very high levels.

Initially, PL growth was driven mainly by discount retailers, but now mainstream retailers are just as active in this area. Although the PL share of classical grocers in Germany is just 14.2 percent, this market segment has the highest PL growth rate. According to Nielsen Markettrack, it was growing at 16.3 percent between 2007 and 2008. Leading retailers in the UK already have a PL share of more than 45 percent. Although PL shares vary by product category, there is a clear growth trend that spans almost all categories (Exhibit 5.2).

To a large extent, this growth is triggered by consumer behaviour. Economic crises usually favour the development of private labels: Consumers buy as much as ever, but at lower prices. In essence, they switch to cheaper alternative products ('consumer downtrading'). Private labels allow consumers to get a very similar product at a lower price – without the added emotional

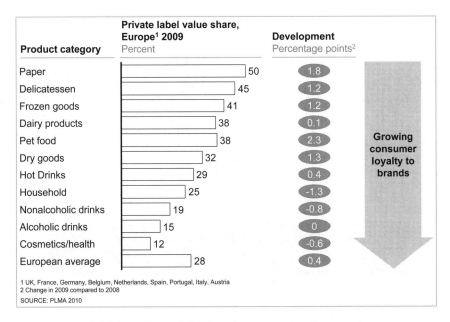

Product category	Private label value share, Europe[1] 2009 Percent	Development Percentage points[2]	
Paper	50	1.8	
Delicatessen	45	1.2	
Frozen goods	41	1.2	
Dairy products	38	0.1	
Pet food	38	2.3	**Growing consumer loyalty to brands**
Dry goods	32	1.3	
Hot Drinks	29	0.4	
Household	25	-1.3	
Nonalcoholic drinks	19	-0.8	
Alcoholic drinks	15	0	
Cosmetics/health	12	-0.6	
European average	28	0.4	

1 UK, France, Germany, Belgium, Netherlands, Spain, Portugal, Italy, Austria
2 Change in 2009 compared to 2008
SOURCE: PLMA 2010

Exhibit 5.2 Private label share by category (2008, percent).

value provided by an A brand. But often, consumers' PL product experience is positive. As a result, they don't return to their original, more expensive, product even when the crisis is over. This effect is evident in a long-term overview of PL share, as presented in Exhibit 5.3 (US food example).

But consumer downtrading is by no means the only reason for PL growth. Historically, growth has been continuous and was driven by many factors, including retailer consolidation, increasing retail marketing sophistication, the growth of hard discounters and increasing consumer acceptance.

For obvious reasons, retailers don't mind. For them, PL growth is a strategic priority because of the multiple benefits it affords:

- margin advantages derived from value chain integration
- coverage of a wide range of price bands to cater to all customer budgets
- the opportunity to use private label products to strengthen the retail brand itself and foster customer loyalty.

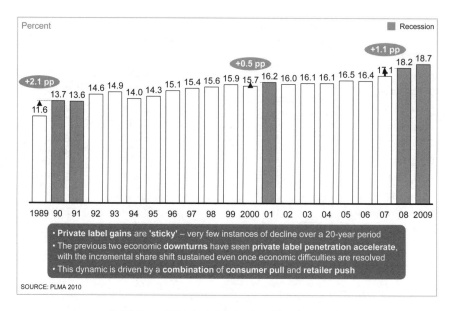

Exhibit 5.3 US private label value share (percent).

When almost every retail chain is stocking the same 'must have' brand name products, private labels increasingly become instruments of differentiation for retailers.

But brand name companies are fighting back. And for the first time, they seem to be making some headway. Recent figures for Germany provided by the GfK confirm that brand name companies have successfully deployed advertising pressure, promotions and new basic ranges to recapture market share from PL after the most recent crisis. For example, Procter & Gamble has successfully introduced 'basic' brands, positioned at lower price points than the established brands in their portfolio, in a range of product categories such as toilet paper, paper towels, diapers and detergents. And since even discount retailers are increasingly using high-profile brands for differentiation, premium brands are currently the fastest growing segment in the German market (Exhibit 5.4).

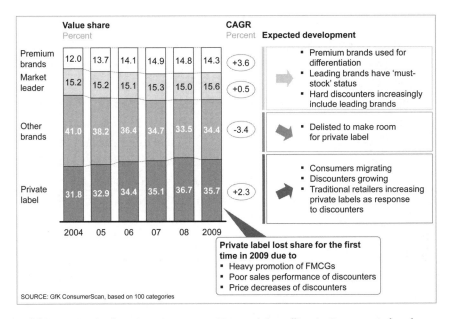

Exhibit 5.4 For the first time since 2004, PL growth is stalling in Germany (value share, percent).

PL – the Achilles' heel of brand manufacturers?

Because of the persistent market share gains of private labels, brand manufacturers are under increasing pressure to take action. This is especially true for mid-segment brands, that is B and C brands that are neither especially innovative nor perceived as particularly strong brands by consumers. Yet most brand manufacturers are hesitant to enter the private label business, be it independently or in cooperation with retailers. They fear a loss of focus and identity, but most of all, they fear the negative impact on their A brands. Will consumers still pay extra for a branded product if they can get what they perceive as similar tangible benefits at a much lower price?

A recent study by the University of Hamburg, overseen by Professors Sattler and Clement, has shown that manufacturers don't have much reason to worry in most cases – at least not about the short-term effect on consumer perception. In fact, most consumers simply assume that brand manufacturers also produce PL products, regardless of whether this is really the case. For example, noted personal care player Beiersdorf, the company behind the Nivea brand, expressly states that it does not produce any PL products. Even so, many consumers believe it does, usually because of the remarkable similarity between Beiersdorf's Nivea brand and the PL brand 'Balea' in terms of packaging, logo and brand name. Yet in reality, Balea is owned by dm, a drug store chain. In particular, Beiersdorf does not manufacture products sold under the Balea brand.

But the good news according to the study is that this kind of assumption, faulty as it may be, doesn't usually damage manufacturers' A brands. There are some exceptions: market segments dominated by emotionally charged brands, consumer target groups characterized by high quality consciousness and product categories with high consumer involvement. In these cases, brand manufacturers would have good reason to be sceptical about being associated with PL brands or products. For details, see Henrik Sattler, ' Was ist in der Handelsmarke?', Hamburg 2009.

PL has evolved beyond its origins in generic products and value segments. *The most recent PL generation is even venturing into the premium segment*

As we noted at the beginning of this chapter, retailers used to position private label product at the bottom of their shelves and at the bottom of their price architecture. But private labels have evolved from cheap alternatives in the entry-level price segment all the way up to the premium segment. Today, PL brands cover almost all product categories and price segments. They have become an integral part of most major retailers' category strategy. As a result of their expanding presence, different PL tiers serve different objectives.

- In the *entry-level price segment*, classical retailers use PL products to defend market shares in their daily battle against discounters.
- In the *higher price-level segment*, retailers use PL to strengthen their retail brand (especially its perception as a provider of 'value for money'), create sustainable competitive differentiation and increase customer loyalty.
- *Across all price segments*, the greater control over the value chain afforded by PL ensures savings in sourcing, marketing and selling costs compared to branded products. These savings are typically split between consumers – in the form of lower prices – and retailers – in the form of higher margins.

This differentiation of PL objectives has spawned four distinct types of PL strategy, also known as the four generations of PL. Although they have entered the market one after the other, they now exist in parallel (Exhibit 5.5).

The *first and second PL generations* mainly help retailers create a competitive offering in the entry-level price segment, thus improving their perception

	1st generation Generics	2nd generation Value	3rd generation NBE[1]	4th generation Premium/niche
Description	Low prices in generic product categories	Lowest possible prices for basic, 'no frills' products	Same quality as brand leader at a better price	Innovative and/or premium quality products
Primary objectives	▪ Provide competitive entry price points	▪ Provide competitive entry price points ▪ Improve retailer's price perception and defend against discounters	▪ Offer consumers better value for money ▪ Increase bargaining power and margins	▪ Differentiate retail brand ▪ Reach new consumer segments ▪ Increase loyalty ▪ Improve margins
Recent development	Generics staging a comeback	Center stage in current activities	Sideshow – some potential left	Breakthrough delayed by crisis
Tesco examples	No example at Tesco	Tesco Value	Tesco	Tesco Finest Tesco Organic

1 NBE = national brand equivalents
SOURCE: Bruhn 1997

Exhibit 5.5 Four generations of PL.

as providers of value for money. This strategy serves to defend a company's market position, particularly against discounters, by offering lower-cost alternatives to the leading brand or brands. In most cases, this strategy seems to be working. Quantitative analyses have demonstrated that PL is one of the top drivers of value-for-money perception in the largest European markets. For these early PL generations, brand perception and image are only of secondary importance. Although there is a long-term trend towards more differentiated PL in higher price bands, the latest economic crisis has engendered a revival of second-generation PL products. Since many consumers are switching to lower-priced products, traditional retailers have launched massive advertising campaigns promoting their own entry-level price brands to prevent customers from churning to discount stores altogether. In Germany, Edeka's low frills 'Gut & Günstig' brand is perhaps the most prominent example of this strategy. In the United Kingdom, Sainsbury's is pushing its 'Basic Range', followed by Waitrose and its 'Essential Range'.

But today, PL isn't only used by retailers to drive their value-for-money perception. The increasing sophistication of retailers' brand portfolio management has given rise to *third and fourth generation* PL products that venture into categories and price bands previously deemed unattainable for private labels. *Third-generation private labels* are those that present consumers with a direct alternative to the national market leader, and that produce higher retail profit margins than A brands – although not always higher absolute profits because of the lower ticket prices. Third-generation PL puts retailers in direct opposition to the leading brand manufacturers. The main strategic objectives of this PL generation are to improve margins, to reduce the dependence on A brand suppliers and create negotiation leverage, and to foster customer loyalty. In general, third-generation PL is a more strategic game than the more tactical earlier generations. Consequently, retailers usually launch third-generation PL products in several product categories and make consumers become gradually more aware of this PL generation as a real brand, not just as a range of cheaper, alternative products. Today, most national brand equivalent (NBE) PL brands are branded with the retailer's own brand name.

The *fourth generation of PL brands* is tapping into the higher price ranges as well as into specific niche target groups. These PL products are usually priced at or above premium products, either because of their superior quality or because of some other special benefit, e.g. organic ingredients. Premium PL brands are often used in categories where there are no strong brands, effectively making the PL the reference brand. Examples include ready meals or fresh products like fruit, vegetables and meat. Most retailers carrying several PL generations have defined a portfolio of PL brands to ensure they cover all the various product and price segments. Take German grocery retailer Edeka, for example. Alongside its classic low-priced own brand 'Gut & Günstig', Edeka uses PL brands such as 'Edeka Bio' to reach selected target groups, while its 'Edeka Selection' brand targets various categories in the premium segment.

PL – only in low-involvement categories?

Until very recently, the most basic assumption about PL read as follows: the higher the brand relevance in a given product category, the lower the share of private labels. In an empirical study conducted by McKinsey & Company and the Marketing Centrum at the University of Münster (MCM), this hypothesis was put to the test. Brand relevance was measured for selected categories in three dimensions: prestige, risk reduction and information efficiency. According to this research and market share data from GfK and Nielsen Markettrack, categories with the highest brand relevance score, e.g. cigarettes and beer, had, in fact, the lowest PL share. Medium brand relevance scores and respective medium PL shares were measured in categories like shower gels and coffee. The lowest brand relevance scores among the categories in scope were observed for paper tissues and wrapping foil. In line with the original hypothesis, these categories also showed the highest PL share in the market. However, the more recent third and fourth generations of PL could change this picture. As consumers increasingly perceive private labels as real brands, these may stand a higher chance of succeeding in categories with higher brand relevance. This is especially true for categories in which retail brands enjoy high credibility, such as food.

So PL is growing across countries, sales channels and product categories. Increasing PL differentiation has given rise to PL portfolios that frequently extend over multiple product categories and comprise more than a single no-frills white label. Many of these brands are connected with the retail brand by way of umbrella branding or endorsement. As a result, PL management has become much more complex than yesterday's tactical selection of SKUs. Under these circumstances, retailers need a much more professional PL management approach. Key questions include:

- What is the most promising private label strategy, price tier and brand?
- Which categories have the highest PL potential?
- Which capabilities are required to deliver on the PL strategy?

These questions are reflected by the simple, yet systematic '3D' approach presented below (see Exhibit 5.6).

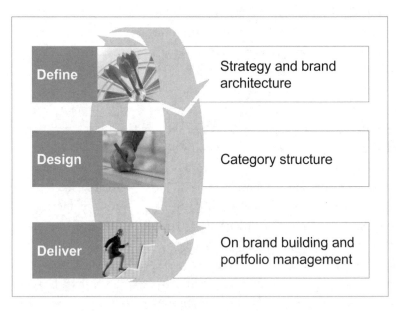

Exhibit 5.6 '3D' approach to PL management: our approach.

- Define brand strategy and brand architecture for PL based on strategic objectives.
- Design category structure: identify the most relevant categories for profitable PL growth.
- Deliver on brand building and portfolio management: build capabilities for excellent implementation.

As the foundation of sustainable PL success, retailers need to define their PL strategy, *particularly an appropriate price and brand architecture*

Successful PL management starts with the definition of the right price tier derived from your strategic intent when launching or extending a PL range. The introduction of a first-generation value range, for example, will help retailers to defend their volume against discounters, whereas the launch of a premium PL range might help to attract previously inaccessible customer groups, drive competitive differentiation and help build customer loyalty. In any case, the purpose and proposition of the PL should reflect your overall strategy.

Once the proposition for the PL range is spelt out, the right branding for this range needs to be defined in the context of your overall PL brand architecture. There are two different basic PL branding strategies, with a range of hybrid strategies in between.

Umbrella brand strategy

The umbrella brand name, often the retail brand itself, is also used as a private label brand name, sometimes with a supplement or a descriptive attribute that explains the sub-brands. The value proposition and image of the umbrella brand is, thereby, transferred to the private label products. The entire brand portfolio profits from the umbrella brand's credibility and sympathy. Umbrella branding offers clear efficiency benefits, e.g. because of communication spill-over effects. In this strategy, the product brand influences the umbrella brand and vice versa. Therefore, umbrella branding is recommended if you have a strong umbrella brand with a positioning that is relevant in the chosen PL product segments. The key challenge results from the fact that the umbrella brand is usually positioned quite broadly without addressing the specific purchase drivers of individual product categories. Tesco is perhaps the most prominent proponent of umbrella branding: they have 'Tesco' on all their PL brands. Only recently have they launched a discount range with no reference to the Tesco brand. Many other retailers use their retail brand as the umbrella brand for their third- and fourth-generation PL ranges, but use a different brand for their value range to protect the retail brand from any 'discount' associations. Albert Heijn follows a similar strategy with 'Euroshopper' as their price entry range and Albert Heijn branded products in higher price tiers.

Individual brand strategy

In this strategy, each brand in the PL portfolio is autonomous in terms of its brand message. Individual PL brands shape the image of the retail brand only indirectly, e.g. through their product value proposition and positioning, depending on how much transparency consumers have about the link between the PL brands and the retail brand. Aldi and Lidl are prominent examples of this strategy, given their portfolios of stand-alone PL product brands that are not connected to the respective store brands. Individual PL brands are particularly useful for market segments in which the umbrella brand carries no discernible benefits that are relevant to consumers. This strategy is also suitable for niches where it is crucial to avoid any association with the retail brand. While individual brands allow for greater differentiation, they are less efficient in terms of communication.

To select the most promising SKUs for a given PL effort, *it is imperative to design the category structure with a profitable growth mindset*

Besides the right branding, retailers need to identify the product categories in which PL will drive profitable growth. This is done by way of a category-by-category assessment based on economic criteria, especially volume and margin potential. For more differentiated niche efforts, such as organic or children's private labels, growth or profit potential in a specific target group might serve as additional criteria. Especially for first-, second- and third-generation private labels, volume is the most important success factor because of its direct impact on costs and sourcing flexibility. As demonstrated by the brand relevance study quoted above, PL consumer acceptance is generally higher in commoditized market segments. However, in highly commoditized markets, the margin potential may be limited, making volume even more important. The more manufacturers of A brands spend on marketing and distribution, the higher the margin potential for retailers through backward value chain integration. But in categories or markets with high brand relevance, it often also takes higher price discounts to drive penetration. This makes it difficult to hit exactly the right price points for a given PL effort. The retailer's challenge is to find the sweet spot between volume and margin potential.

To capture the full benefit of PL, *retailers need to match the sourcing, manufacturing and marketing capabilities of brand manufacturers*

The more PL brands become 'real' brands, the more retailers find themselves in direct competition with brand manufacturers. At the same time, PL management is very different from the purchasing of manufacturer brands. Retailers need to optimize the value chain all the way back to product specification and production. In the case of first- and second-generation PL, low-cost sourcing is the main additional success factor. But third- and fourth-generation PL ranges take retailers much closer to consumer goods companies in terms of tasks and necessary capabilities, e.g. regarding the specification of products, supplier selection, quality control and brand building. Fourth-generation PL brands, in particular, require extra attention to product development and innovation abilities since these brands are differentiated through the novelty of products, excellent quality and strong value propositions for selected target groups.

While end-to-end management of the value chain is a new challenge for most retailers, they also hold a fundamental advantage over consumer goods companies. Successful PL management requires a deep understanding of consumer behaviour, and retailers usually have the best data because of their direct customer relationships. While consumer goods manufacturers will have to conduct costly market research to investigate consumer needs, retailers can simply tap into their pool of transaction and loyalty data.

But retail's structural advantage doesn't stop at shopper insights. Direct customer contact also holds opportunities for higher marketing efficiency. In recent years, it has become more and more difficult and expensive for manufacturers to reach broad consumer groups with their brand messages due to heavy media fragmentation and competitive noise. Retailers, however, own the point of sale and can leverage it as a key element of their marketing mix. This enables them to reach out and touch their customers every day – a valuable competitive advantage in communication.

The overarching strategic challenge for retailers is to stay on top of category management and ensure consumers find a healthy mix of PL and relevant manufacturer brands in their stores. Yet, complex as it may seem, PL is definitely worth the effort for retailers. According to a joint study by AC Nielsen and McKinsey & Company, retailers with above-average PL shares stand out from their peers in terms of market share and customer loyalty. Usually, they also achieve higher profit margins. So don't hesitate to reclaim some of the shelves in your store for your own brands!

Key takeaways – Private label branding

1 Private labels are here to stay: their share is growing across countries, sales channels and product categories.

2 PL has evolved beyond its origins in generic products and value segments. The most recent PL generation is even venturing into the premium segment.

3 As the foundation of sustainable PL success, retailers need to define their PL strategy, particularly the appropriate price and brand architecture.

4 To select the most promising SKUs for a given PL effort, it is imperative to design the category structure with a profitable growth mindset.

5 To capture the full benefit of PL, retailers need to match the sourcing, manufacturing and marketing capabilities of brand manufacturers.

Part II

Optimizing Marketing ROI

CHAPTER 6

Nicolai Johannsen, Lars Köster, Thomas Meyer

'Money changes everything.' At least that is what Cyndi Lauper says, and most people would agree she knows a thing or two about marketing, or self-promotion at any rate. But how much money do you need to change the world of retail marketing and make customers swing your way? It's the million dollar question – quite literally.

Once a retailer's brand strategy is in place, it is time for the CMO and the CFO to talk dollars and cents. While there may be no single algorithm to calculate the optimal marketing budget, we firmly believe that you will get to a robust and realistic figure by combining three proven perspectives:

- outside-in competitive benchmarking
- inside-out budgeting based on marketing objectives
- efficiency modelling, used as a 'sanity check'.

In this chapter, we will discuss these multiple perspectives, as well as the starting point of any sound budget-sizing effort: transparency creation.

Marketing budget sizing is the million dollar question: *it calls for a systematic and comprehensive, yet pragmatic, approach*

In February 2008 consumer electronics retailer Media Saturn embarked on a radical experiment. For an entire month the company – one of Germany's top advertising spenders – cut their ad spend by 60 percent. It was a top management decision, simply to see what would happen. Revenues dropped massively, leaving store managers disappointed at what they felt, in essence, was a corporate betrayal. As they saw their revenue-based bonuses falter, store managers' motivation plunged to an all-time low. (Source; *Lebensmittelzeitung* 12, 20 March 2008.) Simply speaking, Media Saturn proved Cyndi Lauper right: money *does* change everything. Case closed?

Not quite. While the experiment substantiated the direct sales impact of advertising, it still does not say very much about the appropriate budget level; 40 percent of the current budget may be too little, but how much is enough? Not unlike Media Saturn, many retailers look to the past when defining the overall level of their next year's marketing budget. They start with their current budget and make a few adjustments for inflation, major events in the marketplace, changes in cost or shifting priorities according to their own marketing strategy. This pragmatic approach is familiar, and with good reason. It contains several key elements of best-practice budgeting: experience, market dynamics and a glimpse of the future. Yet we believe it is worth the retailer's while to take a somewhat more systematic approach – without becoming excessively analytical.

Cause-and-effect relationships between marketing spend and market success are notoriously difficult to establish, simply because of the wide variety of influencing factors. In June, you may spend at just the right level, but what good does it do if you are a sports goods retailer and June happens to be rainiest month in recorded history? In July, you duly ramp up your spend to promote indoor sports with an award-winning campaign, but it is no match for your key competitor's drastic discounts. August would have been the month of a major co-marketing effort with your biggest vendor, but as it happened, they came under pressure from the financial markets and so slashed their marketing budget to boost the bottom line. And so on.

In light of this complexity, no budgeting tool or algorithm can calculate your budget level at the push of a button. What we propose instead is a systematic, yet pragmatic, approach that starts with transparency creation and moves on to combine three perspectives on overall budget size.

Transparency is key: *conduct a comprehensive budget stock-take to capture the current budget, its components and its organizational owners*

It sounds simple, but in reality it is not: it can be a major challenge for retailers to find out how much they are currently spending. Marketing activities are often managed and accounted for in different parts of the organization: international media planning is in charge of classical advertising, the new media taskforce oversees the company's homepage and PR expenditure is part of the board's proprietary budget. Co-op campaigns are partly funded by vendors and may not be considered as part of the marketing budget at all. A substantial share of the total budget, especially funds for local advertising, can also be hidden in the P&L of local subsidiaries or franchise partners. Yet all these activities affect a retailer's target audience in some way or another, and they all contribute, or fail to contribute, to overall marketing objectives.

So before even looking at the various perspectives on budget sizing, the first step is to compile a comprehensive list of the individual positions in the current marketing budget. Of course the actual number, granularity and naming of these positions will vary from company to company. Conceptually, the marketing budget stock-take should comprise all the investments that are made to move current and potential customers through the purchase funnel from 'awareness and consideration' to 'repeat purchase and loyalty'. For many retailers, classical advertising may be a comparatively small share of the total marketing budget compared to important below-the-line activities such as POS and direct marketing. Any comprehensively defined marketing budget should also account for indirect costs such as agency fees and production costs.

To establish a customer-centric mindset, we recommend making customer touch points the primary dimension for creating budgetary transparency. Ideally, investments should be split according to where and how they reach a retailer's audience: on TV, in newspaper print ads or leaflets, in the store, in the form of an addressed direct mailing, or as part of the retailer's reward scheme or loyalty programme. This kind of split helps the retailer to take a consumer perspective, instead of worrying about budget ownership and organizational responsibility, which may or may not reflect consumer needs. But keep in mind that costs incurred at the same touch point may be split between multiple departments.

For example, a retail company's corporate website may be co-funded by IT, PR, marketing and various other departments. Some activities may not be treated as marketing cost positions at all: sales stimulation campaigns directly funded by vendor allowances can sometimes be managed as profit centres in their own right.

Once you have a basic overview of how much is spent at the various touch points, it is often helpful to add the purchase funnel stage as a secondary dimension. Is the investment made to create awareness, to drive consideration, to increase basket size or to foster customer loyalty? Experience shows that the intended purchase funnel impact of a given investment is often hard to define, especially for long-term activities such as co-branding efforts or sponsorships, since sponsorship is often not handled by the marketing department at all and may be out of bounds for the annual budget review for historical or contractual reasons – or simply because it is a board member's pet project. Yet these 'forgotten investments' either strengthen or weaken the brand, and should thus be included in the initial budget stock-take.

Budget transparency creation

The larger and more complex your organization, the more difficult it is to get hold of comprehensive and reliable marketing spend data. Gathering details on all investments and the corresponding communication objectives can take several weeks – but the effort is worth it. In the end, it not only creates transparency about the current budget and its components but can also trigger debate among executives about meaningful allocation keys, appropriate organizational accountability and effective reporting lines.

Use outside-in competitive benchmarking
to determine the share of voice required to cut through the clutter in your competitive arena

A retailer's marketing activities never take place in a void. They compete with competitors' activities for customer attention. In a noisy environment, it is important for the retailer's own tune to be heard above the general hubbub.

Perhaps the most common indicator of the relative marketing intensity is marketing expenditure as a percentage of sales. This metric varies greatly by segment and country, but it is a quick and easy way of determining whether you are spending within a healthy range. Take Scandinavian grocery retailers, for example: they spend 0.7 percent to 2.5 percent of their sales revenues on marketing (ATL and BTL). A retailer would need good reason to spend significantly below or above this range; such reasons might include the need to drive short-term profitability or long-term growth.

Marketing as a percentage of sales is a highly aggregated figure. Plotting the share of voice versus the share of market (or sales) is usually a more insightful basis for competitive benchmarking. This kind of analysis reveals that the 'fair share of advertising' is by no means a linear function of revenue. Rather, smaller players have to set aside a higher proportion of their sales for marketing in order to get noticed, while bigger players can afford to spend less (see Exhibit 6.1 for a disguised example). In this case, the retailer in question was able to cut its share of voice without compromising market share. When conducting this kind of analysis, be careful to include only companies you consider to be competitors according to your definition of the relevant market. Separate analyses may be required for different countries or even for different categories.

Note that the share of voice (y axis) of Exhibit 6.1 reflects only gross media buy; this is mostly traditional advertising spend. To derive an apples-and-apples comparison of marketing pressure, the share of voice analysis should also cover BTL positions such as leaflets and direct mail. While you will usually know your own BTL expenditure, information on competitors' BTL spend is often hard to obtain. However, providers of advertising data such as AC Nielsen and Thomsen have started to track non-traditional media, and benchmarks for ATL/BTL ratios are starting to emerge in many categories. Alternatively, it is possible to approximate BTL spend by deducting the observed ATL spend from the total marketing expenditure as given in competitors' annual reports.

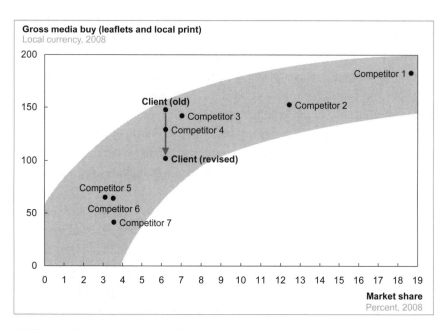

Exhibit 6.1 Share of voice versus share of market scatter plot (European grocery retailer).

Reported ad spend versus actual media cost

Note that advertising tracking agencies such as AC Nielsen report *gross* media spend rather than the advertiser's cash-out expenditure. Gross media spend is calculated by multiplying observed advertising pressure, e.g. number of prime-time 30-second TVCs, with ratecard prices as published by media owners. But media owners grant substantial discounts on these gross prices to media agencies and advertisers, sometimes by as much as 50 percent – or even more. In effect, 100 'observed' advertising dollars might actually have cost the advertiser only 50 dollars. Recognizing these rebates is of particular importance when you combine marketing spend data from multiple sources, e.g. using ad tracking data for some parts of the marketing budget and internal data for other parts.

Employ inside-out budgeting based on marketing objectives *to estimate the investment needed to advance customers on their purchase journey*

Your budget level should be high enough to get you noticed in the market-place but it should also reflect what you are trying to achieve. In light of the differences in marketing strategy and overall business targets, competitive benchmarking alone is insufficient to determine the appropriate budget level. Take the example of US retail: while some players spend less than 1 percent of sales on advertising, others spend up to 5 percent. These variations indicate differences in overall growth ambition, as well as different operational market-ing objectives.

Assume a given retailer is trying to build brand awareness for a new product. Once you know the structure and size of your target group (e.g. all female shoppers in the greater Los Angeles area aged 15–35) and the quantified awareness goal (e.g. 60 percent unaided advertising recall), media agencies can employ so-called Morgenzstern curves to help you calculate the required GRPs (gross rating points) and, subsequently, marketing investments. Most retailers will want to reiterate this process for the multiple objectives they are seeking to achieve in a given year, and then total up the sum of individual investments to arrive at an overall budget figure.

In general, larger companies – or those highly focused on profitability – will spend below their segment's average. In contrast, small players – and compa-nies with extraordinary growth ambition – may decide to outspend the market. This is, for example, what German consumer goods giant Media Saturn did both prior to and after their fateful budget-cut experiment in 2008. In 2009, their share of voice was a remarkable 85 percent in their category, more than four times their share of market at that time. Media Saturn's market share increased to 19.7 percent in 2009, up from 17.8 percent in 2007 – but the jury is still out on whether this growth is sufficiently sustainable to offset their massive marketing investment.

Engage in efficiency modelling, correlating marketing spend with impact *to conduct a sanity check on the efficiency of the overall budget level*

Your competitors might be going overboard in their advertising spend and your ambitious growth targets may also warrant massive investments – but budget sizing isn't only about spending enough. It's also about not spending too much. Even if both outside-in benchmarking and inside-out budgeting lead you to believe a very high marketing investment is required, the figure you arrive at may actually be beyond the efficient range. For example, according to the disguised case in Exhibit 6.2, the marginal utility of additional spend decreases dramatically beyond USD 45 million. Further spending will theoretically yield some gains, but in excess of this point they will be of little practical benefit. Once you reach a certain household penetration, or a certain number of contacts in a given period of time, additional activation simply adds less and less value.

Media agencies conduct s-curve analyses to determine both the lower threshold ('minimum spend') and the upper threshold ('saturation level') of efficient marketing spend. Also see Chapter 10: 'Marketing Mix Modelling' for

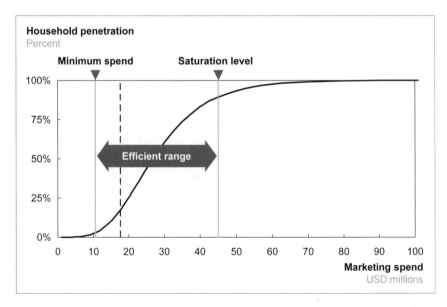

Exhibit 6.2 Marketing spend saturation curve.

further details on how response curves can be used to optimize the allocation of advertising funds.

Combine benchmarking, objective-based budgeting and efficiency modelling *to derive a realistic budget level estimate – refine as needed*

Each of the three perspectives described above – outside-in benchmarking, objective-based budgeting and efficiency modelling – provides you with a number or, more commonly, a budget range. Typically, these ranges show a fair amount of overlap. To take a fictitious example, a given retail company may have to spend EUR 100–120 million to achieve a share of voice in line with their market share and growth ambition. Further assume that to support their purchase funnel objectives, they would need to spend EUR 90–110 million according to their media agency's estimate of required GRPs. Their impact sanity check, however, revealed that the range of efficient spend spanned from EUR 50 million to EUR 100 million. Combining these three perspectives enabled them to arrive at a budget level of EUR 100 million. Exhibit 6.3 shows a visualization of this example.

So you need EUR 100 million. That's it? Not quite. The common ground defined by the overlap of the ranges determined by the three perspectives is only the starting point of budget sizing. On their way from this first estimate to the final cash-out budget, retailers will want to check on the following five issues.

- *BTL spend*: if you have only considered ATL thus far, be it for reasons of data availability or urgency, make sure to set aside funds for BTL activities as well. Even if there is no benchmarking data, the direct and POS marketing plan should provide a good sense of the required budget.
- *Indirect costs*: activation spend is wasted unless there is something worth activating. Make sure to include creative agency fees and production costs, as well as expenditure for testing and research.
- *Third-party contributions*: while BTL spend and indirect cost *increase* the cash-out required to reach the desired effective gross marketing spend,

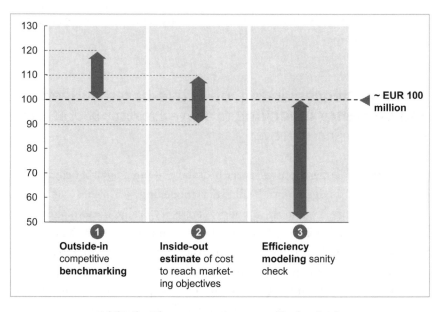

Exhibit 6.3 Three perspectives on total budget level.

co-funding may help to *decrease* it. Be sure to recognize rebates from media owners and agencies, as well as vendor allowances for co-op marketing.

- *Tactical considerations*: while simply matching competitors' activities is usually an inefficient use of marketing funds, spending 'against the trend' can prove a very successful tactic, especially when money is tight and everyone else is cutting their budgets. According to a Credit Suisse study, companies that maintained their spend levels during the 2008/09 recession consistently outperformed their peers in the stock markets in the subsequent 12-month period. Smart retailers may want to zig when others zag.
- *Special circumstances, constraints or unforeseen events*: anything from new market entry and temporary cash-flow bottlenecks to disruptive competitor moves and understaffed marketing departments may necessitate 'manual' adjustments to the budget level, as indicated by the combination of the three perspectives.

Budget sizing, as described in this chapter, is neither an automated process nor a black box. Rather, it is a systematic approach that is based on explicit assumptions, employs transparent criteria and allows for manual adjustments. Much of its value resides in the open and rational debate it will trigger among executives. To stay on top of changes in consumer behaviour, the competitive environment and their own marketing strategy, retailers will in any case wish to review their budgeting approach at least once a year. And at all times, they will want to make sure their budget is a function of their objectives, not vice versa. If they do so, money might not change everything, but it *will* make a big difference.

Key takeaways – Budget sizing

1 Marketing budget sizing is the million dollar question: it calls for a systematic and comprehensive, yet pragmatic, approach.
2 Transparency is key: conduct a comprehensive budget stock-take to capture the current budget, its components and its organizational owners.
3 Use outside-in competitive benchmarking to determine the share of voice required to cut through the clutter in your competitive arena.
4 Employ inside-out budgeting based on marketing objectives to estimate the investment needed to advance customers on their purchase journey.
5 Engage in efficiency modelling, correlating marketing spend with impact to conduct a sanity check on the efficiency of the overall budget level.
6 Combine benchmarking, objective-based budgeting and efficiency modelling to derive a realistic budget level estimate – refine as needed.

CHAPTER 7

Thomas Bauer, Ingeborg Hegstad

In the previous chapter (Chapter 6: 'Budget sizing: the million dollar question') we looked at how to create budget transparency and how to size the budget according to the marketing objectives, business opportunities and competitive benchmarks. In this chapter we introduce proven approaches and tools for allocating the budget to the various spending units.

The chapter is designed to answer key questions about allocation:

- How much should you spend on a given country, region or store – and why?
- How granular does the allocation logic need to be?
- How do you account for unforeseen events?

The chapter addresses such topics as whether to make decisions centrally or locally, how to define the right size of units for your investments and how to create transparency. To help retailers derive or optimize their actual budget split, we also discuss the definition of allocation criteria, criteria weights and spending thresholds.

Find the right decision mode: *deciding centrally or convincing locally*

Many retailers plan their marketing activities by reviewing their activity plans from previous years and then apply adjustments to the plan to account for any changes that have taken place in the intervening period. The types of change that can warrant such a budgetary adjustment include competitors' moves, new insights from market research, fresh input from media agencies regarding media trends – or simply changes in costs for specific activities.

Our experience is that you are unlikely to make big mistakes with this 'last year +/– x' method. If it worked last year, why change it? In the words of Sir Alf Ramsey, manager of the English national soccer team at the time of their triumph during the 1966 World Cup: 'Never change a winning team.' But if marketers follow Sir Alf's advice to the letter, they are likely to miss out on certain market opportunities.

To take one example: a retailer that has always invested in billboard advertising near to its stores to promote special offers and deals. Now, for some reason or other, the cost of billboard advertising has increased dramatically. Applying the 'last year +/– x' approach, the retailer's reaction would be to increase the billboard budget accordingly; however, this will be at the expense of other media and new advertising opportunities. The flaw in this, clearly, is that the resulting budget allocation, because it is driven by historical patterns, could miss the newer and emerging chances to win – like, for example, free newspapers, social media or search-engine marketing. The challenge for marketing managers is to find these pockets of opportunity, compile winning arguments for the budgeting discussion and convince top management to re-allocate funds from established vehicles to the latest and greatest opportunities for maximizing marketing ROI.

According to a recent McKinsey survey of marketing practitioners, in general, high-performing companies prefer a top-down approach to defining their marketing budget. When they encounter any prioritization conflicts, more than two-thirds of the most successful companies look to their CMO, or most senior marketing executive, for resolution. For these companies, this clear top-down budget allocation and prioritization process, led by top management, is a key success factor.

Sticking to this rule is easy if marketing decision power resides centrally: i.e. the CMO decides what to spend – and how to spend it. But things get more complicated in companies where there is a high level of local decision-making power, a feature of many retail organizations. Local P&L accountability usually means that marketing budget allocation is also done at the local level. The same goes for franchise business models, at least for all budget positions other than classical advertising. In these cases, the responsibility of the CMO at corporate headquarters is limited to international or cross-regional brand building activities. But many local marketers even want their say when it comes to brand image campaigns. It is often up to them to support corporate efforts with local activities of their own, e.g. with leaflets, billboards and local newspaper advertising. Such local power makes top-down allocation decisions almost impossible.

Yet there are ways to make sure centrally devised allocation principles are applied consistently across countries and regions, even for the share of the budget that is technically out of central control. For example, the CMO can hand the results of a central prioritization effort to regional managers as a decision-making support. Alternatively, the central marketing function can act as a coordinator for local prioritization efforts. In either case, headquarters needs to convince every regional marketing team that it is in their best interests to apply centrally developed tools and guidelines to their budget allocation process – an exercise that can prove challenging for both parties.

Budgeting prioritization is usually a *four-step process*:

1 Define the right investment units.
2 Create full transparency on spend per investment unit.
3 Define the prioritization criteria and weights.
4 Prioritize your marketing investments.

Define the right investment units: *go granular and find the pockets of growth*

Once the overall budgeting responsibilities are understood or clarified, retailers have to determine the appropriate budgetary allocation between investment units. By 'investment units' we mean the positions, or clusters of positions, into which the budget is split for allocation and tracking purposes. There are several well-established dimensions and levels at which marketing spend can be allocated and tracked (Exhibit 7.1). The appropriate level of granularity depends on the given company organization and structure. But whatever the specific characteristics, the basic trade-offs remains the same: while higher granularity promises additional insights and more targeted spending, it also brings additional complexity for data gathering and marketing management.

In retail, the most common split is by geography and format, i.e. the budget is allocated by region, county or city and for a specific format, e.g. hypermarkets. In non-food retail, assortment category and/or brand(s) are equally important investment units, reflecting the 'halo' effect that certain known-value items, categories or brands have for consumers. At the most granular level of the individual store, all three dimensions – geography, category and format – converge. This gives rise to two crucial questions confronting every allocation: how much should a given store (of a specific format) spend in total, and which categories or products should get the biggest slice of the pie?

To determine the appropriate level of granularity that should be used in the budget prioritization, the retailer will need to establish which of its spending units, or groups of spending units, are sufficiently homogeneous to justify a unified approach – as opposed to those units that are sufficiently different from each other to warrant customized solutions.

When determining the appropriate geographical cut, you will first need to answer a series of questions:

- Are there local differences in the competitive landscape?
- Do consumer preferences differ from region to region?
- Is there a higher growth ambition in certain regions?

In cases where there are major local or regional differences, it makes sense to break down the budget accordingly, so as to be able to adjust its allocation to local requirements. Retailers will need to answer similar sets of questions for each of the other dimensions, for assortment categories, brands, store formats and channels.

The budgeting mill grinds slowly, but it grinds exceedingly fine

High budgeting granularity promises targeted marketing investment. But sometimes a very detailed budget breakdown will create more work than added value. For example, if a retailer does not have detailed information on its regional markets, such as the share of voice or growth rates, then there is no point in differentiating the budget for these regions. Similarly, a highly granular budget allocation is not likely to be worthwhile if the retailer does not have the operational means and processes to derive true value from it. For example, it makes no sense to determine the budget for 300 Italian fashion retail outlets at the individual store level if there is no communication plan in place to make sure these funds are used to the benefit of the individual stores.

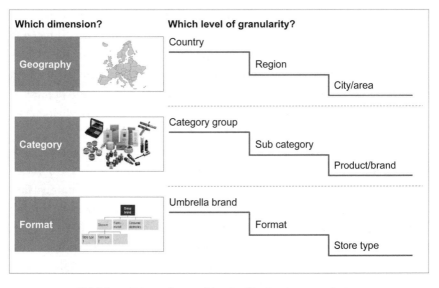

Exhibit 7.1 Dimensions and levels of budgeting granularity.

Create full transparency: *understand where the money goes*

It's one thing to make a conscious choice to stick to historical budgets and allocation keys. It's another thing to be in ignorance of how much you actually spend in the various units. As mentioned in Chapter 6, as much as 20–50 percent of all marketing cost is incurred below the radar of marketing executives, often at the regional or local level, or in departments other than marketing.

There are many reasons for this lack of transparency. In the case of decentralized spending, it is not easy for corporate headquarters to keep track of all that goes on at the local level. In the case of central spending, sometimes costs are not allocated to the units that actually benefit from it. In other cases, central spend is accounted for in central departments outside marketing, e.g. in separate online, CRM, communication or commercial units. Take, for example, the case of POS marketing material designed and commissioned centrally: this can be requested by regional managers according to their demand; often, the central marketing department does not keep track of how much is ordered by region. Reporting back to headquarters about which stores actually used the material is often the last thing on a general manager's mind. This is just one example; the same issues apply to many forms of local advertising, such as leaflets, billboards, radio, local print advertisements or consumer events. In total, these local touch points can account for more than 50 percent of marketing spend of retailers (see Chapter 13: 'Leaflets and local print advertising: how to achieve local media excellence' for further details).

To challenge current spend levels, you need to know how much you currently spend and be able to relate this expense to your business development. But to achieve this level of transparency at the chosen level of granularity takes dedicated effort, often involving substantial data mining. Yet most retailers that do carry out such an exercise find it well worth their while. True transparency often reveals quite a few surprises – as well as ideas for immediate improvements, both in terms of budget allocation and in organizational accountability.

Once there is full budget transparency, retailers need to decide which part of the total budget should be made available for the actual allocation process (Exhibit 7.2). Though certain central activities, such as training or agency fees,

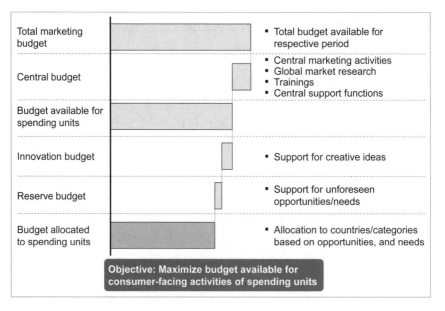

Exhibit 7.2 Key elements of marketing budget structure.

may not be consumer facing, they are nevertheless key enablers of consumer communication. For details on purchasing and non-working costs, please see Chapter 17: 'Smart sourcing'.

Keeping it flexible

Certain retailers, though they allocate the bulk of their budget to the spending units at the beginning of the year, hold back a fraction as a central 'opportunity budget' in order to ensure short-term flexibility. One international company, for instance, has introduced an internal 'innovative communication challenge', in which it asks its national marketing heads to provide creative ideas for direct marketing activities. The best three ideas are rewarded with their share of the 'innovation budget' that has been held back in the initial budgeting round. Competitions like this come with a double benefit. They encourage executives to weigh the costs and benefits of specific activities carefully, and they encourage marketing departments to try out new and innovative media formats that might otherwise not find their way into the marketing plan.

Define the prioritization criteria and weights *based on what really matters in your budgeting decisions*

Once you have determined the total budget, chosen the granularity of the investment units and finalized the budget structure, the next step is to decide upon the criteria by which the budget will be allocated to the investment units. For want of a more systematic approach, many companies take a percentage of sales or use similar allocation keys to make this allocation.

The main challenge in making the allocation is to ensure that the criteria used support the overall business objectives of the company. For example, if the ambition of the retailer is to grow sales in a few selected regions while maintaining current sales levels in all others, it would make sense to use regional growth targets, or budgeted revenue, as the allocation criteria. If, in addition, a number of local markets are planning new store openings, another meaningful factor might be the number of new stores per market. As a rule of thumb, the greater the business complexity, the greater the number of criteria required; in all cases, however, a weighted average should be used as the ultimate allocation key.

The most common allocation key is revenue per format, region or store. In general, this makes a lot of sense; its weakness is that it does not take into account relative competitive intensity or specific local opportunities. Because of such factors, it may make sense to fine tune investment manually. A region with high market share (and high store density) typically needs less marketing support to be visible in the market place than a region where the retailer has a low market share. Pia Marthinsen Mellbye, Head of Marketing at ICA Norway, says, 'When looking at revenue per region and linking it back to marketing spend, it became clear that we over-invested in regions with high market share and under-invested in regions with low market share. This wasn't in line with our growth ambitions for some of these regions. So we made adjustments, primarily by defining regional budgets with leeway for local media in some of the regions.' As a result of this optimization, ICA achieved budget savings of the order of 15 percent and was able to re-align its marketing spend with its business goals. For further details, see the interview later in this chapter.

In order to pick the right budget allocation criteria, it is critical for the marketing department to have a deep understanding of the company's business objectives:

- What is the long-term goal of the company, and what is its store portfolio?
- Does the company aspire to expand in a certain region?
- Have new competitors entered the marketplace?
- What are the implications for sales stimulation activities and brand building?

Best-practice retailers make life a lot easier for the marketing department by disaggregating their business objectives by country, format and region. Among the well-established metrics for marketing investment decisions are: sales, sales growth, sales growth versus market rate (share gain), market share,

	Criteria	Operationalization (example)
Financial	• Revenue	• Net revenues of business unit by region
	• Revenue growth	• Net revenue growth of business unit by region
	• Gross profit on sales	• Net revenue minus cost of goods sold by business unit by region
	• Gross profit growth	• Delta net revenue minus cost of goods sold of business unit by region
Strategic	• Growth opportunity	• Market size not captured in EUR, e.g., (1 – market share) x factor addressable share (considering local competition)
	• Industry competition	• Brand building and promotional spend of competitors
	• Relative individual growth	• Company or segment growth (e.g., discount) of business unit in region
Marketing-oriented	• Marketing cost factor	• E.g., local cost for typical marketing basket
	• Brand status	• Brand awareness according to market research
	• Event communication	• Store openings, etc.

Exhibit 7.3 List of potential criteria for budget prioritization.

profitability, competitive intensity (e.g. measured as competitor ad spend, or share of voice, in a given segment or area) and media cost (see Exhibit 7.3).

But even when a set of relevant criteria have been agreed upon there is still room for error. Often, there is no common understanding of how a specific metric is or should be defined. Take growth ambition: most marketing managers will agree that units with more ambitious targets will need and deserve more funds. But what is growth ambition? Is it percentage revenue growth? Using this metric would lead to a bias towards those units with low current sales levels. Alternatively, is it the absolute growth in EUR or USD? No matter how high this amount, the level of growth could still be at or even below market growth – which should not justify extra funds. So in this case, absolute growth above market level, or above market share gain, would be the best choice. This is just one example that shows how different interpretations of the same metric can lead to fundamentally different budgeting decisions.

Ranges to be discussed between countries and headquarters		Financial			Strategic		Marketing-oriented	
Weighting options	Budgeting objectives	Sales	Profit contribution	Long term growth opportunity	Relative growth plan	Events	Competitive intensity
Ⓐ Maintenance orientation	Strengthen current "sales stars"	20 - 40	20 - 40	5 - 15	5 - 15	5 - 15	5 - 15
Ⓑ Growth/ portfolio orientation	Expand growth areas	5 - 20	5 - 15	10 - 20	20 - 30	10 - 20	5 - 10
Ⓒ Competition orientation	Match competitive situation	5 - 15	5 - 15	5 - 15	5 - 15	20 - 40	20 - 40

Exhibit 7.4 Weighting of criteria according to strategic focus (percent).

Once there is a shared understanding of which criteria should inform the prioritization, the relative importance of these criteria can be defined. Exhibit 7.4 provides a simplified overview of the different strategic options. The basic choice is whether to focus on stability or growth. If the primary objective is to defend current sales, the greatest weight should be given to past or current sales as allocation criteria. If the primary objective is growth, greater weight should be attributed to growth targets or metrics capturing opportunity, e.g. the size of the market not yet captured.

In addition to the weighting of allocation criteria, spend thresholds need to be defined for the different investment units. Thresholds fulfil several roles. They can create leeway for tactical or strategic investments beyond mere financial objectives. An example would be allowing a greater budget than would be indicated by the pre-defined criteria in cases such as, for instance, where there is a strategic directive to attack a certain competitor in a certain market. Also, a threshold can act as an emergency cap. If, for example, the predefined criteria indicate that a substantial investment increase should be made in an emerging market, but the marketing team in that particular country is unlikely to be in a position to handle the additional funds effectively – because, for example, it is still in the process of being set up – a temporary budget threshold could help prevent the company from wasting its money.

Avoid automatic decisions: *prioritize your marketing investment in the light of the full facts*

All the subjects we have talked of so far in this chapter – top-down budget making, the selection of budgeting units, the assessment of current spend, the choice of decision criteria, weights and thresholds – need to be combined and integrated to derive a robust allocation recommendation. Best-practice retailers use a scoring model to create full transparency regarding the reasons behind the proposed reallocations (Exhibit 7.5).

By all means, avoid 'black boxes'. Full transparency about the reallocation rationale is essential, especially to secure the support of stakeholders who are

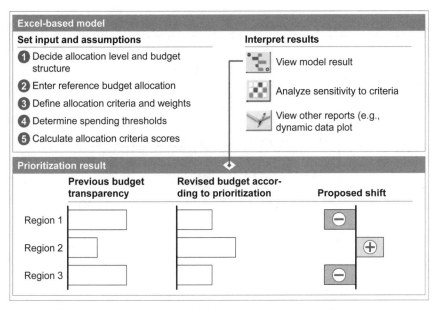

Exhibit 7.5 An easy-to-use model helps to derive a prioritization proposal.

at the receiving end of proposed budget cuts. To make the reasons for reallocations even more tangible, leading retailers use sensitivity maps that detail the
criteria used to shape the decisions about whether an investment unit should
lose or gain funds compared to the status quo (Exhibit 7.6).

To make sure such prioritization tools are easy to use, their design should
allow for convenient changes to the input factors (e.g. in terms of the total
budget, the criteria, weights or thresholds being used). Once the tool is in place,
it can even be used 'live' in decision-making meetings in order, for instance, to
illustrate the sensitivity of the allocation to particular changes in the input factors. Its use can make the relative impact of the different factors on the actual
allocation recommendations more tangible and transparent. Like every piece
of software, however, the effectiveness of such a prioritization tool will depend
on the quality and validity of the data it is based upon. In any case, its purpose
is not to replace executive decision-making about budgetary allocations, but to
inform it.

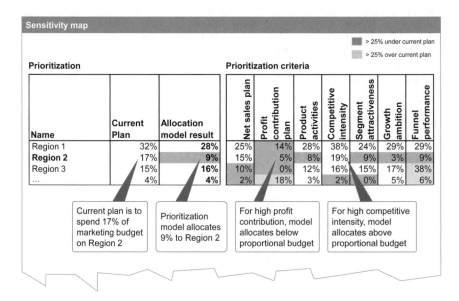

Exhibit 7.6 Sensitivity maps help to explain the re-allocation rationale.

Interview: Pia Marthinsen Mellbye
Chief Marketing Officer, ICA AB

ICA AB is one of the Northern Europe's leading grocery retailers. They have some 2200 stores in Sweden, Norway and the Baltic countries, some of which are operated under franchise agreements. Pia Marthinsen Mellbye is ICA's Chief Marketing Officer.

Pia Marthinsen Mellbye talked to Ingeborg Molden Hegstad, a retail marketing expert at McKinsey & Company, about ICA's approach to marketing budget sizing, budget allocation and marketing message definition.

Q: What was your traditional approach to budget sizing like?

Pia Mellbye: The budget was set based on last year's spend levels, adjusted for inflation and changes in the market place. For example, if we spent EUR 10 million on one of our formats last year, we would increase the amount by 2 percent to compensate for inflation. On top of this, we typically made changes to the budget based on a qualitative assessment of the implications of competitors' moves, such as store openings or seasonal campaigns.

Q: Why did you change the budgeting process?

Pia Mellbye: At the time, the company was in a challenging situation, losing market shares and showing low profitability. In addition, our two brands were in a transition phase. The CEO asked me to review our marketing spend to see whether there were any efficiency and effectiveness opportunities. We initiated a project to take a more systematic approach to managing the return on marketing investment.

Q: How did you go about it?

Pia Mellbye: First of all, we created spend transparency. Once we started digging, we found that there was quite a big amount of marketing spend incurred outside marketing, e.g. in the communications department, in the commercial unit and in local stores. In total, this amounted to more than 20 percent of the marketing budget. This was due to the business model we had in the company, with multiple profit centres, and the fact that some of the marketing spend vanished in the accounting process because it was offset by marketing funds we receive from suppliers. This made it extremely difficult for the marketing department to have a full overview.

Q: What were the benefits of transparency creation?

Pia Mellbye: Even at the surface level, it was clear we would have to make some changes to the budget. The biggest change was to move accountability for all spend to the marketing department. Also, we started treating marketing activities as true investments. Separating our investments from suppliers' funds enabled the company to optimize the marketing plan according to what is best for the company, not the suppliers.

Q: How did you define the total level of the budget?

Pia Mellbye: We implemented a systematic approach, relating the marketing budget to revenue and comparing our 'share of voice/share of market' ratio with that of competitors to understand the spending levels in the market. This benchmarking analysis confirmed our hypotheses about the market, e.g. that the marketing intensity in the hypermarket format was much higher than in the soft discount segment. On average, hypermarket chains focusing on groceries spent 2–4 percent of revenues on marketing activities, whereas soft discount chains were closer to 1 percent of sales. The biggest players spend less relative to sales, given the scale benefits derived from a large store network.

Q: What was the impact of the new budget sizing approach?

Pia Mellbye: Because our brands were in a transition phase, we scaled down the ATL communication significantly compared to previous years. We reduced our budget by as much as 30 percent compared to previous years, resulting in an average marketing-to-sales ratio of approximately 1 percent across our hypermarket, supermarket and soft discount formats. We did this because we realized that over-investing compared to competitors had not helped us capture additional market share, and because we needed to improve our value proposition in the stores before investing in brand-building campaigns.

Q: Traditionally, how did you allocate the budget to the various activities?

Pia Mellbye: Our budget was developed on a country level – by format and media channel – as opposed to local geographical units. This was a result of our mindset at the time, working closely with the media agency to optimize the efficiency of individual media on a national level.

Q: How did this change?

Pia Mellbye: After assessing this in detail, we decided to allocate and track our spend on a regional basis, instead of by channel on a national level. When we looked at revenue per region and linked it back to marketing spend, it became clear that we over-invested in some regions (regions with high market share) and under-invested in others (regions with low market share). By defining regional budgets with the opportunity to use local media in some of the regions, we improved the situation. We now set the regional budget, e.g. in soft discount, in the range of 0.6–0.9 percent, depending on our local market share, as opposed to, for example, 0.8 percent across the country. Today, we hold a central budget for research, store openings and special circumstances, such as unexpected competitor store openings or campaigns.

Q: What was the impact of the new allocation approach?

Pia Mellbye: We are developing activity plans that are tailored to the local markets. In effect, we get more bang for the buck. We also choose our media mix based on local and regional reach. Also, the new approach has resulted in a common language, as well as in more transparency about the steps in the budgeting process. This makes internal discussions so much easier.

Q: Historically, how did you define your marketing messages?

Pia Mellbye: Traditionally, we have based our communication messages on different insights about the customer. Up until 2009, we ran various market studies to understand customer preferences, as well as how our formats performed. The range included big surveys on perception, brand equity measurements, ad hoc analyses and focus groups. A synthesis of the different surveys was the foundation for our marketing messages, enhanced by input from our group and format organization. The challenge was that the insights from the studies were sometimes pointing us in different directions.

Q: How did this change?

Pia Mellbye: We have implemented the BrandMatics approach. This research basically replaces several of our previous studies and enables us to understand what is important to the customer, and how we perform in the purchase funnel (from 'awareness' to 'loyalty') compared to our competitors.

Q: Why is this more insightful than your previous studies?

Pia Mellbye: Our insight is much more crisp and granular. We have defined 120 parameters related to price, service, in-store experience, convenience and assortment. We measure our performance on these parameters for each stage in the purchase funnel, compared to our competitors. These measurements serve as a unique fact base; it helps us focus on the parameters that are important to the customer. The research also provides the rest of the organization with deep insights on how to improve in areas other than communication, e.g. commercial management and in-store operations. For instance, in our latest study, we found out that high-quality fresh herbs are a key loyalty driver in the 'high end' segment, and that a high-quality private label offering is a key driver for trial in the 'value' segment.

Q: What is the overall impact of the new approach?

Pia Mellbye: The systematic and analytical way of looking at the world has two types of benefit.

One, we have changed our communication objective: after running the funnel analysis, we realized that we had very high awareness, but low conversion rates from 'awareness' to 'trial', as well as from 'trial' to 'loyalty'. It became clear that we needed to invest more in sales stimulation, e.g. in newspapers and leaflets, and less in brand building campaigns on TV.

Two, we became more fact based in our messaging: the funnel analysis gave us unique insights into the drivers of the various transfers. We now focus our communication on the attributes that are most important to the customers. This way, we know we are relevant.

Key takeaways – Budget prioritization

1 Find the right decision mode: deciding centrally or convincing locally.
2 Define the right investment units: go granular and find the pockets of growth.
3 Create full transparency: understand where the money goes.
4 Define the prioritization criteria and weights based on what really matters in your budgeting decisions.
5 Avoid automatic decisions: prioritize your marketing investment in the light of the full facts.

CHAPTER 8

Jesko Perrey, Dennis Spillecke

Admittedly, most advertising vehicles are a lot less glamorous than the vehicles that grace the pages of *How To Spend It*, the monthly magazine on lifestyle and luxury that comes with the weekend edition of the *Financial Times*. However, 'how to spend it?' happens to be the very question that governs media mix optimization: once you know which messages to convey and what the total size of the budget should be, it is all about how to spend it. While this may not be the most entertaining exercise, there is nothing as effective as a perfectly balanced media mix for driving a retailer's marketing ROI. If you play it right, you may have the means to read *How To Spend It* with a more urgent sense of interest than before.

To support retailers in their efforts to spend their marketing funds in value-creating ways, this chapter outlines recent changes in the media landscape and introduces the three principal media mix optimization approaches:

- testing and learning
- comparative heuristics and
- econometric modelling.

The media landscape is in rapid transformation
and the media mix used for advertising differs substantially across industries and between countries

The media landscape is changing at breakneck speed. For example, while the average German household had access to fewer than ten TV channels in the late 1980s, today, they have a choice of over 300. The number of radio stations has quadrupled over the same period, now also numbering more than 300. The same is true in most other European countries and elsewhere. And there is no end in sight.

So, is this a golden age for advertisers? Not quite. Today's environment is characterized by multiple media and hybrid usage: as a result, targeted marketing is anything but a walk in the park. The average consumer is subject to 1300 commercial stimuli every day, up from a mere 170 in 1980. Advertisers are battling for the consumer's limited reservoir of attention and involvement. As in any battle, there are winners and losers. While digital media are on the rise, the impact of traditional channels is dropping. According to an analysis conducted by McKinsey & Company in the US, TV commercials have lost much of their effectiveness within the last 20 years. (Source: David C. Court, Thomas D. French, Trond Riiber Knudsen, 'Profiting from Proliferation', *McKinsey Quarterly*, March 2006.) In general, consumers have become more educated in their media usage and more critical of commercial messages. Also, they have started to grow accustomed to multimedia campaigns, making them potentially less receptive to traditional communication plans. At the same time, retailers have experienced an explosion of shopper data, collected both offline and online. Based on insights derived from these rich sources, new and more targeted retail marketing instruments are taking hold: customized electronic newsletters, personalized direct mail or leaflets distributed with the help of high-resolution geo-marketing tools, to name but a few.

Because of the dynamics of their business and the privilege of their direct access to customers, retailers typically use a media mix which differs discernibly from that of advertisers in other top-spending industries. In classical above-the-line communication in Germany, retailers rely mainly on print advertising (62 percent), while the food industry favours TV commercials (86 percent). Car manufacturers, by comparison, use a more balanced media mix

(Exhibit 8.1). Similar splits for below-the-line advertising are, unfortunately, hard to come by, since most research agencies do not track non-classical vehicles systematically.

Even within retail, there are significant differences across formats and territories. For example, many discount retailers typically rely almost exclusively on print advertising, while many high-profile retailers are increasingly using TV commercials to build their brands. But the regional differences are no less distinctive. A comparison of the mix of classical media used by retailers in Germany, France and the United Kingdom shows that Germany favours print (62 percent), France is unusually fond of radio (34 percent) and British retail advertising is split almost equally between TV (44 percent) and print (40 percent) (Exhibit 8.2). Retailers operating in multiple countries will want to reflect these patterns in their local media mix.

In light of the continuous rise of new media, it comes as no surprise that the average retail media mix is evolving (see Exhibit 8.3 for an example from Germany). During the period 2000–09, online media has seen by far the biggest growth of any vehicle and now accounts for 6 percent of total spend.

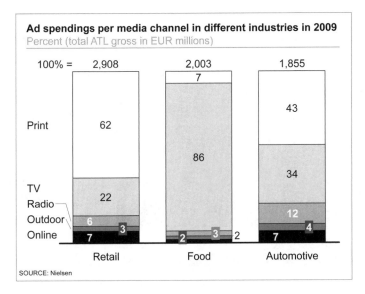

Exhibit 8.1 Advertising spend by media channel in different industries.

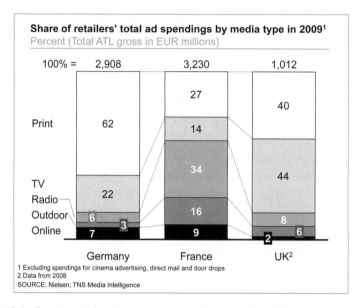

Exhibit 8.2 Retail advertising spend by media channel in different countries.

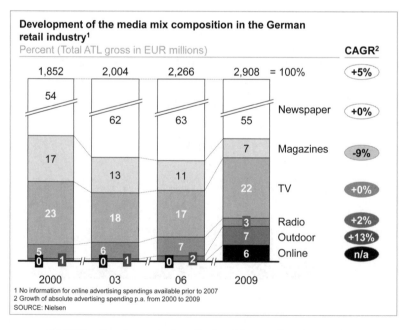

Exhibit 8.3 Development of retail advertising media mix over time.

Engage at eye level with your media agencies
to ensure the media mix is tailored to your needs

Given this diversity and the rapidly changing nature of the marketing environment, retail marketing managers have a lot to worry about. Is the current media mix still in step with the latest trends? Is the budget distributed optimally between classical advertising, digital vehicles, POS activities and direct marketing? Are your messages being delivered effectively and efficiently – at the right time, to promising target groups, using the most appropriate channels and at reasonable cost? Without conclusive answers to all these questions, the hunt for marketing ROI will always be a shot in the dark.

But isn't this why retailers hire media agencies? Yes and no. It is true that media agencies are the experts when it comes to the evaluation and selection of marketing vehicles. But they can only help you if you know what you want and understand the constraints of their advice. We believe agencies and retailers should discuss media mix decisions at eye level. Media agencies can't read your mind, nor you theirs.

Most media agencies cover only a part of the whole media landscape. They often have little experience with channels outside their scope, and even less interest in recommending them to advertisers. The same is true for those instruments that are within their scope but which carry low commissions or incentives for the agency. In addition, agencies typically do not have full cost transparency about the advertiser's real costs for each channel. In many cases, they will have a tendency to focus on the cost of media buying, but neglect creative agency fees and production costs. This means that they can only approximate the advertiser's real investment, an effect that will inevitably blur the marketing ROI perspective.

There are three distinctly different approaches to media mix optimization: *testing and learning, comparative heuristics and econometric modelling*

Testing and learning is the most basic approach: this allows the assessment and refinement of individual activities, rather than providing a comprehensive optimization of the entire media mix. Comparative heuristics enables retailers to compare all media on an apples-and-apples basis, but does not yield absolute ROI figures. This is the purpose of the most sophisticated, but also the most time-consuming and expensive approach: econometric modelling.

We will now take a look at how each of these three approaches work, their advantages and disadvantages and their applicability.

Testing and learning

- *How it works*: testing and learning is about tracking the effects of specific campaigns or other marketing activities. Perhaps the most established example of this technique is the analysis of direct marketing activities that include a response element, e.g. a coupon. The ROI assessment of such activities is calculated as 'sales (or profit) triggered by response element' over 'campaign cost'. To refine the campaign, retailers test multiple executions of the same concept on a small scale. The winning execution will be selected for wider rollout. Sometimes this approach is also used to track activities that are not directly geared to sales stimulation, such as brand image campaigns. In this case, the retailer would assess the pre-campaign image perception and compare it to the image observed after the campaign. The delta will express the campaign's 'return'; see Chapter 14: 'Excellence in classical media' for further details.
- *Advantages/disadvantages*: the advantage of testing and learning, because it typically uses customer responses to directly assess the impact of a campaign, is that the refinement of the campaign in question can be very hands-on and detailed – and this does not require complex arithmetical methods. You simply go with what works best and then build on that. But the approach has its limitations; for example, it is often difficult to isolate the effect of the test campaign because of the impact of other marketing activities that are being carried out in parallel.
- *Applicability*: testing and learning is appropriate for optimizing individual activities, as opposed to the entire media mix, as it is usually impossible to test all campaigns in all channels at the same time. The approach works best for direct marketing activities: if these feature prominently in the marketing mix, or the retailer operates in a market characterized by push marketing,

then testing and learning should be the tool of choice. Also, testing and learning makes fewer demands on analytical capabilities than the other approaches featured in this chapter.

Comparative heuristics

- *How it works*: comparative heuristics is a way of comparing the relative return of marketing investments at different touch points founded on simple linear algorithms. Based on the definition of a common currency ('apples-and-apples comparisons'), comparative heuristics enables retailers to compare the performance of multiple marketing vehicles. Based on this comparison, you can make fact-based trade-offs when allocating marketing funds to the various channels and vehicles. The 'Reach–Cost–Quality' (RCQ) approach, perhaps the most prominent type of comparative heuristics in use in media mix optimization, makes use of 'cost per actual reach' as the single currency across all touch points and channels. RCQ will be described in detail in Chapter 9.
- *Advantages/disadvantages*: comparative heuristics provides a pragmatic approach for optimizing multiple media, or even the entire media mix, but it does not yield a 'dollar-for-dollar' ROI. Specifically, it will not pick up touch points generating negative ROI. However, it does provide an efficiency ranking across all touch points within the scope of the analysis.
- *Applicability*: comparative heuristics is the approach of choice if testing and learning is too narrow to achieve the desired insights but full-scale econometric modelling is considered too time-consuming or expensive. It allows for robust yet analytically straightforward trade-off decisions between different vehicles. Comparative heuristics is usually the best choice if the market environment is highly volatile and, hence, not suitable for the statistical analysis required by econometric modelling. The same is true if new media, on which there is little or no historical data, are part of the optimization effort.

Econometric marketing mix models (MMM)

- *How it works*: econometric marketing mix models (MMM) use advanced statistics to determine the impact of advertising expenditure on sales at different touch points (or on other dependent variables, like volume or profit). Developing s-curve estimates is an important part of MMM: the s-curves help to identify the windows of highest marketing spend efficiency for specific vehicles. MMM not only includes an assessment of the past and current ROI of multiple media but also serves as the basis for an optimized future marketing mix. MMM is described in detail in Chapter 10.

- *Advantages/disadvantages*: although marketing mix models provide the most precise ROI output of the three approaches, a true comparison of the sales or profit impact of the various marketing vehicles can only be made reliably in relatively stable market environments. MMM usually requires a large amount of data collection, both for internal spend figures and market data. Because of their high level of analytical sophistication, many marketing mix models are in effect 'black boxes' with little transparency about the rationale of the recommendations they produce; often, this inhibits the acceptance of MMM efforts among marketing executives. Note that while MMM gives you dollar-for-dollar ROI based on sales impact, it does not capture marketing impact on brand equity.
- *Applicability*: as already pointed out, for it to be effective, MMM requires a stable market situation in which historical data can safely be assumed to be representative of current business and marketing dynamics. It is the most appropriate approach in cases where the retailer has the requisite data and analytical capabilities necessary for running the modelling and where it plans to introduce few if any new advertising vehicles in the future. If the retailer has to rely on external experts to conduct the data collection and modelling, the costs of this analytical approach can be significant, typically in excess of EUR 100,000.

There are, of course, many variants and hybrids above and beyond these three types of approach. For example, heuristics can be combined with econometric MMM to support a trade-off between short-term sales effects, measured using MMM, and long-term brand effects, measured using comparative heuristics. Before they commit to one of these approaches in a given situation, retailers should also consider their organization's readiness to accept and implement the methodology in question, as well the availability of the required supporting tools and IT systems. The best analytical method may not always be the best solution in practice – e.g. if organizational or technical constraints prevent it from being used to its full capacity.

The next two chapters will explore comparative heuristics (Chapter 9: 'Reach–Cost–Quality') and econometric modelling (Chapter 10: 'Marketing Mix Modelling') in more detail.

Key takeaways – Media mix optimization

1 The media landscape is in rapid transformation and the media mix used for advertising differs substantially across industries and between countries.
2 Engage at eye level with your media agencies to ensure the media mix is tailored to your needs.
3 There are three distinctly different approaches to media mix optimization: testing and learning, comparative heuristics and econometric modelling.

CHAPTER 9

Thomas Bauer, Ingeborg Hegstad, Nicolai Johannsen

- 'There is nothing like a TV commercial to build brand image.'
- 'If you want to drive sales, you should spend your marketing budget where customers make their choices: at the POS.'
- 'I've never seen so much impact at such low cost. Our online viral campaign was a real bargain. Why don't you try it, too?'

You have heard it all before. Tips like these are a dime a dozen. Yet they often contain a grain of truth. For a given retailer, with a given budget, in a given country and competitive environment, they are all most probably true at some point in time. But that doesn't mean they are true for you, here and now.

In this chapter, we present the 'Reach–Cost–Quality' (RCQ) approach, a quantitative method for evaluating, comparing and selecting different media on a like-for-like basis. It relies on the concept of a common currency across all marketing touch points: real cost per actual reach. Thanks to RCQ, you won't have to rely on trial and error, gut feeling or plain rumour any longer. We will walk through this approach step by step, highlighting how it helps you generate a robust fact base for media mix and budget allocation decisions.

Optimizing individual vehicles one by one is challenging enough, *but cross-media optimization is next to impossible without a universal metric*

- 'Why don't we run more sales stimulation ads in local newspapers and fewer fuzzy brand campaigns on TV?'
- 'What is the most cost-efficient media channel in region X?'
- 'Why don't we use the internet to strengthen the loyalty of our customers?'

These questions sound simple, but they are hard enough to answer even in isolation – since the data on the success of past marketing activities is often incomplete. In many cases, a retailer's central marketing department has no transparency on local marketing activities, and lot of research agencies do not track below-the-line activities at all. At the same time, media agencies are not always incentivized equally across different media. As a result, the best solution for the advertiser may not be in the agency's best interest.

While individual optimization of a given channel, or of a group of media, is challenging enough, optimizing the entire mix is even harder. There are few widely accepted performance indicators that apply across all media. What is more, most retailers are pursuing multiple marketing objectives in parallel, such as sales stimulation, brand building and customer retention. So which tool or method should you use to bring consistency and analytical rigour to your media evaluation and selection?

RCQ is one of the more promising answers to this question. Of course, it is by no means the only one (see Chapter 8 for an overview of alternatives). RCQ will enable you to increase actual reach at no extra cost (i.e. to increase effectiveness) or reduce costs without compromising advertising impact (i.e. to increase efficiency). The approach combines the core criteria of reach, cost and quality to create a ranking of communication vehicles, using 'cost per actual reach' as the common currency. The RCQ concept is summarized in Exhibit 9.1.

Over the course of this chapter we will look at a concrete, if simplified, media mix question in order to illustrate this approach: 'Which of the following touch points works best for us: classical TVCs, POS promotions or online viral marketing campaigns?'

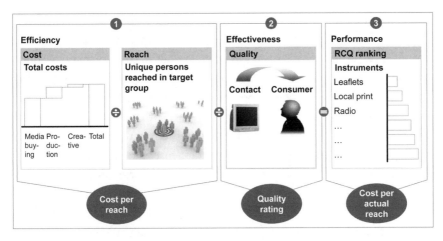

Exhibit 9.1 Reach–Cost–Quality approach.

Compare apples and apples: *use 'cost per actual reach in target group' as the common currency for evaluating and selecting different media*

We will now look at each of the components of 'cost per actual reach in target group' one at a time. You will find that while cost and reach are more or less straightforward and easily quantified, quality takes a little more creativity to get your hands around.

Cost

The first step in RCQ is to define 'cost' in a comprehensive way. To obtain a valid indication of the true return on investment, you need to capture the entire investment linked to each touch point ('total cost of ownership'). Media buying is the first item that comes to mind, but it is by no means the only one – agency fees, production costs and research expenses also need to be included. This step often proves quite an eye-opener. Some vehicles will immediately look less expensive than previously thought, while others may well turn out to be a lot more costly. Commonly held assumptions like 'email is free' do not survive the sweep of full cost transparency.

A complication is that suppliers often contribute to the costs of retail advertising, as when handset manufacturers pay network operators to push their cell phones in advertising. This makes the creation of full cost transparency quite difficult, particularly because of the opportunity-cost effect: supplier funding may make certain touch points look more attractive than they really are. For example, suppliers may favour and subsidize local print advertising because of the opportunity to have their products featured prominently in the ads, but this might not be the most effective touch point for reaching the retailer's marketing objectives. For instance, it might be that in-store promotions or out-door advertising near to the retailer's outlets could create a higher sales uplift per euro investment. Retailers should maintain an independent perspective on the true cost of ownership of individual media. Ideally, the creation of cost transparency should initially disregard all supplier funding. Once the retailer has true transparency on its costs, it is always possible to renegotiate supplier co-funding arrangements in order to support the retailer's overall marketing and media mix strategy.

To see what this means in practice, let us revisit our example.

- TV: for TVCs, you will need to make sure the analysis not only covers the media cost but also the creative agency fees for developing, shooting and producing the commercial. If you intend to use the same TVC in multiple countries, you will also need to take account of the additional costs of adaptation and the local rights charged by models, composers and other artists.
- POS: for POS materials, you will not only need to recognize the design and production (or procurement) costs, but also the costs incurred for distribution and maintenance. If there is a response element (e.g. a voucher handed out at the POS), the calculation should also reflect the variable administration costs incurred in handling the responses.
- Viral online: the concrete cost positions depend on the exact setup of an online campaign. For example, placing a 'cool' clip on YouTube typically requires significant investment in terms of creative agency fees, production and license fees. The retailer might also wish to enhance access to the clip, for example, by using the services of a professional tremor network to try and start a snowball effect around the clip; these costs also need to be included.

Reach

For it to be reliable, any definition of reach should be based on the actual number of people reached by a given vehicle among the retailer's relevant target groups. Depending on the overall marketing strategy, these groups might include teenagers, affluent senior citizens or LOHAS ('lifestyle of health and sustainability'). To establish its actual reach among its target group, you first need to remove all those consumers who do not match the target group characteristics. This is especially important for diffusion media such as TV and radio, as well as for contacts made through local marketing instruments distributed outside a retail outlet's own patch.

How do you measure reach? Typically, it is not possible to get data on reach for all media from a single source. Media agencies or tracking agencies provide reach data for above-the-line activities, while your own local or regional organization should be able to supply data on reach for in-store activities. Once you have a full set of data, a two-step approach needs to be followed to obtain reach in your target group:

- *Step 1*: net reach in target group. Start with the gross reach in the population, then subtract the number of contacts outside your specific target group. To complete this step, you may have to conduct market research on the media usage of your target group, unless the media agency, research agency or consumer insight department is able to supply this information. To derive the net reach from the gross reach, divide the gross reach by the average contact frequency. Finally, exclude all consumers residing outside the catchment area of your stores.
- *Step 2*: actual reach in target group. This step accounts for the fact that not everyone who has theoretically been reached by a given vehicle actually receives the message. For example, TV net reach only gives you the reported number of viewers of a given programme; this fails to take account of whether an individual viewer was actually watching the TVC, or had just stepped outside for a smoke during the commercial break. Actual reach, therefore, equals net reach minus the number of people who are 'tuned out'. The 'tune-out' percentage varies greatly across different media; while it is low for personal interactions, it is typically very high for billboards.

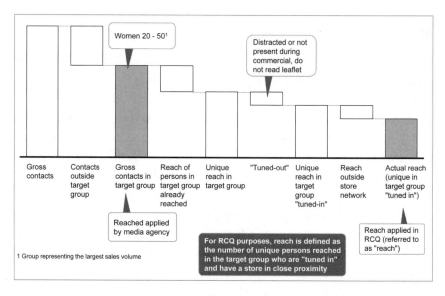

Exhibit 9.2 Definition of actual reach in target group.

Frequency is another factor: the higher the 'opportunity to see', the lower the probability of 'tune-out'.

'Actual reach in target group' gives you the number of people reached in your target group who live near to one of your stores and who have actually had meaningful contact with your ad or message (Exhibit 9.2).

Dividing the full cost per vehicle by the actual reach of that vehicle in the target group yields the actual cost per relevant reach. This number is far more insightful than the commonly used cost per mille (CPM). However, you may nevertheless need to use CPM for certain media if you don't have all the data required to make the calculation outlined above. In these cases, you might be able to make rough adjustments to the full cost and actual reach based on the input of marketing experts.

Let us now look at how the calculation of actual reach pertains to our case example.

- TV: TV is among the media that need the highest adjustment in terms of reach. On the one hand, many viewers who are subject to your TVC will not match your target group criteria, and not all of those who do will be tuned in. Of those who remain, quite a few will live outside the local catchment area of any of your stores, especially in the case of nationwide broadcasting. To get a reliable estimate of the relevant radius, you need to understand how far people are willing to walk or drive to your stores, or whether there are competitors nearby that make it unlikely to attract visitors in these neighbourhoods. The best way to establish the number of households that match the target profile within a certain area is to use a geo-marketing tool (see Chapter 13: 'Leaflets and local print advertising: how to achieve local media excellence').
- POS: reach data is especially hard to find for POS activities. There is currently no agency that tracks footfall by retail format, let alone shopping frequency and target group fit. To approximate POS reach, retailers typically observe footfall in selected shops and extrapolate from the results to their entire network.
- Viral online: for viral campaigns, there are two kinds of reach: primary contacts generated through exposure to the actual advertising or clip, and secondary contacts generated through word-of-mouth among those who do not themselves view the ad or the clip. Measuring gross primary reach in online media is relatively easy: this is equal to page impressions. But net reach is more difficult to derive. To obtain full transparency, a response element is recommended, e.g. 'send to a friend'. This serves a double purpose: it identifies unique visitors and also serves to generate email addresses. In contrast, secondary reach can only be captured through consumer surveys. Estimates of both primary and secondary reach are necessary in order to capture the full value of viral online marketing.

Quality

Contact quality is defined as the impact of a given advertising activity on each consumer reached. As campaigns usually pursue several marketing goals at the same time, measuring quality is undoubtedly the most challenging aspect of RCQ. For example, you will often want an ad to stimulate sales, convey the benefits of the product featured and build the retail brand – all at the same time. However, very few vehicles serve all goals with the same effectiveness. For example, you would expect a digital campaign that links consumers directly to an online shop to have a major impact on sales, while most print ads primarily convey rational reasons to buy, and TVCs, in contrast, strengthen viewers' emotional attachment to the brand.

So how do you measure quality in a comprehensive and balanced way? Based on the proven psychological assumption that changes in attitude precede changes in behaviour, quality measurement needs to assess three different components:

- the ability of a touch point to convey *information*, such as the price and features of a product ('cognitive attitudinal quality')
- the suitability of a touch point to evoke *emotion*, such as the attachment to a trusted brand ('affective attitudinal quality')
- the ability of a touch point to trigger *action*, such as increases in traffic or basket size ('behavioural quality').

It is hard to isolate the nature of a vehicle itself from the quality of a given execution in terms of its creativity and production. However, not all award-winning campaigns result in high sales and brand impact. For further details, see Chapter 14: 'Excellence in classical media'. Suffice it to say, RCQ evaluates touch points irrespective of the quality of a given execution. If you expect systematic uplift or downturn in specific channels, you would need to adjust the respective quality scores of that touch point. The judgement of experienced marketing practitioners, both within the organization and in the lead agencies, is usually the best basis for making this kind of adjustment. Prior to major campaigns, you might also wish to use advertising pre-tests to control for the quality of a given execution.

See Exhibits 9.3 and 9.4 for sample outputs of RCQ efforts conducted in retail. Please note that the numbers given in these charts are specific to the context in which they were created and are not necessarily applicable in other environments. The nature of these examples is purely illustrative.

A shortcut to media quality

Because disaggregated data for the three different components of media quality presented in this chapter may not be available for all vehicles in the scope of an RCQ analysis, it is common practice for retailers to use only two quality indicators: the propensity of an instrument to push sales (behavioural quality) and the ability to build the brand (attitudinal quality). For example, while leaflets and POS activities are known to push sales, their ability to build the retailer's brand in areas other than price perception is limited. In contrast, TVCs are ideally suited to conveying emotional brand messages, but their direct sales impact is usually lower. In light of these differences, you may want to adjust or weight your quality assessment of the various vehicles, depending on your overall communication objectives.

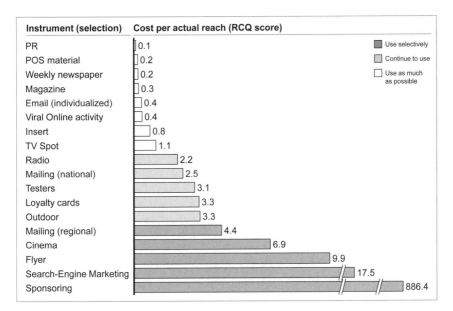

Exhibit 9.3 Overview of cost per actual reach (RCQ score).

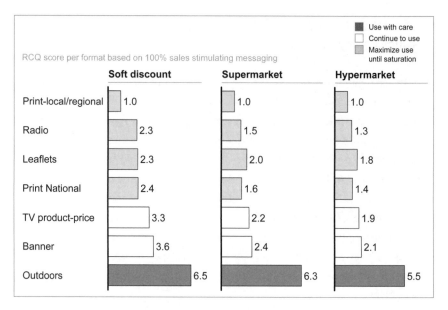

Exhibit 9.4 Cost per qualified reach (RCQ score) for different retail formats.

RCQ scores can be used to increase efficiency as well as effectiveness, *both within and across communication channels*

The 'Reach–Cost–Quality' approach has proven particularly helpful in three areas of marketing ROI optimization.

- *Increasing efficiency though internal benchmarking of advertising activities*: for example, a manufacturer of consumer goods found that the cost per actual reach of their online banners ranged from EUR 0.04 to 1.45. By cancelling the more expensive banner placements, the company cut their cost for this vehicle by 60 percent without reducing its actual reach. Similarly, a grocery retailer compared its cost per actual reach for different TV campaigns and observed a cost range from EUR 0.15 to 0.55. In light of this, it reviewed and adjusted its campaign plan, effectively increasing its proportion of high-impact campaigns on TV.

- *Tailoring media selection to drive efficiency*: based on RCQ scores, you can rank all media vehicles, for example, to select the best local marketing instruments based on their real cost and actual reach in the given region. As an example of this application, a European grocery retailer discovered that in one specific region the cost of placing ads in a local newspaper was significantly higher than for distributing leaflets. The spread was even higher in areas with low population. Based on this knowledge, the retailer developed customized regional media plans reflecting the RCQ scores observed in its different local markets.

- *Optimizing the overall media mix to increase marketing returns*: to optimize its entire media mix, you should combine RCQ scores with thresholds of efficient spend for the different touch points. This avoids overspending on vehicles that, while they might look highly attractive because of the low cost per actual reach, will nonetheless lose efficiency beyond a certain saturation point. Similarly, spend thresholds help ensure that you invest above the minimal level necessary for your communication to be heard despite the competitive noise at a specific touch point.

In effect, RCQ is an approach for measuring and optimizing the ROI of each media vehicle. It does this by relating the marketing investment ('cost') to the number of persons reached ('reach') and the impact per contact ('quality'). Leading companies from industries as diverse as retail, automotive, FMCG and telecoms have all used RCQ to optimize their media mix; some of them reallocated as much as one-third of their total marketing budget to instruments that have greater impact. The efficiency and effectiveness potential they have discovered ranges from 10 to 30 percent of total marketing investment. Surely, with this kind of saving, the executives in charge of RCQ efforts deserve their bonus? How much did you say that racy, red two-seater was, again?

Key benefits of the RCQ approach

1 Common currency: the RCQ score is based on 'cost per actual reach'; it can be used to measure and compare marketing effectiveness and efficiency across all touch points.

2 Cross-media approach: RCQ takes account of all marketing vehicles, including TV, print, direct marketing, events, online and PR.

3 Integration of qualitative and quantitative factors: RCQ incorporates and weights data sources ranging from web tracking to expert assessments.

4 Comparability of online and offline: RCQ compares traditional and digital marketing activities on a like-for-like basis.

5 Target group focus: the RCQ score is based on relevant and actual reach, i.e. on only those contacts that matter to the advertiser.

6 Combination of multiple marketing targets: RCQ reflects various advertising purposes, from sales increase to brand building.

7 Data transparency: RCQ creates full transparency about the reach, cost and contact quality of all the marketing vehicles in scope of the analysis.

8 Freedom of choice: the RCQ ranking serves as fact base for the advertiser's decision making; it is not a black box for budget allocation.

9 Plausibility of output: all recommendations in regard to the selection of specific vehicles can be traced back to the components of the RCQ score.

10 Universality: RCQ can be applied to a variety of processes to optimize the media mix, and it can be made to work with different types of source data.

Interview: Thomas Koch – Germany's 'Media Person of the Year, 2008', and founder of TKM

Q: What do you make of the increasing trend towards image campaigns in retail?

Thomas Koch: This clearly differs by category. In DIY, for example, this is already used successfully – just think about the 'Hornbach' campaign, which recently even won the Klappe-Award in Germany – whereas in groceries, the trend is just starting. Edeka is playing this card quite successfully to strengthen their premium position; Lidl has just stopped its test. I assume it will continue it after having done the analysis.

Q: What other media trends do you see more generally?

Thomas Koch: In times when sales are under pressure, you see a trend towards more direct media. Online advertising is profiting most from this trend at present, also driven by the general trend towards digital media. But flyers will also profit – at least as long there is no significant digital substitute, such as localized online ads or mobile advertising. Classical print advertising will stay under pressure from online ads, but increasingly, even TV advertising money will be shifted to online media as multimedia formats become available. Outdoor might be stable, especially when it's able to leverage some additional effects from digital add ons. Radio, in general, may profit from its sales push effects, but in Germany, it suffers from the limitations brought about by the regulation of public stations.

Q: What are the most important communication channels for retailers?

Thomas Koch: In the past, retailers focused on flyers and daily newspapers, sometimes enriched by local papers. But here, too, dailies are coming under pressure, as the younger generation no longer subscribes to newspapers that much. Interestingly, shopping newspapers like '*Einkauf aktuell*' seem to be more accepted among young people, and so it is no wonder that some retailers are experimenting with their own shopping newspaper formats – though their success has yet to be proven ... A second channel to reach younger audiences is the online channel, where new regional targeting features are being introduced.

Q: Do the relevant channels differ by category?

Thomas Koch: Yes, of course! Groceries rely greatly on shopping newspapers and flyers, whereas in consumer electronics, you see inserts and – after having tested online banners with mixed results – once again, online ads with rich media formats. It remains to be seen to what degree this will cannibalize their TV spending going forward. Home and textile players are also very active online. IKEA, for example, has offered a creative service where one can upload a picture of one's flat and then integrate new furniture online to see what it will look like.

Q: How are retailers choosing their media mix?

Thomas Koch: Today, trial-and-error tests predominate. You regularly see these tests in the market, but once the test is over, most players go back to their previous advertising behaviour. There is seldom a routine in place for systematic testing and fine-tuning of the media mix. But some players are starting to ask their agencies for econometric models to optimize sales impact. Interestingly, such exercises often show that a certain share of TV, in combination with dailies, can be very successful. But since only few players are applying sophisticated models rigorously, there is clearly plenty of opportunities in media mix optimization that have yet to be captured.

Key takeaways – Reach–Cost–Quality

1 Optimizing individual vehicles one by one is challenging enough, but cross-media optimization is next to impossible without a universal metric.

2 Compare apples and apples: use 'cost per actual reach in target group' as the common currency for evaluating and selecting different media.

3 RCQ scores can be used to increase efficiency as well as effectiveness, both within and across communication channels.

CHAPTER 10

Francesco Banfi, Rishi Bhandari, Jonathan Gordon, Michele Porcu

Retailers have privileged and powerful access to consumers – especially through promotional activities and loyalty programmes. These instruments are direct purchase decision drivers, but they are also highly targeted communication channels since both the message and execution can be tailored to the needs of individual regions, clusters, outlets or even consumer segments. Their effectiveness makes them key elements in any retailer's marketing mix.

In Chapter 9 we discussed the Reach–Cost–Quality (RCQ) approach as an established and pragmatic way to evaluate and balance the role of a wide range of traditional touch points, comparing them on an 'apples-and-apples' basis. By comparison, Marketing Mix Modelling, or MMM, is a more comprehensive and analytically sophisticated tool – albeit a more complex one – for creating a fact base for advanced marketing allocation and activity decisions. Based on a purely quantitative methodology, MMM enables retailers to optimize not only their media advertising but also their entire marketing mix, including unique retail levers such as promotions, loyalty programmes and shelf price management.

What it is: *Marketing Mix Modelling tells you how to spend it*

It's all about the look. You want your ads to look good on the TV screen, your products to look good on the shelf, your brands to look good in the consumer's mind – and the bottom line to look good on your company's income state-ment. Of course, retail management is more complex than that. But precisely because it is complex, executives in both marketing and sales are looking for a comprehensive, yet straightforward, fact base that helps them with the wealth of strategic and tactical choices involved. How do I split my investments be-tween branded and private label products? Which commercial levers are the most effective for driving traffic and revenue? What is the impact of different promotional schemes on price perception?

Marketing Mix Modelling is geared to helping executives in charge of strategic as well as tactical retail management – usually the CMO and the com-mercial director or head of sales – providing them with a fact base to help them make the trade-off decisions they face, especially regarding the allocation of funds and resources across the various marketing and sales levers. The tool typically provides answers to three types of question the CMO and commercial director would ask.

- *Performance driver analysis*: what are the true drivers of top-line performance and consumers' price perception? Which of these are under our direct influ-ence, as opposed to external factors?
- *Impact analysis*: what is the top-line (revenue and/or traffic) impact of our marketing investments? How does the ROI compare for different line items in the marketing budget?
- *Price perception sensitivity testing*: what is the effect of specific marketing mix decisions on price perception? How do we balance short-term impact with sustainability?

A state-of-the-art MMM tool is able to capture the influence of a wide range of marketing levers on revenue, traffic and price perception in order to identify the true drivers of performance. Its output helps separate external factors, such as the overall market growth or demographic trends, from the levers that you can pull yourself, such as shelf price positioning, promotional strategy or advertis-ing investment. MMM also provides revenue and traffic impact measurements across all marketing levers in order to assess their relative business contribu-tion. This type of impact analysis provides an understanding of whether, for example, advertising is a more effective top-line driver than promotions – in a specific market and situation. Finally, MMM enables executives to keep an eye on price perception. Lowering average applied discounts may be a great way of boosting revenue, but how does this affect consumer price perception in the long term? This sensitivity test enables the executive team to balance short-term tactics with long-term strategy.

Ultimately, MMM provides retail managers with the means to investigate the likely consequences of their actions before they act, enabling them to steer a much clearer course without the need for constant fixes and corrections.

How it works: *MMM compares the relative impact of a wide range of growth levers*

The logic of MMM is simple and straightforward, but its mechanics require a sophisticated blend of science (i.e. leading-edge statistical modelling) and art (i.e. deep, commercial retail expertise). In a nutshell, MMM captures two types of input factor: on the one hand, the marketing mix under the retailer's control (such as average prices, loyalty schemes, promotions and advertising pressure) and external parameters on the other (such as demographics, economic trends and seasonality). The heart of MMM, its analytical engine, models the relative impact of these levers on revenue and traffic, as well as on consumer price perception (Exhibit 10.1).

Since many relevant characteristics of retailers, such as data sources and degrees of freedom, differ across markets, across sectors and between individual companies, MMM is not normally available as an off-the-shelf solution, but is usually developed as a proprietary tool. However, three key elements are common to all versions and varieties: MMM always comprises an integrated input database ('data sources'), an econometric statistical engine and a user interface (Exhibit 10.2).

The database integrates a variety of sources of data, from client reporting and publicly available market data, right down to proprietary research and general trend information. The database is set up to handle integration, cleaning and validation of large data sets. The database is typically built on a standard IT platform such as SAS. The econometric model itself is designed to fit the optimal statistical methodology to the commercial dynamics of the situation at

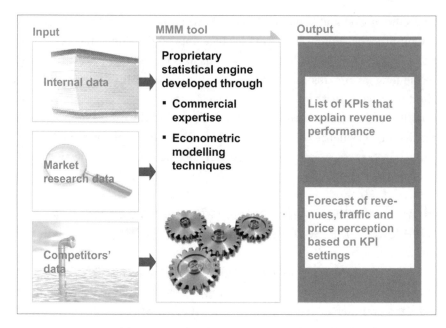

Exhibit 10.1 MMM: high-level logical architecture.

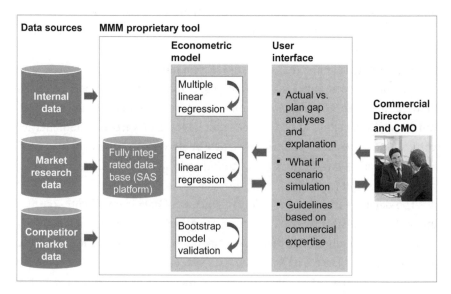

Exhibit 10.2 MMM: high-level technical architecture.

hand. The user interface makes the full power of the tool accessible to executives through features that are directly relevant to marketing decision-making: gap analyses of actual versus plan, 'what if' scenario simulations and interpretation guidelines based on commercial expertise.

If retailers want MMM to be more than a one-off, stand-alone project, it is vital that it is integrated into the retailer's established systems and processes. Specifically, its interface should be fully compatible with the retailer's existing IT architecture, while the model's output should have a well-defined role in standard management and reporting procedures.

What it does: *MMM has strategic as well as tactical applications*

Given its hunger for data and analytical sophistication, MMM is not a 'quick fix' – but neither is it a once-in-a-lifetime effort. Its true power lies in its continuous and consistent application. As an integral part of a retailer's management information system, it is a comprehensive decision support tool that yields transparency at a holistic level, as well as at the granular level of individual marketing activities.

At the holistic level, MMM informs the retailer's strategic positioning, including the retailer's quality/price position, its competitive differentiation, its cross-format policy and its private label strategy. For instance, the CMO may wonder whether the company's traditional positioning as a budget retailer focused on speed and affordability is really more promising than an upmarket strategy driven by convenience, quality and a high share of branded SKUs. While MMM can help to generate insights that can inform strategic deliberation, such as the relative importance of the retailer's average shelf prices compared to its key competitors, it is also a useful tool in day-to-day operations, assisting the commercial director's team in answering such questions as: how should a given type of SKU be priced? Which types of SKU should be included in promotions? What is the average discount that should be applied to a given range or product group? By analyzing the effect of these various levers on revenue and traffic growth on the basis of historical data, MMM enables the commercial director's team to run various scenarios and compare their prospective top-line impact.

What it yields: *MMM creates transparency across multiple marketing levers*

The specific benefits of MMM in day-to-day marketing mix management include increased transparency about the drivers of performance, the return on investment of different marketing levers and their impact on consumer price perception.

Exhibit 10.3 shows how MMM can help executives to distinguish between the impact of their actions and the effects of general trends in the market. They may find that, for example, a large proportion of the observed sales uplift was driven by extraneous factors like overall market growth, sunny skies or the closing down of a competitor's outlet, while only a small part of the growth was actually driven by the retailer's marketing mix in a given reporting period. This extra transparency gives retailers the ability to build a more realistic and unbiased platform from which to evaluate and optimize their commercial performance.

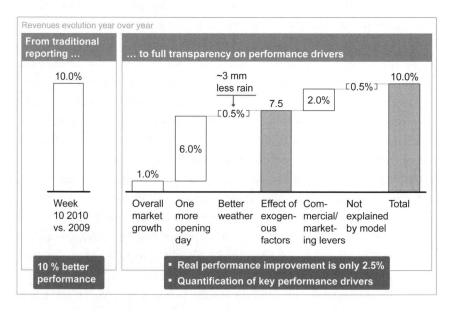

Exhibit 10.3 MMM enables retailers to identify the drivers of performance.

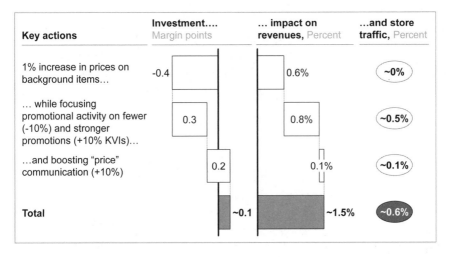

Key actions	Investment.... Margin points	... impact on revenues, Percent	...and store traffic, Percent
1% increase in prices on background items...	-0.4	0.6%	~0%
... while focusing promotional activity on fewer (-10%) and stronger promotions (+10% KVIs)...	0.3	0.8%	~0.5%
...and boosting "price" communication (+10%)	0.2	0.1%	~0.1%
Total	~0.1	~1.5%	~0.6%

Exhibit 10.4 MMM brings transparency to ROI across all marketing levers.

Not only does MMM tell executives which performance drivers they *should* pull, it also identifies the return on investment for the ones they *do* pull (Exhibit 10.4), or have pulled in the past. While some activities generate solid profits and others are bottom-line neutral, though required for tactical reasons, the activities commercial directors really lose sleep over are the ones burning money. MMM enables them to spot these – and stop them.

Last, but not least, MMM helps retailers to keep track of how their marketing activities influence consumers' price perception. Exhibit 10.5 illustrates how the insights on the impact of different marketing activities on revenue and price perception can be combined to inform decisions about the trade-off between tactical, short-term moves and long-term strategy. While some activities are beneficial from both perspectives (described as the 'best moves' in Exhibit 10.5), others are either long-term investments designed to fuel consumers' perception of the retailer as a provider of good value, or purely tactical moves to drive revenue and traffic in a given market environment.

While MMM lays bare the impact of various marketing activities on sales and price perception, it cannot capture potential changes in brand image brought about by these same activities. To avoid any damages to brand equity,

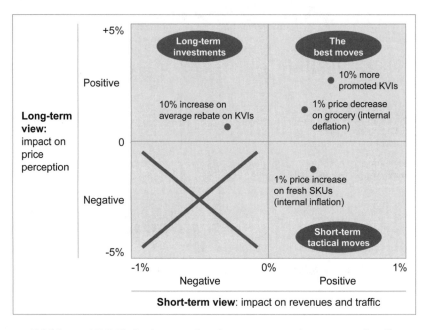

Exhibit 10.5 MMM helps in managing short-term versus long-term trade-offs.

you should not rely on MMM exclusively for your marketing mix optimization efforts. Rather, you will want to treat the MMM output as the basis for a wider discussion that also reflects other sources, such as consumer market research.

What to watch out for: *the devil is in the details of the database; cross-functional teams of marketing and IT experts help to ensure its integrity*

The heart and soul of MMM is its econometric engine; this is a robust tool built on solid science that has been widely tested. It incorporates decades of international marketing and commercial experience, as well as the latest econometric expertise tailored to the retailing environment.

Working with a wide range of input factors, the engine recognizes each variable that has a statistically significant influence on sales and traffic uplift, whether it be the CMO's latest loyalty initiative or the changes to a competitor's store network. It automatically chooses the most appropriate algorithm and regression model from a range of options to produce the most mathematically accurate and practically instructive comparison of how the marketing levers influence the dependent variables – revenue uplift, traffic uplift and consumer price perception.

From this description is should be clear that the accuracy of the model is dependent on how well the database of input factors has been built and maintained. To ensure its output is both valid and actionable, the database has to satisfy a wide range of criteria – some of which are, in part, conflicting.

- *Sufficient scope and granularity*: statistical analysis shows that two to three years' weekly historical data is necessary to stabilize the model. The data set has to be sufficiently detailed to encompass all the relevant influencing factors necessary to describe the retailer's commercial policies. The data also has to be sufficiently granular to capture all the relevant differences between regions and categories. For example, retailers may want to use multiple POS clusters – e.g. of sufficiently homogeneous regions – rather than the entire universe of all its stores. Similarly, using product categories, such as 'dairy products', 'sweets' and 'salty snacks', will often produce more informative results than using generic sectors like 'food'.
- *High reliability and accuracy*: 'garbage in, garbage out' applies to MMM as much as it applies to any other advanced modelling effort. Extra care is required to detect and fix any gaps or inconsistencies in the database. For example, data on competitors' activities is often unavailable or incomplete. But even in-house reporting systems are often susceptible to error and corruption, be it because of manual procedures at the POS or because of incompatible data formats. Meticulous merging, cleaning and validation of data sources are indispensable measures to safeguard the reliability and accuracy of the output.
- *Constant care*: to ensure MMM remains meaningful and relevant in the longer term, the database needs to be fed with new input data on a regular basis, be it through automated or manual interfaces. Up-to-date input metrics enable the model to capture the market's evolution and changes in competitive dynamics. If data is uploaded automatically, extra care is required to ensure

that the source matches the formats and units of the pre-defined metrics used in the model in order to maintain the integrity of its impact analysis. After all, it makes every difference whether sales figures are in 'm' or 'bn'!

To generate and maintain a sufficiently detailed, reliable and up-to-date database, both functional and technical trade-off decisions are required. In our experience, only a cross-functional team is capable of tackling the challenge of MMM database creation and maintenance. Take the example of advertising spending: while the marketing or media director might know which vehicles are relevant, it takes a market research specialist to figure out whether it is possible to obtain the ad-spend data of competitors, and only a financial controller will know how third-party ad tracking information can be made comparable to in-house figures. And without the help of the IT systems manager, there is no telling which formats and file names are required to fit the model's operating platform. While a cross-functional team can manage such challenges, finance, marketing or IT on their own could not.

MMM applied: best practice, example 1

Telecoms
Telecom faces great pressures in advertising spend: this has led the industry to push the limits of tools such as MMM for optimizing ad-spend ROI. These companies work closely with their media agencies to find out where they achieve the best value in terms of consumer contacts (and subsequent revenue) for their ad spend. Their goal is to determine which time slots, channels and sellers provide the best contact-to-ad spend ratio in their target group. See Exhibit 10.6 for a daytime optimization example and Exhibit 10.7 for an example of how the share of different channels and sellers is adjusted. Based on this kind of information, advertisers are able to fine tune their choice of advertising opportunities to maximize the effectiveness and efficiency of their media spend.

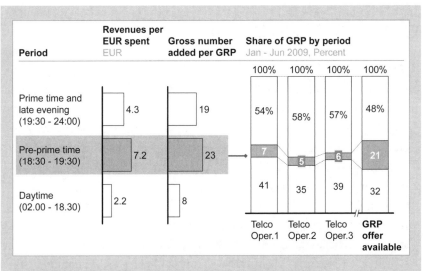

Exhibit 10.6 Daytime optimization for effective media planning – telecom example.

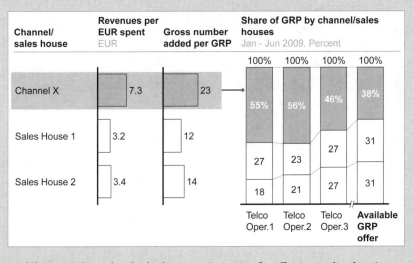

Exhibit 10.7 Channel and sales house optimization for effective media planning – telecom example.

MMM applied: best practice, example 2

FMCG

Consumer goods companies are notorious high rollers when it comes to advertising spend. As an industry, FMCG spends the most of any industry on advertising, investing some USD 100 billion worldwide every year. According to *The Wall Street Journal*, Procter & Gamble's observed annual advertising volume totals almost USD 3 billion – in the US alone. P&G's rival Unilever spends similar amounts.

In light of the large amounts retailers invest in advertising, marketers will want to be sure that every dollar is doing its job. But allocation issues are almost as old as the industry itself. The trouble is that GRPs, the universal currency of classical advertising, are insufficient for optimizing advertising ROI. For one thing, GRP data is often fragmented and usually not exhaustive. But even if the data is consistent and reliable, there is no obvious link between a given contact and its impact on revenue or profit.

In this situation, MMM acts as a shortcut to help FMCG companies optimize their budget allocation (Exhibit 10.8). The input factors in these deliberations include their current budget allocation, their business objectives and marketing targets, and, most importantly, the response curves for different media and regions. These response curves plot the revenue impact of GRPs and help to determine the marginal utility of additional ad spend: for example, while one TVC per week may go unnoticed by the target group, more than five spots per day might be a waste of money. Based on these input factors, in combination with other relevant corporate guidelines, such as budget caps for specific regions, the MMM tool produces an allocation proposal and simulates its effect on the revenues and market shares of the company in the different regions.

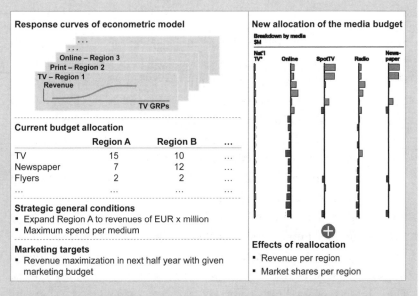

Exhibit 10.8 Budget allocation optimization based on media response curves.

MMM applied: best practice, example 3

Grocery retail

In many countries, mainstream grocery retail is a low-margin business. Ever since the rise of discount retail some 50 years ago, grocery retailers have not been able to afford to let a single penny slip. As a result, they want the price of each SKU to be exactly on their customers' price sensitivity curve – no higher, lest shoppers churn to competitors, but certainly not lower either, lest precious profits go unclaimed. Unfortunately, consumer price perception is not the only factor in the equation. Chiefly because of competitor reactions, pricing has become one of the most dynamic of all marketing levers. If retailer A cuts prices for a given item, retailer B might match the new price practically overnight. As a result, the impact of changes in pricing is highly volatile and very hard to predict. Most traditional simulation models underestimate the speed of competitive reactions, especially in mature markets with high retail marketing sophistication. What is more, leading retailers even adjust their reactions depending on the importance of the SKU for consumer price perception. While retailer B may not care about retailer A's price cut for private label commodities, it is likely to react much more swiftly and decisively if the article in question is a known value item (KVI) that has direct impact on consumers' general perception of the retailer as a provider of good value for money.

The increasing speed and differentiation of competitive reactions to pricing changes usually lead to vastly exaggerated impact estimates for potential price cuts. In reality, price leadership that lasts only a few days has a very limited impact on shopper behaviour. The market share that can be captured from competitors through price reductions isn't what it used to be. State-of-the-art Marketing Mix Modelling tools recognize these effects. Exhibit 10.9 shows a sample output of an MMM tool that uses recent data on price changes, consumer price perception and competitive reactions

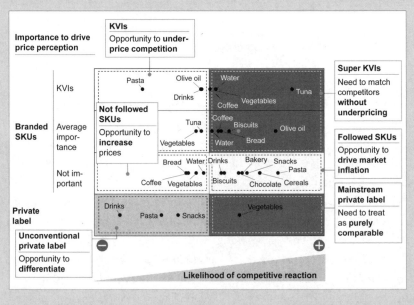

Exhibit 10.9 Simulation of competitive reactions to pricing changes.

to predict the effects of potential price changes for various categories and SKUs. Based on this type of output, retailers can produce much more realistic estimates for the impact of the price decreases or increases they are considering.

With this worry off their backs, retailers can finally start crafting sustainable strategies that will stop the discount craze and make grocery retail less of a cut-throat business. Once shoppers are willing to pay for quality, convenience and service, price wars will be a thing of the past. Even marketers can dream, can't they?

Despite its analytical allure, MMM is by no means meant to take the place of experience and common sense. Rather, it acts as a complement and potentially a corrective to the gut feeling and good judgement of seasoned marketing and sales professionals. It is a decision support tool, not a retail management robot. Like any management information system, it depends on the wisdom of its users.

Key takeaways – Marketing Mix Modelling

1 What it is: MMM tells you how to spend it. It generates a straight-forward, yet sophisticated and comprehensive, fact base for retailers' commercial decisions.

2 How it works: MMM compares the impact of a wide range of growth levers by modelling their influence on revenues, traffic and price perception.

3 What it does: MMM has strategic as well as tactical applications. Its uses range from overall strategic positioning to daily operations.

4 What it yields: MMM creates transparency across multiple marketing levers, including performance drivers, the ROI impact of different marketing levers and sensitivity to price perception.

5 What to watch out for: the devil is in the details of the database; cross-functional teams of marketing and IT experts help to ensure its integrity.

CHAPTER 11

THE DIGITAL EVOLUTION OF RETAIL MARKETING

Adam Bird, Linda Dauriz, Mathias Kullmann

To stay relevant in the digital world, you need to be in Second Life. No, wait a minute! – that's the way we might have started this chapter five years ago. While Linden Lab may now be a thing of the past, Web 2.0 is, more than ever, the primary stage of the digital present and possibly the centre ground of all our futures. New media, new platforms and new usage patterns are taking hold, especially among the young.

To stay relevant to tomorrow's shoppers, retailers need to understand the mindset and the behaviour of these digital natives. But that does not mean that each and every technological fad should become a part of their marketing mix. Paying tribute to the vagrant nature of the virtual world, this chapter will focus on the five megatrends we believe are here to stay: constant connectivity, social interaction, two-way marketing, consumer control and total recall.

Today's digital natives are tomorrow's mainstream shoppers: *to stay relevant, retailers need to understand their mindset and behaviour*

Ten years ago, a casual reference to the 'information superhighway' or 'cyberspace' was the nerds' way of telling us they knew something we didn't. Today, the interactive web and live mobile access are a clear and present part of

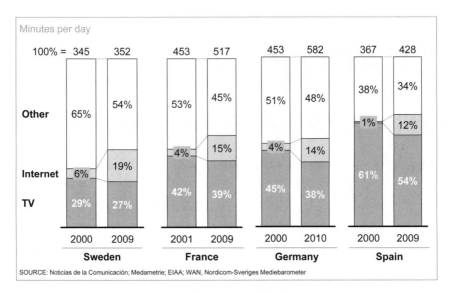

Exhibit 11.1 Increased internet usage.

most consumers' daily lives. Anyone born after 1980 is a digital native and this broadband brigade has left its mark on average media consumption. In 2000, the internet accounted for just 5 percent of consumers' daily media usage. By 2009, this had more than tripled in most countries (Exhibit 11.1). Experts believe this trend will persist. Analysts at Carat expect digital media – defined as comprising the internet, digital TV, wireless, games and digital radio – will account for 80 percent of our media consumption by 2020 (Exhibit 11.2).

In reaction to this development, advertisers and media agencies are shifting sizable chunks of their marketing budget to new media. According to a 2009 Forrester report, search engine marketing is the most important digital touch point for advertisers in the US, followed by display advertising. Overall, interactive advertising is expected to grow by 17 percent CAGR over the next 3 years, with social media as the most important driver of this growth (Exhibit 11.3).

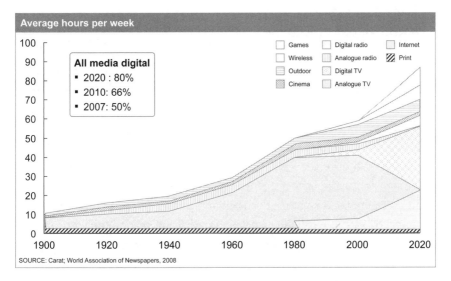

Exhibit 11.2 Global media consumption per week.

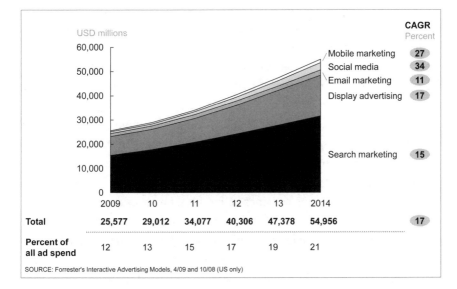

Exhibit 11.3 US interactive marketing spend.

More than you bargain for

When reviewing publicly available or proprietary reports on digital advertising spend, keep in mind that these figures usually only account for the 'bought' part of digital communication, i.e. activities paid for by advertisers and handled by media or online agencies. These reports do not usually show either 'owned' or 'earned' digital communication. 'Owned' communication is defined as the content delivered through a company's own websites. 'Earned' communication refers to the powerful user-generated stream of content and communication found in chat rooms, blogs and social media networks, partly in reaction to a company's pre-existing 'bought' and 'owned' content, partly as a result of the users' own independent initiative.

Has this digital flood reached the safe haven of retail yet? The answer is yes. Parts of it anyway. While traditional vehicles such as leaflets remain important for retailers, online and multichannel players are moving quickly to adapt their marketing mix. And even traditional retail giants are starting to feel the need to fortify their digital presence. Hans-Otto Schrader of Otto Group, a corporation comprising brick and mortar retail and catalogue-based mail order, as well as some online ventures, says: 'We aspire to be innovation leaders in mobile commerce and communication.' (FAZ #167, 22. Juli 2010).

Yet many marketers are uncertain about how to handle new media. In a survey among Chief Marketing Officers, we found that CMOs face two main challenges when it comes to digital marketing: a lack of standardized measurements and a lack of in-house skills. CMOs find it difficult to measure the impact of digital marketing activities on key brand metrics or purchase intent, and they struggle with the fact that there are no widely accepted performance indicators or universal providers of tracking data. Many marketing departments also find it difficult to find the right talent. Advertising agencies are not always helping this situation either: many are slow to embrace the challenges of 360° communication that includes both traditional and new media. (Sources: Blair Crawford, Jonathan W. Gordon, Susan R. Mulder, 'How consumer goods companies are coping with complexity', *McKinsey Quarterly*, May 2007; David Court, 'The evolving role of the CMO', *McKinsey Quarterly*, August 2007.)

Constant connectivity: *digital natives are online 24/7 – wherever they go, using everything that has a screen*

Five years ago the smart money was on Second Life. Companies, advertisers and agencies were placing major bets on a scenario that had users strapped to their chairs, staring at their desktop computer screens and remote-controlling clumsy avatars, shuffling in virtual sneakers on virtual dance floors. Today's digital reality is nothing like that. Usage of the web is neither an isolated nor a dedicated activity, but a constant and casual part of daily life.

In 2002, the launch of the BlackBerry marked the beginning of mobile internet connectivity. Since the first iPhone hit the streets in 2007, smart phone penetration has skyrocketed. According to Gartner, 94 percent of mobile phones sold in 2010 in Western Europe are capable of internet access (Exhibit 11.4).

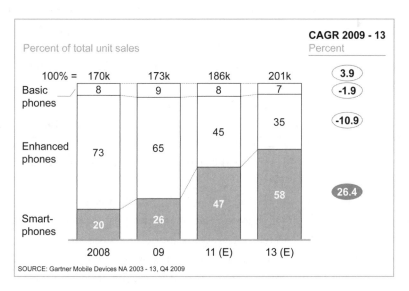

Exhibit 11.4 Penetration of web-enabled mobile phones.

But mobile access is more than a technological capacity. It's a consumer reality. Some 40 percent of iPhone users say they prefer to connect to the internet via their mobile phone, even when they are close to a PC (source: Geoff Duncan, 'Pew: 60 Pct of Americans Use Wireless Internet', www.digitaltrends. com, 8 July 2010). And it's more than just basic emailing and googling, too. For an increasing number of users, it is about staying in touch with their friends and peers. In January 2010 alone, more than 100 million visitors accessed Facebook – via their mobile phones. Consumers use constant connectivity to share their lives with the ones they hold dear – and everyone else who cares to listen. Why should retailers care? Because shopping is an important part of the lives of digital natives. Constant and instant connectivity make word of mouth a more powerful touch point than ever before. If a smart phone user happens upon a single rotten apple in a supermarket's fresh produce section, chances are that a global community of smart shoppers will know about it before the store manager does. But it works both ways: if an attentive salesperson walks up to that same shopper and takes their concerns seriously, the world will know this as well.

Of course, the implications of constant connectivity are not limited to word of mouth. Amazon is now so well established and ubiquitous that it has almost taken the place of the department store of yesteryear. Apple's AppStore is, effectively, an entire business model built around constant connectivity. Within 9 months of its launch, users downloaded more than one billion apps. (Source: 'Thanks a Billion. Over 1 billion downloads in just nine months. Only on the App Store', http://www.apple.com/itunes/billion-app-countdown/, entered 15 September 2010.) The ticket price may be low, but at that kind of scale, it still pays the bills. In May 2010, Apple's market capitalization exceeded that of Microsoft, a company three times the size of Apple in terms of the number of employees.

But the internet is more than a new retail format. It is also the source of considerable unease for traditional retailers. Some apps, for example, enable shoppers to scan the barcodes of products found in a store and access price comparisons and user reviews in real time, effectively curtailing the retailer's traditional in-store information monopoly. If this trend persists and retailers fail to develop compelling new propositions, tomorrow's stores may be little more than display windows for products that are researched – and purchased – online.

But constant connectivity also holds considerable opportunity for retailers. Smart sensors enable billboards to send text messages to the phones of users as they walk by. Products equipped with RFID (radio frequency identification) chips can communicate with shoppers' mobile devices, smart shopping carts and automated check-out systems, providing access to rich browsing and transaction data. NFC (near-field communication) capabilities enable mobile phones to take the role of credit cards. As usual, Japan leads the pack in this area. They were the first country to roll out mobile internet connectivity almost a decade ago – remember i-mode, anyone? – and now they have introduced a new currency based on mobile devices, Edy (Exhibit 11.5). By mid-2010 Edy was already accepted by more than 200,000 stores.

In effect, constant connectivity has made the internet a platform for information exchange, commercial transactions and payment. But there are more ways for retailers to put constant connectivity to good use. If properly incentivized, users are quite willing to reveal information such as their location

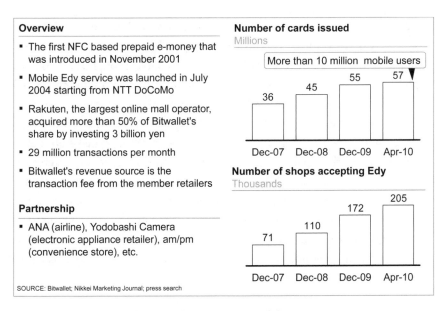

Exhibit 11.5 Edy, Japan's new mobile currency.

and preferences online. Take the example of Foursquare: if consumers use the website's service to share their current location with their friends, they consent to receive 'individual' advertisements with discounts from nearby venues such as restaurants, movie theatres or hotels. Although most retailers currently make little use of this kind of targeted marketing, the possibilities seem endless. Tomorrow's leaflets may well be personalized, localized – and virtual.

Social interaction: *the web is where digital natives meet, chat and play with their friends and peers*

Social networks and platforms are the killer applications of the interactive web. Two-thirds of the global internet population are using social network sites. Every day, some 200 million people log onto Facebook alone; the site's total number of subscribers had reached 500 million by July 2010. Every second, more than a thousand short messages, or 'tweets', are sent through Twitter's micro-blogging service, peaking at more than 3000 per second during NBA and soccer world cup finals. In the US 'tweet' was voted word of the year in 2009.

While social media started as a way of connecting and communicating with others, they have now become a space where people spend time – and money. Zynga's simulation game 'Farmville', which is available through Facebook and applications for Apple's iPhone and iPad, had more than 80 million registered users by May 2010 (*The Independent*, 2 May 2010). Many subscribers use their credit cards to purchase the Farmville coins they need to purchase land, equipment or buildings in the game. Facebook subscribers also make abundant use of the network's 'like' button to share their site and product preferences with other registered users. News about cool applications or products spreads swiftly and effectively through social media – at no direct cost to companies and advertisers. Leading companies actively take advantage of this kind of technology. Italian apparel heavyweight Diesel, for example, set up cameras in its stores so that shoppers could share photos of themselves, wearing a new pair of Diesel jeans, with their friends on Facebook.

Two-way marketing: *in the digital realm, consumers and companies connect at eye level*

Digital natives not only liaise with friends online but also reach out to companies to provide feedback and input. They even become 'friends' of these companies, often incentivized by first-hand news or special discounts. US electronics retailer Best Buy, for example, has made significant efforts to become a major force on Facebook. They hired and trained staff to answer questions from consumers almost in real time, staged exclusive presentations of new products and developed special offers only available to the 'friends' of the brand. As of July 2010, Best Buy had amassed a Facebook followership of 1.2 million users.

New opportunities also give rise to new types of company and business model. Groupon, for example, has taken advantage of the swarm-like

Nothing travels more quickly than bad news

Marketers need to keep in mind that consumers do not always wait for the company to start the dialogue. Often digital natives are the first to break the news, be it good or bad. Costco, for example, had to deal with a shopper who, after coming into their stores, made a habit of behaving in annoying ways, waiting to be kicked out. YouTube videos of his pranks achieved more than 300,000 hits per film. Examples like this show that two-way marketing can easily spin out of control. The voice of a single consumer can reach thousands of others in little more than a heartbeat. It is therefore all the more important that retailers should listen to their customers – and react in credible and authentic ways. Token replies or posts in the style and spirit of press releases are frequently the object of online ridicule. Grocery giant and marketing innovator Tesco says that it follows micro-blogging services like Twitter closely, albeit in 'listening mode'. (Sources: *ENP Newswire*, December 2009; *New Media Age*, April 2010; *Retail Week*, May 2010.)

characteristics of internet users, offering a 'deal of the day' that only becomes valid when a certain number of users are willing to buy it – a fast and safe track to marketing ROI, if ever there was one. This approach incentivizes users who have learnt about the offer to tell their friends, creating critical mass much more quickly than through traditional channels.

Consumer control: *digital natives are selective; they actively manage their media consumption*

While companies used to *send* and consumers used to *receive* marketing messages, digital natives increasingly act as their own editors. Traditional audience aggregators such as media companies are losing their influence as gatekeepers and intermediaries. Instead of tuning into TV and radio stations, or reading papers and magazines, digital natives are creating their individual content streams. Search engines and portals such as Google or Yahoo let users customize their starting pages with newsflashes, tweets, applets, widgets and games from a wide range of sources and providers. Using services such as Apple TV or Hulu, users buy videos and TV shows on demand to watch, pause, rewind and review at their own discretion on computers, smart phones, tablets or even game consoles. Amazon's Kindle, Sony's Reader and Apple's iPad have introduced a similar value proposition to the realm of print publishing. Consumer electronics companies such as Phillips, Samsung and Sony are currently developing set-top boxes and TV portals that will allow consumers to customize their media consumption in ways that will result in further erosion of mass-market vehicles and widespread audience fragmentation.

When it comes to shopping for physical products, specialized search engines, portals and price comparison services – such as guenstiger.de or pricerunner. co.uk – are increasingly important for shoppers at the pre-purchase stage, especially for big-ticket, non-recurring items. As a result, the importance of all but the most dominant online shops is likely to decrease. To pre-empt any commoditization of their offering, retailers have to find new ways to create lasting connections with their customers.

Total recall: *the web doesn't forget, and its inhabitants generate more data than most retailers have use for*

Digital natives value customization and interactivity. In return, they offer details of their lifestyle, as seen in their preferences on Facebook, wish lists on Amazon or their present location on Foursquare. It is up to retailers and their online agencies to absorb and leverage this wealth of information. The consumer's liberal hand even extends beyond individual bits and pieces of information. Through Facebook's 'Connect' service, for example, they log onto third-party websites using their Facebook login data without registering at the destination page. The service offers convenience to its users – and almost unlimited audience tracking opportunities to Facebook and its partners. In 2010, some 60 million Facebook members were using the service, enabling the site to track their visits and purchases on more than 250,000 third-party web pages from participating sites. This emerging log may soon be the world's richest consumer journal, offering new and manifold opportunities for targeted marketing and ROI optimization. Amazon is already leveraging users' entry points and track records as direct ROI drivers. If a given user comes from a price comparison website and has an Amazon history of low-price purchases, prices will be lower for them than for those users who have come to its site directly from a Google search.

For retailers who are overwhelmed by the wealth and disparity of data generated online, specialized aggregators and providers are helpful intermediaries for establishing which information really matters. Who cares about hourly updates on third-level page impressions, after all? If a piece of information cannot be translated into input for a relevant business decision it is useless to the company. Services such as NM Incite can help you slice and dice data for different business functions, including assortment management, pricing, communication and customer service.

To stay on top of the data, companies positioned along the same value chain (e.g. OEMs, retailers and research agencies) have also started forming alliances to increase the efficiency of their data gathering and leverage. There is no harm in talking to vendors and providers of tracking data to find out whether it makes sense to pool your digital marketing resources.

Think evolution, not revolution: *retailers should stay on top of digital trends, but balance new and traditional marketing vehicles carefully*

Technological innovation has given today's consumers new and exciting powers. They expose retailers and their products to close public scrutiny. But they also reach out to their favourite brands and companies with unexpected fervour and dedication. Customers will continue to demand more attention, commitment and care from retailers. However, yesterday's assets, such as a convenient location, an attractive assortment, a low price or a warm smile from sales staff will still be important, but not sufficient in this world.

So what is it that you will need to do differently to succeed as a retailer in the digitalized environment? The first and most fundamental mindset change is to think of retail marketing in a more holistic, integrated way. Tomorrow's communication channels are manifold, interactive and dynamic. You cannot afford to lose touch with the consumer of tomorrow, so you need to start expanding your marketing mix today. Even if you feel you are not up to a digital big bang, there is no harm in reserving a small part of your marketing budget to take controlled risks with selected digital communication vehicles. This way, you will learn quickly what works for you and your audience – and what doesn't.

Yet it is also safe to say that there will still be leaflets in tomorrow's retail marketing mix. Digital touch points currently play only a relatively minor role for most retailers. According to a survey conducted by the Allensbach Institute in July 2010, for instance, Germans still have a clear preference for traditional media as their prime source of information on current affairs. While 69 percent rely on TV and 50 percent on newspapers, only 16 percent say that the internet is their primary source. What retailers are witnessing is digital evolution, not a revolution. While touch points such as push email, online advertising or web feeds will inevitably become increasingly important, they will not replace leaflets and local print advertising anytime soon.

The rise of new vehicles does not mean that trusted tools and approaches have become obsolete; in fact, the contrary is true. In order to avoid hasty reactions to the apparent changes in consumer behaviour, retailers would be well advised to treat digital marketing like any other touch point, at least when it comes to budget allocation and effectiveness monitoring. The Reach–Cost–Quality

(RCQ) and Marketing Mix Modelling (MMM) approaches introduced in Chapters 9 and 10 are fully applicable to digital media. As in the case of all other touch points, the quality of such analyses will depend on the availability of reliable information about the reach, cost and quality of the different digital instruments, such as banner ads, video streaming and social media posts.

Interview: Alastair Bruce
Director, Google Germany

'The end of the digital age: "No line" is the new retail mantra'
We spoke with Alastair Bruce, Director of Google Germany, about the future of retail marketing. Google advises leading national and international retail companies on digital strategy, particularly relating to e-commerce, branding, and mobile platforms.

Q: How important is digital marketing in retailers' current marketing strategies? How do you think this will change?

Alastair Bruce: One of the CMO's key tasks in any business is to ensure maximum return on total marketing investment. Retail is no exception. Marketing and communication strategies typically reflect media usage, since marketing experts seek to reach their target consumers efficiently. 'Dollars follow eyeballs' is an old adage, but still true in the digital age. CMOs need to respond to changing media consumption patterns and adapt their marketing plans accordingly if they want to maximize return on marketing investment. The media landscape has changed fundamentally. YouTube didn't even exist 5 years ago!

Today, we see a shift in media usage towards online. Just take a look at the young target group, aged 14–19 years: 97 percent of them use the internet. (Source: AGOF Internet Facts 2010, June 2010.) This means that the internet will become the new lead medium in the not too distant future. E-commerce is already a common feature of most European markets. Indeed, the pace is picking up. Whilst traditional 'bricks and mortar' retail business volume in Germany stagnates, e-commerce turnover grew year on year by 14 percent in 2009. (Source: GfK Webscope, 2008 and 2009.) The dynamic is similar across most of Europe.

Media budgets will continue to shift from offline to online, where MROI can be quantified more precisely. Consequently, online marketing will play an even more central role in the marketing mix than is does today. Mastering the skills of online marketing will be a key prerequisite of future success. Organizations will need to develop and nurture the appropriate skill sets.

We live in exponential times, where change is the new norm. Retail will be impacted strongly, as will other industries. It no longer makes sense to talk about digital and analogue, traditional and new, online and offline – it's simply the real world, and we are all challenged to think beyond just e-commerce.

Q: What are the key opportunities and challenges for retailers?

Alastair Bruce: Since more and more people can now only be reached online, the key importance of the internet will be amplified: both as a sales channel and as a customer acquisition tool. Online marketing has a higher degree of measurability and flexibility compared to the offline world. It is highly transparent. Users can be targeted accurately, and the success can be measured with high precision. Let's take an AdWords campaign as an example: you have full flexibility. You can turn the volume of the campaign up or down at anytime, and refresh your content as frequently as you wish. Indeed, some advanced retailers even connect their inventory management systems to their online campaigns. This enables them to integrate real-time information (e.g. stock availability and price changes) into their online marketing campaigns automatically.

During the next 2 years, a key challenge for advertisers will be to optimize their marketing mix by taking into account all marketing channels and key performance indicators. 'In which medium should I invest?' is the 'sixty four thousand dollar' question that will occupy both CMOs and CFOs. Forget simple bidding strategies like 'last cookie counts'. It is no longer sufficient to analyze marketing channels in splendid isolation. Channel interdependencies and 'knock-on' effects will need to be factored in. Value attribution modelling will become increasingly important. Capturing and reflecting, for example, the 'full value of search' will emerge as a central marketing discipline. Marketing and finance experts will cooperate more closely than ever before – both by design and by necessity.

Mobile marketing is a major disruptive trend. The potential for retailers is enormous. Few have recognized this yet. Mobile can have impact at all stages of the purchase funnel. Traditional AIDA paradigms remain relevant, but will require new interpretation in the context of an 'always online' mindset. We are just at the beginning of this phenomenal behaviour shift. Currently, we have 12 percent smart phone penetration in Germany, and the share of smart phone users is predicted to grow by a staggering 83 percent by 2012. (Sources: Otto Group, Google, tns infratest, Trend Büro: Go Smart 2012. Always-In-Touch. Studie zur Smartphone-Nutzung 2012, May 2010.) We can only begin to speculate about the likely impact on consumer behaviour. As mobile phones connect the offline to the online world, retailers will need to think 'mobile first'. Today, many lag well behind.

Q: How well are European retailers prepared to take on these challenges?

Alastair Bruce: E-commerce readiness varies from retailer to retailer. Broadly speaking, virtually all retailers have included e-commerce into their overall business strategy. But the degree of sophistication varies greatly. Few are leading-edge practitioners. Even fewer fully understand the mobile opportunity and have embraced it within their online strategy.

E-commerce pioneers of the 1990s, like Amazon, and of the recent past, like asos.com, are perfectly positioned to capitalize the most recent trends. On the other hand, more traditional mail order retailers or high street retailers with a strong heritage in the offline world first have to adapt to new business models and structures. Progress here may be slower.

In my view, there are two prerequisites for businesses seeking to win in the online space. The first is to secure board-level buy-in to the digital strategy. This is absolutely critical. It is the key success factor, driving – or hindering – everything else. The second is to build online competence and capability, such as search engine marketing and data mining expertise, appropriate organizational structures, flexible IT technology, modern back-end systems, and so on. Boards have the strategic choice between 'make or buy'. There are no right answers.

Online used to be a topic for IT experts only. Today it is a key strategic issue for the board.

Q: What differences do you see across countries and between retail categories?

Alastair Bruce: There is a wide variation in e-commerce capability and performance across Europe. Today, we still see a strong north–south divide. While the internet represents 9.5 percent, 6.9 percent and 4.9 percent of total sales in the UK, Germany and France, respectively, Italy and Spain rank among the lowest-scoring countries with just 0.8 percent and 1 percent of online retail sales. (Source: *eMarketer*, Retail E-Commerce in Western Europe, May 2010.) Lagging markets will catch up rapidly in the coming years and may even overtake countries that are currently more advanced.

The same applies to retail categories. We observe mature categories, like books or consumer electronics, on the one hand, and rising categories with substantial growth, like fashion, on the other. While computers and electronics still account for a 43 percent share of sales in Germany, the fashion segment was the only category which was able to grow its share of sales from 20 to 24 percent from 2008 to 2009. (Source: GfK Webscope, 2008 and 2009.) Categories to look out for in the future will be furniture and DIY products.

Q: Which retail categories will derive the greatest benefit from digital marketing opportunities?

Alastair Bruce: I firmly believe that you can sell almost anything online nowadays. Technical innovation and sales channel convergence are driving true multimedia online retail experiences. Take fashion as an example: product videos, augmented reality apps, or zoom functionality are increasingly able to compensate for the lack of the sensual experience. Coupled with excellent logistics services, e.g. credit card payment, free shipping and simple returns, and attractive pricing, the online retail experience often stacks up well against 'brick-and-mortar' shopping.

Previously, retailers distinguished clearly between offline and online and were keen to defend footfall and turnover in physical stores. Increasingly, this demarcation is blurring. The landscape is changing, driven by the powerful combination of technical innovation and consumer behaviour. Digital is rapidly becoming integral to multi-channel retailing. Future winners are already embracing this development actively.

'No line' is emerging as the new retail mantra.

CHAPTER 12

Nicolò Galante, Alex Perez-Tenessa de Block, Toni Schmidt

The point of sale (POS) is the most powerful marketing vehicle available to a retailer. No other marketing vehicle can match its ability to influence consumers at the time of purchase. And while all retailers control their POS, very few reap the full benefit of POS marketing.

POS marketing includes any marketing activity a retailer can unfold in its stores, be it through visual merchandising or through the service and performance of frontline employees. Both elements are potential levers for retailers to differentiate themselves from the competition. POS marketing, when well done, has real and tangible business impact: it drives traffic, improves conversion and increases basket size. Yet many retailers consider POS marketing as just another cost position, rather than as an investment in one of the most effective consumer touch points imaginable. This chapter covers a wide range of tools and methods to help retailers unleash its full power and to bring analytical rigour to the art of POS marketing. We have also included a number of practical hints and examples of best practice.

For retailers, the POS is the most powerful marketing vehicle

The point of sale is not just a place where goods are sold: it is a major marketing vehicle that retailers should use to create a unique consumer experience, communicate with their target audience, build their brand image and, ultimately, drive sales. Visiting a store is a multi-sensorial experience: as shoppers enter and walk through a store, they see a myriad of goods, smell the scents, listen to the sounds, touch and try out products, meet sales staff and other shoppers and, finally, interact with the cashier. No other medium can match the richness of this interaction.

Because of its direct impact on the consumer's brand experience, POS marketing should be an integral part of every retail branding effort. What is more, its reach exceeds that of most traditional mass-marketing channels. According to media experts, an end-cap at Wal-Mart reaches more people in a week than a 30-second commercial on prime-time television. As the number of advertising vehicles grows and the traditional media landscape becomes increasingly fragmented, the store is, potentially, the last single touch point that can reach 'the masses' – after all, everybody has to shop. And most of the people you reach in the store are there with the intention of making a purchase, ensuring that in-store marketing is particularly valuable to retailers and their suppliers.

In-store marketing beats every other medium in terms of its 'brain hours' (see Exhibit 12.1) – a measure of marketing intensity that combines the number of people a medium can reach with the length of time they are exposed to

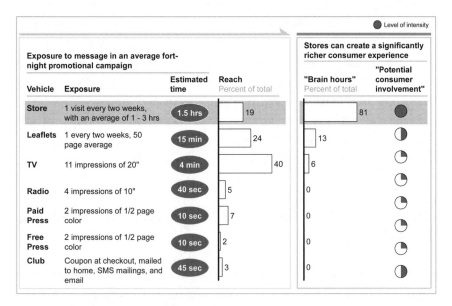

Exhibit 12.1 Ranking of marketing vehicles by 'brain hours'.

that medium. It shows that in terms of its high-intensity interaction with the consumer, the store is an unbeatable marketing vehicle.

But the power of POS marketing is not limited to its high level of exposure and involvement. POS marketing also carries a 'halo' effect that extends beyond the shopping experience and touches fundamental aspects of the consumer's perception of a retailer. A McKinsey survey of several hundred shoppers in a large multi-category retailer in North America highlights clearly the impact of POS marketing on their overall perception of the retailer (McKinsey US consumer survey, March 2009). The participants were asked to assess two stores. The outlets only differed in their POS marketing; all other aspects – assortment, pricing, promotions, etc. – were the same (about 400 participants qualified to answer this question). Not only did the store with the improved POS marketing score 10–20 percent higher on all shopping experience attributes; it also helped improve the retailer's brand image, including attributes such as 'quality of the assortment', 'breadth of the assortment', 'quality of the private brand' and 'value for money'.

Despite its importance, many retailers don't leverage the store effectively

According to estimates, 70 percent of all purchasing decisions are taken at the point of sale. Even when making basic or repeat shopping trips, most people do not use or do not follow a shopping list. POS marketing reaches consumers just at the decisive moment when it can have a huge effect on their purchasing decisions – in a more direct way than any out-of-store marketing activity. POS marketing has the potential to drive traffic, improve conversion and increase basket size. Given this potential, you would expect POS marketing to be a top-priority item for retailers. But surprisingly, POS marketing is often neglected, both in terms of budget and in terms of management attention.

In a McKinsey survey of executives from various functions at six leading North American retailers, 'in-store experience' was ranked as the least critical capability necessary for running their business (out of a list of 13; McKinsey survey, May 2010). In consequence, POS marketing is often in the hands of inexperienced, time-constrained buyers who are given loose guidelines – 'make it compelling' or 'surprise and delight the shopper' – but who have no tools available to help them make the right decisions. The resulting POS marketing decisions are based on gut feeling and fail to deliver a consistent ROI. One result of this is that many executives entertain fundamental doubts about the value of POS marketing as a whole. And so the vicious circle continues.

Over the course of our work with retailers across multiple subsectors we have found five symptoms typical of sub-optimal POS marketing management:

- A lack of transparency about the return of POS marketing investments, or experience of inconsistent and often negative returns.
- A split in POS marketing responsibility between different functions, with some decisions left to junior employees in addition to their 'regular' work.
- POS-related decisions are based on intuition and creative talent, rather than on facts and the evidence from past successes.
- Discussions on POS marketing are overly focused on physical elements, such as signage or lighting, rather than on the overall consumer experience.
- The decision-making process does not have systematic links to merchandising, marketing, consumer insight or store design groups.

The effect: consumer confusion. Stores to which the above observations apply will have a hard time creating a consistent consumer experience in line with the brand proposition of the retailer. So while their control of the POS puts retailers in a powerful position, many do not make the most of it.

Systematic POS management *can advance both long-term brand building and short-term business success*

To extract the full value of POS marketing, retailers need to set up a disciplined process that covers both sales generation and brand building, as well as the appropriate analytical tools.

Any effective use of POS marketing as a brand building instrument starts with a clear definition of the message retailers want their stores to convey. Like any other touch point, the store is a communication vehicle that can and should carry the retailer's overarching message. It can either contribute to the holistic delivery of that message, or it can do a very effective job of confusing it! Even a clear message can be delivered unclearly: 'The road to hell is paved with good intentions,' as a sixteenth-century proverb says. By analogy, it is safe to say that the store from hell is plastered with signs and posters. The arch-enemies of clarity in POS communication are inconsistency and clutter.

Inconsistency – of styles and messages – is mainly the result of too many POS marketing decisions being pushed down to the buyer level. This inconsistency is often increased by POS material that suppliers, eager to promote their own brand message and style, manage to push into the stores. Best-in-class retailers set and enforce strict guidelines on style and communication that apply to their entire network, covering three levels: the 'sky level' (directional, overhead signage), the 'eye level' (top-of-shelf signage) and the 'buy level' (on-shelf signage).

But even if the signs and labels are consistent, there can still be too many of them. Clutter is usually the result of retailers trying to compensate for their lack of a clear POS marketing strategy with a proliferation of POS materials. One consumer electronics retailer in North America was able to reduce its POS costs by 20 percent after identifying that 30 percent of its POS materials were ineffective – ineffective being defined as materials that were noticed by less than 1 percent of shoppers. Best-practice retailers use signage sparingly and only when and where it is truly needed, preferring to let the merchandise speak for itself as often as possible.

But POS marketing does not only mean defining an overarching message and making sure it is consistently communicated in the store; it can also help to achieve concrete business objectives. The general situation of the retailer, or of a specific category, should determine which business objective is the most relevant in guiding POS marketing investment decisions. Surveys, in-store observations and analyses of POS data can help retailers gain a good sense of their strengths and weaknesses. Based on these insights, they can define their areas of focus for POS marketing and then set hard targets for investments. Typically, POS marketing can serve three types of business objective:

- drive traffic, frequency and loyalty
- improve conversion
- increase average basket size.

Imagine a multi-category retailer that wants to drive sales in its underperforming children's apparel category using POS marketing. The company's first move is to conduct a shopping funnel analysis to identify gaps in the category relative to external benchmarks (Exhibit 12.2). It then combines this benchmarking information with insights derived from consumer research on the importance of POS marketing in the different stages of the shopping funnel. In this example, the shopping funnel analysis indicated both that repeat purchase traffic is in line with external benchmarks, and that the retailer's basket size is clearly better than that of the benchmarks. The underperformance of children's apparel appears to be rooted in the retailer's inability to drive more first-time planned and unplanned traffic into the department, and then to turn these visitors into buyers. The insights of this analysis indicated to the retailer that it needed to focus its POS marketing investments on driving unplanned traffic and conversion. Levers other than POS marketing were shown to be more effective in driving first-time planned traffic into the department.

	Traffic (Percent of shoppers/ total visitors)			Conversion Percent (purchasers/ total shoppers)	Basket size (Percent of shoppers with 2+ items in the basket)
	Planned		**Unplanned**		
	First time	**Repeat purchase**			
Children's apparel	3	18	14	65	37
Best competitor	7	16	16	69	29
Potential sales lift in reaching benchmark USD millions	11		9	25	
POS marketing relevance index[1] (1 - 5)	0.9		2.6	3.9	

1 Based on derived importance in customer research

Priority visual investments

Exhibit 12.2 Shopping funnel analysis used to identify category gaps.

Limitations of POS at early purchase funnel stages

Clearly, consumers are influenced by many factors other than POS marketing – such as classical advertising or coupons – at every step of the purchase funnel. So before deciding to fix a given gap in the funnel with POS marketing investments, retailers are well advised to check whether the in-store experience is really a relevant driver of the transfer in question. In the example shown in Exhibit 12.2, a deeper analysis of the purchasing drivers showed that while POS marketing was a key driver of conversion, it was not a driver of first-time traffic. In other words, a superior in-store experience helps to turn visitors into buyers and justifies respective POS marketing investments. But POS marketing does not – and perhaps cannot – lure first-time visitors into the store or the respective department. In consequence, you will need to make investments in other activities to drive first-time traffic, such as traditional advertising or billboards placed near the store.

The tangible and intangible elements of POS marketing *have to work in tandem*

Essentially, we believe that POS marketing is composed of a tangible part and an intangible part. The tangible part comprises all types of visual merchandising in the store, e.g. improvements to the look and feel of the store, cross-merchandising and visual promotions. The intangible part is the human factor: the mindset and behaviour of the retailer's frontline employees, such as sales staff and cashiers, who play a vital role for the success of POS marketing. While successful POS marketing depends on the integration and coordination of tangible and intangible elements, a given retail company may want to prioritize either one, depending on its business objectives (Exhibit 12.3).

Visual merchandising, the tangible part of POS marketing, is a major marketing lever and sales driver for retailers. Using advanced statistical analysis we have developed an approach that ties decisions about the look and feel of the store, its use of cross-merchandising and its display organization and signage to specific business objectives.

The basic logic is as follows.

- An appealing *look and feel* is primarily intended to attract shoppers to the store or department. This especially applies to categories within larger stores, where the goal is to leverage existing traffic – that is, to entice shoppers who came into the store for other reasons to visit the department in question.
- *Display organization and decision-support signage* exists to make it easy for shoppers to find the products they want; these are therefore good investments, if the objective is to increase conversion.
- *Cross-merchandising* is an effective way to increase average basket size by driving unplanned purchases (see Exhibit 12.3).

One store's look and feel is not necessarily 'better' than another's. It is simply a matter of creating an experience that matches the target consumer's needs and expectations. The right question to ask is: how do we come up with the right experience for our target audience? To answer this question and to

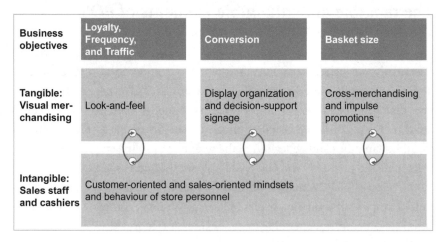

Exhibit 12.3 Successful POS marketing combines the power of tangible and intangible elements.

help retailers create the look and feel that will attract their target audience, we have developed an approach to visual merchandising that shifts the retailer's attention from hard assets (such as fixtures, lighting or signage) to the overall consumer experience.

We recommend a two-stage approach to optimizing the look and feel of a store. Start by brainstorming about which attributes could potentially be important for the target audience, and then test your long list in a comprehensive consumer survey. Making sure that this consumer survey is truly comprehensive is a critical aspect of this stage. The 'visual merchandising triangle' (Exhibit 12.4) is an aid that can help retailers to design an exhaustive survey. The triangle's three sides represent the three main attributes of visual merchandising communication: emotional, rational and reputational. Carrying out statistical analysis of customer behaviour to determine the ranked importance to the consumers of the various attributes will enable the retailer to identify the aspects that are most likely to drive traffic, frequency and loyalty.

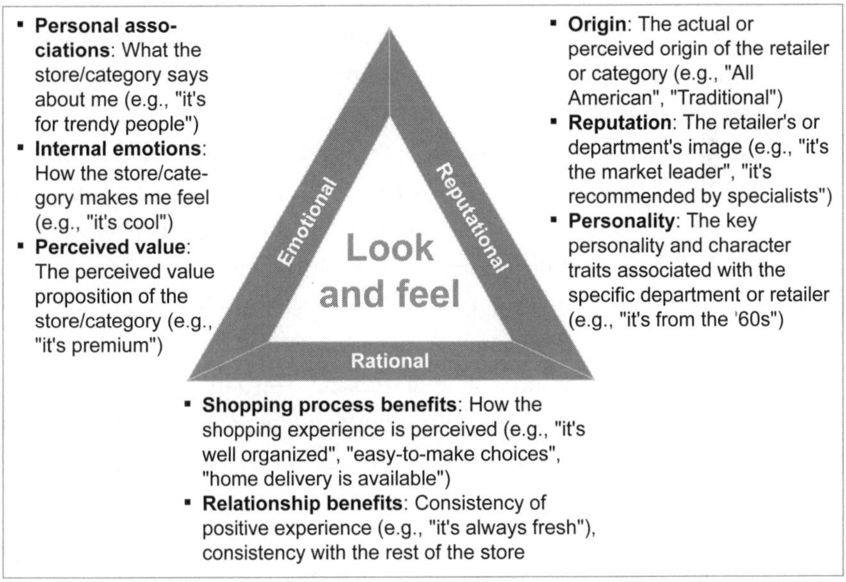

- **Personal associations**: What the store/category says about me (e.g., "it's for trendy people")
- **Internal emotions**: How the store/category makes me feel (e.g., "it's cool")
- **Perceived value**: The perceived value proposition of the store/category (e.g., "it's premium")

Emotional

Reputational

Look and feel

Rational

- **Origin**: The actual or perceived origin of the retailer or category (e.g., "All American", "Traditional")
- **Reputation**: The retailer's or department's image (e.g., "it's the market leader", "it's recommended by specialists")
- **Personality**: The key personality and character traits associated with the specific department or retailer (e.g., "it's from the '60s")

- **Shopping process benefits**: How the shopping experience is perceived (e.g., "it's well organized", "easy-to-make choices", "home delivery is available")
- **Relationship benefits**: Consistency of positive experience (e.g., "it's always fresh"), consistency with the rest of the store

Exhibit 12.4 The visual merchandising triangle.

Don't let me be misunderstood

When conducting consumer surveys to identify the drivers of traffic, frequency or loyalty, retailers should be mindful of what the specific attributes actually mean to the survey participants. For example, in one case, 'modern-looking' came up at the top of the list of the desired look-and-feel attributes. However, when the company tested this attribute against reference pictures, they found that what consumers considered to be 'modern-looking' was the use of wooden fixtures and natural plant decorations, whereas geometric shapes in bold colours and simple lines were considered 'old-fashioned'. Obviously, a written statement or attribute can mean different things to different people; it is vital to double-check that the common interpretation is the one the survey designer had in mind.

Once the key design attributes for the store are clear, the retailer should then work with design firms to translate these attributes into alternative look-and-feel options. Each of these options should be tested with consumers, and the top options piloted. While this approach might at first sight seem somewhat cumbersome, it actually leaves a great deal of room for creativity. Instead of reducing visual merchandising to a set of purely physical guidelines, it creates leeway for the creativity of designers and other specialists. Instead of specifying the colours, sizes and styles of physical fixtures, it provides general direction for the desired consumer experience, empowering the designers to create new and original solutions. While plunging straight in and testing various physical aspects of a new store design might seem like a faster route, it is far less likely to deliver a unique store experience.

Best-practice retailers use planogramming software to create planogrammes, i.e. diagrams that show the various product types and locations in each aisle. These planogrammes can be optimized using four principal types of input:

- the overarching organization scheme (e.g. by brand, colour, etc.)
- the retailer's product goals (e.g. private label products to be given prime positioning)

Best-practice example

Visual merchandising driven by consumer needs: Best Buy
Once a compelling look and feel has attracted consumers into the store or department, the next task is to drive conversion through intuitive display organization and helpful signage. While the former helps determined shoppers to find the product they want, the latter helps those who are still undecided to choose the right product.

Consider the look and feel of the TV department at a Best Buy store. The setup is built around two critical attributes for buyers of TV sets.

Consumers like to see their future TV set the way it will look at home. Based on this insight, Best Buy redesigned its entire TV department to give it a look and feel more like that of a home living room, rather than a traditional electronics showroom.

Consumers want no-nonsense information to support easy choices. In response to this desire, Best Buy has put in place signage that visually explains the key features of TV sets using everyday language. Few consumers know, for example, what '720p' or '1080p' means, but 'HDTV-ready, ideal for watching sports' or 'Blu-ray-ready, great for movies' will help them make their choice.

- the products' physical characteristics (e.g. size, colour) and
- sales expectations.

The overarching organization scheme is maybe the most critical input factor, as it determines whether or not the shopper will have trouble finding the product they are looking for, an aspect that has a direct influence on conversion rates. In our experience, the planogrammes that drive the greatest conversion rates are organized according to consumer decision trees. Each decision tree shows the order and importance of the various factors shoppers consider when making a purchase in a specific category. For instance, when buying a writing instrument, a given shopper might first decide on a broad category (e.g. pen or marker), then the brand, followed by the pack size (if appropriate) and, lastly,

Beware of skewed consumer decision trees

Multi-category retailers typically rely on suppliers to provide them with an understanding of the various consumer decision trees; but supplier information is not always reliable. Suppliers will tend, for obvious reasons, to emphasize brand as the most important factor, even when this is not the case and other factors are, in fact, more important. It therefore often makes sense for the retailer to investigate consumer decision trees independently. Exhibit 12.5 outlines two proven approaches for building accurate consumer decision trees.

A statistical analysis of household baskets, relying on internal POS data (see left-hand side of Exhibit 12.5), can enable retailers to recreate decision trees with great accuracy. In non-recurrent categories, retailers must turn to consumer survey data as the basis for creating a decision tree (see right-hand side of Exhibit 12.5).

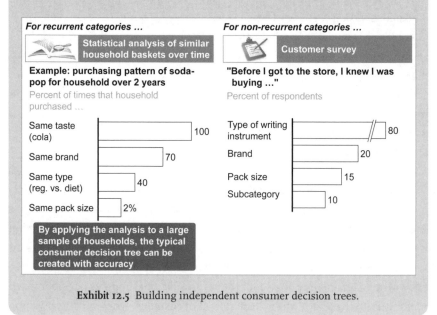

Exhibit 12.5 Building independent consumer decision trees.

the specific type of instrument (e.g. rollerball or gel pen). Once the retailer is aware of this decision-making process, it is easy for them to organize the products on the shelf accordingly.

In addition to considering the look and feel of the store and the location of products, the retailer also needs to consider the role of decision-support signage. Good signage can help shoppers make better buying decisions. The first step is for the retailer to use market research to identify the top four or five product features that are most important to consumers (e.g. sound quality, battery life) for a given product range. Once the top features have been identified, these can be highlighted in ways that are easily absorbed.

You can have too much of a good thing, however. Each sign needs to justify itself by adding real value. A North American apparel retailer introduced a sign in its underwear category stating that a given product was 'available in multiple colours'; however, shoppers were able to see for themselves the range of colours available on the shelf. In this case, the sign was clearly unnecessary; in addition to carrying a cost, it reduced the visual clarity of the display. As a general rule of thumb, we have found that 'less is more' when it comes to decision-support signage, particularly in recurrent purchase categories.

Once visitors have been turned into shoppers, the third challenge for visual merchandising is to maximize their average basket size through cross-merchandising. The difficulty typically lies in the way store and merchandising staff are incentivized, and in the multitude of possible combinations for cross-merchandising. This challenge is made all the greater because the combinations of cross-merchandising items need to be changed regularly in order to keep the store fresh. This quickly becomes a complex optimization problem.

Many retailers collect data on product affinities (i.e. the product categories that regularly appear in the same household basket), but few are able to use the data effectively. Though this information is often stored in huge and intricate databases, few have developed the analytical capabilities required to use this wealth of data in a systematic process that can identify affinities at the department level, the sub-category level and item level. The power of such a system is that it can throw up the unexpected. It might, for example, recommend selling sticky notes alongside three-ring binders – maybe not an intuitively obvious pairing but one that is commonly found in household baskets (see Exhibit 12.6).

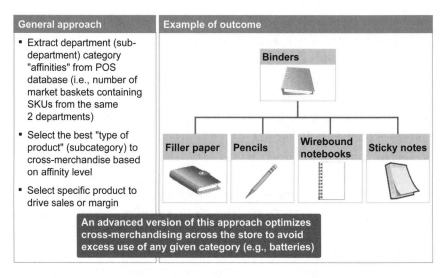

General approach	Example of outcome
• Extract department (sub-department) category "affinities" from POS database (i.e., number of market baskets containing SKUs from the same 2 departments) • Select the best "type of product" (subcategory) to cross-merchandise based on affinity level • Select specific product to drive sales or margin	(diagram)

An advanced version of this approach optimizes cross-merchandising across the store to avoid excess use of any given category (e.g., batteries)

Exhibit 12.6 Optimization of cross-merchandising based on basket affinity.

Innovative cross-merchandising case example

Albert Heijn 'Choose & Cook'

Cross-merchandising based on basket affinity can prove tricky in practice. For instance, in a number of Western European countries, a typical meal features meat or fish, together with vegetables, noodles or rice, and some kind of sauce. Consumers shopping for such a meal will usually have to visit any number of different aisles to find all the necessary products. Dutch supermarket giant Albert Heijn has come up with a simple but highly consumer-centric solution: in its '*Kies & Kook*' (Choose & Cook) range – it places all the components of a number of simple meals on a single shelf. Hungry shoppers in a hurry who are looking for a well-balanced and affordable meal can therefore pick and choose all the ingredients they need from the *Kies & Kook* range, without having to roam the store looking for them.

Go with the flow

Not all square metres in a store are equal to one another. Most stores have high and low traffic areas. While this fact may seem obvious, many retailers underestimate their power to control the traffic. Low traffic in some areas and potential overcrowding in others is often the direct result of store layout issues. To fix these issues, retailers need to know the 'hot' and 'cold' areas of their stores. A store heat map analysis is a simple but effective way of achieving this (Exhibit 12.7). To create a heat map, walk briskly through the store or department and count the number of customers in each aisle. To avoid skewing the data, repeat this several times over the course of a typical day to account for changes in traffic intensity and patterns. Then map the heat levels, calibrated to the maximum number of visitors in the most populated aisle, i.e. if the maximum level is 15, then the relevant brackets could be 1–3 for cold, 4–10 for medium, 11–15 for hot. Based on the heat map, the store managers – or retail executives, if multiple stores are involved – can then make improvements to the floor plan, shelf layouts and displays to optimize the traffic flow.

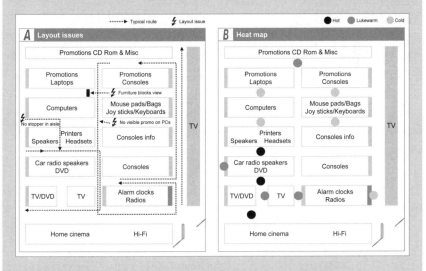

Exhibit 12.7 Store heat map example from Image & Sound department of an electronics retailer.

The human factor is make or break for the consumer's POS experience; *frontline employees are a retailer's foremost ambassadors*

Even the best visual merchandising efforts will only be successful if the store personnel are playing their part. The behaviour of store personnel, the intangible element of POS marketing, is at least as important as the tangible elements discussed above: this human factor is especially important in turning visitors into purchasers. In the real-life case of an apparel retail store, for instance, the conversion rate for those consumers who met a salesperson while shopping was about 70 percent; this figure plunged to 15 percent for those who did not meet a salesperson.

Most retailers are clear about how their frontline employees should behave: the defining element of their work should be the consumer, not the task at hand. They are supposed to be friendly, greeting the shoppers when they enter the store or department, provide advice, encourage them to try on clothes or try out a product, and bid them farewell when they leave. Sales staff ought to provide follow-up recommendations and highlight complementary products; cashiers should be friendly, fast and efficient, ensuring short check-out times. And so on.

While much of this is uncontroversial, many retailers struggle to ensure that this kind of behaviour is adopted consistently in their stores on a day-to-day basis. Retail chains with a large number of outlets try hard to get the best of both worlds by realizing the scale of big-box format while maintaining the quality and individuality of frontline execution found in 'mom-and-pop' stores. But these objectives are hard to combine successfully. Scale comes at a price: compared to mom-and-pop stores, which can maintain personal relationships, large retailing enterprises have very limited control over their outlet interaction. As a result, sales productivity often varies greatly across outlets and employees. In our experience, the top 10 percent of stores are often twice as productive as the bottom 10 percent. Among employees, productivity regularly differs by a factor of five. Executives in charge of frontline management cite several reasons for this variation. They argue that given the large number and dispersal of outlets, it is only natural for productivity to vary. They say that the skill level of personnel is generally medium to low and that it is difficult to improve skills adequately through training, partly because of the high rate of staff turnover.

But the biggest obstacles to frontline sales excellence are more fundamental: the lack of clearly defined responsibilities on the one hand and the lack of knowledge and tools on the other. As a result, many outlet managers are often not even aware of the performance gaps in their stores. The way forward is to improve communication between the retail headquarters and its outlets. Managers at the regional and individual store level need a clear sense of their roles and responsibilities, and they need the tools to track and improve the performance of their stores and teams. It is essential that clear metrics on the impact of frontline performance should be in place (ideally, above and beyond mere sales performance), that store staff are organized and incentivized accordingly, and that regional and store managers act as role models.

A top-down approach is often not the right solution, however. If the corporate board develops the company's sales strategy, in doing so it will squander the knowledge of its frontline personnel. Such an approach will undermine the entrepreneurial spirit of the organization: managers and sales personnel who feel they have no clear stake in a store's success will simply do what they are told to do – hopefully no less than that, but definitely no more!

A proven way to correct these performance gaps – balancing the need for common quality standards with that of tapping into local expertise and initiative – is to conduct on-site workshops that welcome and encourage the initiatives of frontline staff. If aided by centrally developed tools and guidelines, frontline staff participating in such workshops will be able to identify and execute improvement measures quickly and easily. Often, they will start to take effect the day after the workshop.

Such explicit empowerment also fosters local entrepreneurship. Giving credit to the sales staff's ideas strengthens their commitment to becoming part of a high-performing sales organization. One welcome side effect of the training and empowerment of the frontline staff is that it also maximizes the value that can be extracted from the tangible elements of POS marketing: well-trained and highly motivated salespeople will put the visual merchandising and other POS materials to their best use – and in the process become powerful ambassadors of the retailer's brand.

Key takeaways – POS marketing

1 For retailers, the POS is the most powerful marketing vehicle.
2 Despite its importance, many retailers don't leverage the store effectively.
3 Systematic POS marketing can advance both long-term brand building and short-term business success.
4 The tangible (visual merchandising) and intangible elements (mindset and behaviour of store personnel) of POS marketing have to work in tandem.
5 The human factor is make or break for the consumer's POS experience; frontline employees are a retailer's foremost ambassadors.

CHAPTER 13

LEAFLETS AND LOCAL PRINT ADVERTISING: HOW TO ACHIEVE LOCAL MEDIA EXCELLENCE

Thomas Bauer, Hanno Fichtner, Jan Middelhoff

Leaflets are to retailers what flyers are to parties: invitations to those you want to come. If they don't know, they won't show. So it's imperative to get the word out. Local media is much more than just a sideshow in the retail marketing mix. It is the link between classical nationwide advertising and POS marketing.

We will discuss direct mail in Chapter 16: 'Boosting customer value through CLM' (customer lifecycle management). In this chapter we focus on leaflets and print advertising in local publications. We provide evidence for the importance of local media excellence and present guidelines to help retailers answer two key strategic questions: what should be promoted and where should it be promoted? In contrast, we will leave the more operational question of 'How should it be promoted?' to specialized agencies and service providers such as media agencies, media houses, integrated production companies, freelance designers, print shops and distributors.

Local media is the true point of sale: *consumers' love for leaflets drives sales and profits*

Local media creates a blizzard of paper. In France, Germany and the UK, more than 70 billion leaflets are distributed each year. In France alone, every household receives about seven leaflets per week. (Source: DVV.) In Germany, a single company, the discounter Lidl, distributes up to 28 million leaflets a week

(*Lebensmittelzeitung*, 29, 17 July 2009, p. 8). In a country of about 40 million households, Lidl's coverage is almost absolute – week in, week out.

This blizzard of paper is the result of the substantial budget share retailers allocate to local media. According to Germany's EHI Retail Institute, local media accounted for 52 percent of retailers' gross media spend in Germany in 2009. The real share may be even higher, since many research agencies do not include local media expenditure in their tracking and share of voice analyses. And there is no stopping the blizzard: experts at yacast.fr estimate that the leaflet spend of French food retailers grew by 11 percent in 2009. And while local marketing is traditionally the province of grocery retailers, other sectors are following suit. Consumer electronics, DIY, furniture and fashion retail are all fighting for consumer attention – so it is likely that we will see even more leaflets and local print ads in years to come.

But is the congestion in the consumer's mailbox, the considerable effort on the retailer's part and the multi-billion expenditure all worth it? The answer is clear and simple: people read leaflets and leaflets work. Specifically, they influence consumers' purchasing decisions. In 2008, TNS and Mediapost conducted a survey of French consumers' local media consumption and subsequent behaviour. The results were astonishing: 92 percent said they read the leaflets they receive by mail, many of them twice; 74 percent go to the store that sent the leaflet, and 68 percent make a purchase because of the leaflet (*TNS Mediapost* survey, March 2009). If you take promotional SKUs as a proxy for local media impact, then up to 30 percent of sales are driven by leaflets and local ads. Martin Jacobi of the Direct Marketing Union (DVV) says: 'The mailbox is the true point of sale for many retailers.'

Local marketing is a complex challenge: *to succeed, retailers need to cover all bases from consumers to media owners*

To achieve local media excellence, or LoMEX for short, retailers need to manage considerable complexity. They have to cope with large amounts of data, differentiate their approach for different countries and store types, deal with the fragmented landscape of media providers and account for the differences in reach and quality of the individual media. Because of their importance to retailers, we will now address each of these issues in some detail.

Large amounts of consumer data

Targeted local marketing has to absorb and leverage a wealth of consumer data from a variety of sources. In order to identify and reach the most attractive target groups, you will want to use the most granular geo-marketing data available. However, the resolution of this data varies significantly from country to country. In Germany, for example, data on the average category spend per household is available at the street section level for more than two million cells. In other countries, the data is far less granular. In Italy, for example, privacy laws prohibit providers of geo-marketing data from going to a deeper level than the postal code. Other relevant sources of data for targeted local marketing include transaction data and personal preferences gathered from consumer loyalty card programmes.

Different local marketing formats across countries

In different countries, consumers are used to different types of local media. While leaflets are important in Germany, for instance, print advertising plays a bigger role for retailers in the UK. But even leaflets show considerable variety. In the US, for instance, flyers typically carry coupons and are taken to the store (see the Walgreens example in Exhibit 13.1). In continental Europe, in contrast, coupons are far less common and leaflets tend to reflect the overall discount mentality, highlighting percentage price promotions for a large number of SKUs or 'buy one, get one free' offers (see the Carrefour examples in Exhibit 13.1). In the UK, grocery retailers build their flyers around product packages, e.g. special 'meal deals' (see the Tesco example in Exhibit 13.1). The great range of these variations suggests that multinational retailers should depend on the experience and expertise of their local subsidiaries and agencies to handle these local differences.

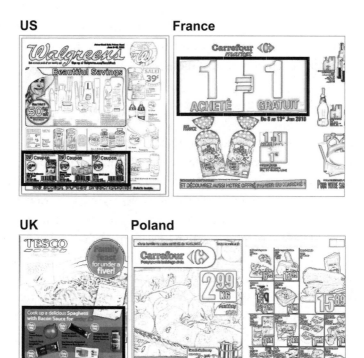

Exhibit 13.1 Leaflets from different countries.

Different store types require different promotions

Even within a single country, there can be many differences between stores types, regions and product categories. The German hypermarket giant Real, for instance, uses 180 leaflet variations to account for different store types and regions. Rewe, another large German supermarket chain, uses some 80 different flyers (*Lebensmittelzeitung*, 39, 26 September 2009, p. 44). In France, Carrefour in effect introduced the mass customization of leaflet production when they launched '*Promolibre*', a leaflet concept that lets the customer decide which products they want promoted.

Fragmented landscape of local media providers

Every city has its own advertising papers. In large cities, there are often several different and partly competing players covering individual districts and boroughs. Most direct delivery providers are also local or, at best, regional players with limited reach. Last but not least, the products, solutions and tariffs of national postal companies differ from country to country. The resulting local media landscape is immensely complex. The German Association of Advertising Paper Publishers (BVDA), for example, lists 41 direct delivery organizations and 232 publishers as its members, the latter producing a total of more than 900 advertising papers. To make things worse, there are unique formats like *EinkaufAktuell*, a German specialty format bundling a no-frills TV guide with a range of leaflets wrapped in foil. The final factor in this landscape complexity is that the granularity of reach differs significantly across providers. While most traditional newspapers solely cover the entire municipality or geographical district, some advertising sheets allow differentiation even below the postal code level.

Variation in reach and quality of media

Delivery options differ in the reach and the contact quality they achieve. This makes it difficult for retailers to compare their effectiveness and cost efficiency. Newspapers are probably the easiest to assess. An ad in a newspaper usually generates a lot of attention among those who buy a copy or choose to subscribe to the paper. As an extra benefit, newspaper ads also get through to those who refuse to receive leaflets in their mailbox. However, a newspaper's penetration is necessarily limited by the extent of its circulation, and the number of products that can be promoted through it is also limited, given the high cost of print ads. In contrast, leaflets can comprise multiple pages, each of which is an opportunity to highlight many products, and can reach every household that accepts promotional mail; however, they are much less likely to be read than newspaper ads. The sector or category the retailer operates in is another factor that determines the potential reach of local media. While leaflets from hypermarkets and supermarkets are the most likely to be read, other sectors, like apparel or DIY, have a harder fight to acquire consumer attention (Source: *LSA* magazine survey of 500 French consumers, 9 July 2009). Assembling such a comprehensive picture of the local media landscape is clearly challenging; but such information can prove invaluable in building an effective local media strategy. For example, based on insights such as these, Aldi Süd, a leading German discounter, has tested the direct delivery of leaflets instead of using print ads, enabling it to reach more households than previously (*Lebensmittelzeitung*, 15, 16 April 2010, p. 1).

Fine-tuning pays: *optimizing local marketing can increase its efficiency by 30 percent*

Local marketing is both large and complex, so managing it effectively can be challenging. Not surprisingly, there are big rewards in making it more efficient. Retailers investing in the optimization of local media find that this can significantly increase its effectiveness and efficiency. In our experience, dedicated local marketing optimization efforts can increase its reach by more than 30 percent – with the same budget. An alternative objective to increasing reach is to reduce cost. IKEA, for example, reports that geo-marketing has helped it to cut the circulation of their catalogues by 500,000 copies in Germany alone (*Der Handel*, 09, 2 September 2009, p. 24).

Exhibit 13.2 highlights the three questions that govern local marketing optimization: what should be promoted, where should it be promoted and how

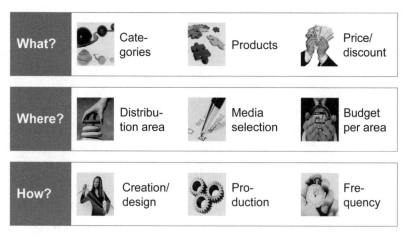

Exhibit 13.2 Governing questions of local media optimization.

should it be promoted? While answering the 'how' question frequently benefits from the kind of craftsmanship found in specialized agencies and service providers, the 'what' and 'where' questions are questions of functional business strategy that require the attention of a retailer's experienced executives and their most trusted advisors. We will, therefore, focus exclusively on the 'what and where' in the rest of this chapter.

What to promote: *what's on it determines what's in it for you! Highlight products with high expandability and low substitutability*

Which categories and products should be featured in leaflets and local print ads? The two key criteria featured products should meet are high expandability and low substitutability. Expandability is defined as the expected impact on sales; this is calculated through an analysis of the sales increases resulting from earlier promotions. Substitutability is an indicator of the degree to which the expected sales increase of the promoted SKU will cannibalize the sales of other products in the same category. Selecting categories and products based on these two criteria promises much higher promotional ROI than simply promoting the same kinds of items all the time.

Exhibit 13.3 provides an example of how these two dimensions can be applied to the grocery sector in selecting products for promotion. This sector has not been chosen at random – in general, local marketing is dominated by food. According to GfM&H (Gesellschaft für Markt & Handelsforschung mbH), food accounts for 84 percent of all products featured on the front pages of leaflets, with soft drinks and coffee ahead of all the rest.

Once you have selected the categories and products to be featured in the leaflet, the next task is to decide upon how many products to display, especially on the front page. The overall number of products promoted in leaflets is decreasing, reflecting consumers' requests for clarity. In France, for example, the number of products featured has dropped by 5.2 percent between 2008 and 2009 across retail sectors (*Editialis*, 10 May 2010). Though the general trend is clear, there is still considerable variation in the number of products featured on the front page – ranging from 3 to 14, according to an analysis by GfM&H.

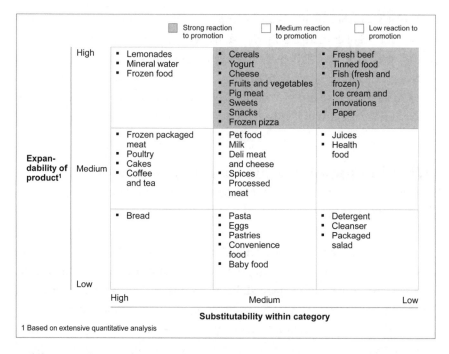

Exhibit 13.3 Selection of promoted products based on expandability and substitutability.

Displaying only a handful of SKUs makes it easier to position the individual products clearly, but harder to answer a wide range of individual consumers' needs.

Where to promote: *use granular geo-marketing to reach your most valuable customers*

Once you know *what* to promote, the next question is *where* to promote. By optimizing the distribution area, media selection and budget allocation of local media, retailers can increase their reach to attractive households by 25 percent – as seen in our experience in multiple consulting projects in various countries and sectors (see Exhibit 13.4 for an example).

The more granular your data, the more effective your local marketing activity. To determine the appropriate distribution, you need to evaluate each

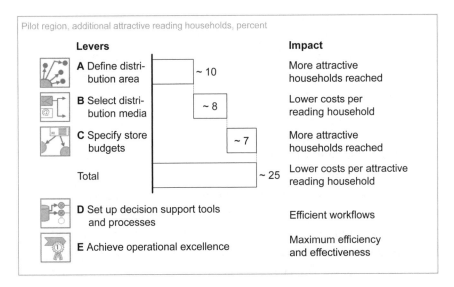

Exhibit 13.4 The local media excellence (LoMEX) approach – example.

area's attractiveness at a highly granular, geographical cell level, ideally by street section. The relevant criteria to be used in this evaluation can include: purchasing power, average age of residents, proximity to the nearest store and local competitive intensity.

Advanced geo-marketing

When evaluating the attractiveness of geographical cells for leaflet and print ad distribution, keep in mind that the granularity of the information used is a direct driver of ROI. For example, purchasing power should be category specific (if possible). If you are a speciality retailer focused on garden and outdoor products, high overall purchasing power can well be irrelevant if a given cell is dominated by apartment buildings without gardens. To control for this particular issue, the right evaluation focus would be category spend for garden products. Similarly, the distance to the nearest store should not be calculated as the crow flies, but should reflect the actual driving time, taking into account, for instance, rivers, bridges and highways.

Once you have identified the most promising distribution area, the choice of media should be optimized; this should be based on the cost of reach per attractive household. The definition of attractive households follows the same general pattern as distribution area selection, reflecting factors such as purchasing power, store proximity and so on. Ideally, multiple criteria are combined to create an overall attractiveness score – this proves to be more reliable than using a process in which multiple data sources are reviewed sequentially. To establish a realistic figure for the cost of reach per relevant household, retailers and their partners need to take into account media-specific indicators, such as area and household coverage, distribution quality and reading rates.

Distribution companies do not operate at the highly granular level of this analysis, so in order to meet their requirements retailers should combine a number of households into 'geo-cells', each geo-cell comprising 400 households or more. The geo-cells level is sufficiently granular to allow for cherry picking based on household attractiveness scores, while also being large enough to enable direct targeting by most leaflet distributors and many advertising paper publishers at competitive cost (see Exhibit 13.5). A decision support tool is often needed to handle data complexity and ensure efficient workflows (Exhibit 13.6).

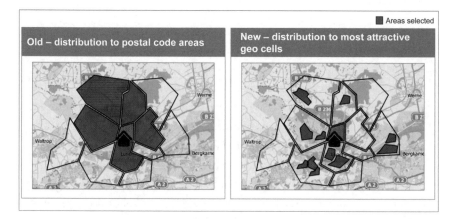

Exhibit 13.5 Geo-cells enable cherry picking.

Exhibit 13.6 The LoMEX tool – illustration of menu and map function

Key takeaways – Local media excellence

1 Local media is the true point of sale: consumers' love for leaflets drives sales and profit.
2 Local marketing is a complex challenge: to succeed, retailers need to cover all bases from consumers to media owners.
3 Fine-tuning pays: optimizing local marketing can increases its efficiency by 30 percent.
4 What to promote: what's on it determines what's in it for you! Highlight products with high expandability and low substitutability.
5 Where to promote: use granular geo-marketing to reach your most valuable customers.

CHAPTER 14

Thomas Bauer, Boris Mittermüller, Björn Timelin

Video hasn't killed the radio star, and new media will not kill classical advertising. Although many retailers have started to shift parts of their marketing budget from offline to online vehicles, traditional media still plays an important role in their marketing mix – and will continue to do so in the foreseeable future. Admittedly, a significant share of retail advertising budgets is allocated to local media: leaflets and local print ads are indispensable for ensuring targeted communication (see Chapter 13 for details). But to build strong retail brands and involve consumers on an emotional level, most will turn to a 'big bang' ATL campaign.

In this chapter we present a selection of some of the most successful classical campaigns in retail, and provide a structured approach that will help ensure retailers get their money's worth from traditional media advertising. The success factors discussed here have been developed over many years in cooperation with leading European retail marketing practitioners.

For many retailers, classical advertising remains a key element in their marketing mix, *despite the importance of local media and digital vehicles*

Across Europe, retailers make ample use of traditional advertising vehicles. Traditional media include TV, newspapers, magazines and radio. They have been around for many decades and are still used by a vast audience as trusted sources of information and entertainment. Small surprise that advertisers make ample use of these established audience aggregators. Traditionally, the retail industry ranks among the top three in terms of advertising spend in France, Germany and the UK. According to Nielsen Media Research, three out of the top five advertisers in Germany were retailers in 2008: Media-Saturn, Aldi and Lidl. In total, German retailers in 2009 allocated some EUR 2.6 billion, or 90 percent of their above-the-line spend, to classical media such as print, TV and radio (see Exhibit 14.1). Similarly, the top three retailers in the United Kingdom, Tesco, Asda and Sainsbury's, spent EUR 217 million, or 96 percent of their ATL budgets, on classical vehicles. Even IKEA, despite their traditional focus on catalogues, recognizes the importance of classical advertising: 'Today's marketing landscape still calls for traditional media to play a role', says Magnus Gustaffson, IKEA's head of marketing. (Source: Andrew Hampp, 'IKEA Support for "Easy to Assemble" May Direct Future of Branded Video', *Advertising Age*, 11 January 2010.)

Some of the biggest success stories in retail advertising rely heavily on classical vehicles. To find out what works well, let's look at the Cannes Lions International Advertising Festival, the largest and most prestigious get-together

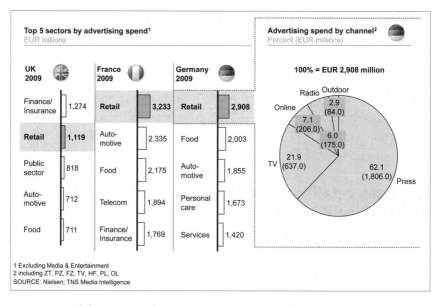

Exhibit 14.1 Net advertising spend by traditional media channel.

of advertising professionals and advertisers from around the world. More than 22,500 ads are showcased here every year. The winners are awarded the highly coveted Lion trophies in 11 categories, including film, press and radio. Table 14.1 lists the most successful campaigns by retailers, restaurant chains and fast food outlets from the last 5 years. From this list it is clear that retailers are not only big spenders but, in the eyes of the advertising industry, are also very successful users of traditional ATL media.

A closer look at some of the Cannes Lion winners shows that retailers' classical campaigns do not only win awards. They are also successful in shaping consumers' perceptions of retail brands and value propositions. Take Dixons, for example, a 2010 Gold Lion winner for print. With their 'The last place you want to go' campaign, the British electronics retailer took two risks simultaneously: they used offline media to promote their online distribution channel (dixons.co.uk) and they tackled the long-standing perceptions of their brick-and-mortar outlets with a humorous twist. Exhibit 14.2 gives a few examples of how this campaign brought out the advantage of the combination of an established high street brand and the convenience of online shopping. The campaign builds on the consumer trend towards multichannel shopping and it recognizes the importance of price as a key purchase driver for increasingly opportunistic shoppers.

Get off at Knightsbridge, visit the discerning shopper's fave department store, ascend the exotic staircase and let Piers in the pinstripe suit demonstrate the magic of the latest high-definition flatscreen then go to dixons.co.uk and buy it.

Get off at the fashionable end of Oxford Street, drift into the achingly cool technology hall of London's most happening department store and view this year's must-have plasma courtesy of the sound and vision technologist in the Marc Jacobs sandals then go to dixons.co.uk and buy it.

Step into middle England's best loved department store, stroll through haberdashery to the audio visual department where an awfully well brought up young man will bend over backwards to find the right TV for you then go to dixons.co.uk and buy it.

Advertising Agency: M&C SAATCHI London, U.K.
SOURCE: www.canneslions.com

Exhibit 14.2 2010 Cannes Gold Lion winner for press: dixons.co.uk.

Table 14.1 Cannes Lion winning retailers 2006–10

Year	Media	Company	Advertising agency	Lion
2010	Film	IKEA	Hjaltelin Stahl & Co. Copenhagen, Denmark	Bronze
		John Lewis	Adam & Eve London, United Kingdom	Silver
		McDonald's	DDB Chicago, USA	Bronze
			Leo Burnett London, United Kingdom	Silver
			TBWA\Chiat\Day New York, USA	Bronze
	Press	Dixons.co.uk	M&C Saatchi London, United Kingdom	Gold
		Harvey Nichols	Y&R Dubai, United Arab Emirates	Bronze
		Hooters	Ogilvy Guatemala, Guatemala	Bronze
		Shock and Soul	Rainey Kelly Campbell Roalfe/Y&R London	Silver
	Radio	McDonald's	DDB Sydney, Australia	Bronze
2009	Film	Fakta	Uncle Gray	Bronze
		Migros-Genossenschafts-Bund	Jung von Matt/Limmat	Bronze
		Visionlab Opticians	Publicis Comunicación España	Silver
	Press	Harvey Nichols	DDB London	Gold
		IKEA Deutschland	Grabarz & Partner	Silver
		Nykke & Kokki GmbH	Scholz & Friends Hamburg	Silver
	Radio	Domino's Pizza	INDIE	Bronze
2008	Film	Boots	Mother	Bronze
	Radio	IKEA	DDB Germany Berlin	Bronze
		Sport Factory Outlet	Ruf Lanz	Bronze
2007	Film	Marktplaats.nl (eBay)	DR FILM	Bronze
		The Big Yellow Self Storage Company	Blink	Bronze
	Press	Harvey Nichols	DDB London	Gold, Bronze
		Mac/Val Restaurant	CLM BBDO	Bronze
		Texto Editores	Leo Burnett	Silver
2006	Film	IKEA	SCPF	Bronze
		IKEA UK	Robert/Boisen & Like-minded	Silver
		McDonald's	DDB Amsterdam	Bronze
	Press	Harrods	Ogilvy & Mather	Silver
		Harvey Nichols	DDB London	Bronze
		Nike Town Berlin	DDB Berlin	Bronze
	Press	Norlis Antique Book-store	Leo Burnett	Bronze

Awards are not everything, of course. Even the more mundane classical campaigns often help retailers to strengthen their brand image, achieve competitive differentiation and drive sales. But what does it really take to create a good classical advertising campaign, and how do you make it stand out from the crowd?

Creativity matters, but it's not enough: *content fit is equally important, especially in campaigns advertising low-involvement, fast-moving products*

'Next year, I want to win even more creativity awards!' This statement, made at the 2007 International Advertising Festival in Cannes, did not come from an aspiring art director, but from Jim Stengel, the former CMO of one of the world's largest advertisers, Procter & Gamble. Winning 14 awards in Cannes was a crowning achievement for the consumer goods giant from Cincinnati. Procter & Gamble's marketing executives obviously believe that creative excellence and advertising success are linked. But does creativity really make all that much difference? And if it does, is creativity all it takes to create a successful classical campaign?

These questions are as old as advertising itself, but today marketing executives are under more pressure than ever before. Their products have to stand out from competitors – in a world already full of advertising, flooded with information and inundated with products that seem ever more alike. In this crowded media landscape, consumers are unmoved by brute advertising muscle: the proliferation of TV channels and the power of the remote control nullify the effect of mainstream advertising – and advertisers' exploding marketing budgets. The only way for campaigns to succeed in increasing sales in this fragmented environment is not through creating massive presence, but through high quality.

In a pioneering study, McKinsey & Company's Marketing and Sales Practice, in collaboration with the Art Directors Club for Germany (ADC) and the Berlin School of Creative Leadership have defined quantifiable metrics for both creativity and content fit to determine their relative impact on advertising effectiveness.

Elements of creativity

Originality

Is the advertisement new, original and innovative? Does it go against conventional norms? Is it surprising?

Clarity

Is the story, copy or imagery easy to grasp? Do you understand the content right away?

Conviction

Are the arguments in favour of the product persuasive and compellingly communicated? Is the campaign coherent?

Quality

Is the campaign well crafted in technical terms? Do its individual parts fit together well, and do they form a homogeneous whole?

Want-to-see-again factor

Is it fun to watch the advertisement? Is it entertaining? Do you want to see it again?

Elements of content fit

Relevance

Is the campaign relevant for the target group and message? Does it fit with the company strategy and the product, brand or proposition?

Differentiation

Does the advertising message stand out from competing messages?

Consistency

Does the advertising fit with previous campaigns? Is it in line with the general communication of the product, brand and company?

Credibility

Are the arguments convincing? Do you trust the product, the brand or the company to deliver the value proposition presented?

Activation

Will the advertising motivate the target group to go out and buy the product or go to the store?

Using these criteria, the jurors assessed a sizeable sample of advertisements on a scale of 1 (poor) to 5 (excellent). A panel of art directors voted on the creativity criteria, while a group of McKinsey marketing experts, including the authors of this book, assessed the content fit of each advertisement.

Exhibit 14.3 shows the results for Media Markt's 2004 campaign 'Don't get screwed'. It scored very high on almost all criteria on both dimensions, creativity and content fit. Unsurprisingly, the campaign turned out to be one of the company's most successful advertising efforts ever, boosting total sales by more than 10 percent and increasing its market share by more than one percentage point.

Clearly, content fit and creativity both have a substantial impact on advertising success. But is one more important than the other? What is the prime determinant of the effectiveness of an advertisement: creative design or content fit – or a combination of the two? In the past, this question was hard to answer. The assessment of creativity, in particular, was hampered by the lack of objective criteria. In most studies creativity was measured only by the number and prestige of awards won in industry competitions, with juries often voting simply on the basis of what they liked and disliked.

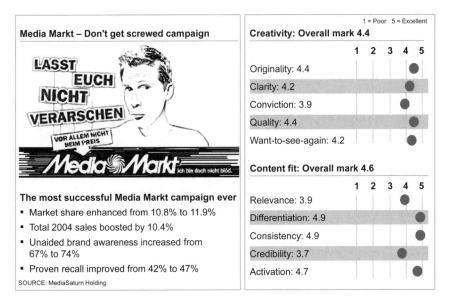

Exhibit 14.3 Media Markt campaign with high scores for both creativity and content fit.

The study shows that, overall, campaigns that score well on both creativity and content fit are the most effective: they drive sales in almost all cases. But the relative importance of the two ingredients depends on the advertiser's industry. For example, in financial services, creativity and content fit are equally important, as consumers make their choices of insurance or investment products based on both emotional and rational factors. For manufacturers of products with low ticket prices and limited consumer involvement, content fit is especially important because of the consumers' somewhat more rational purchasing behaviour in such cases. However, any marketer of highly emotional products, such as jewellery or designer sunglasses, will want to prioritize creativity over content fit. Across all industries, we have observed three guiding principles.

- *Creativity and content fit both have a major impact on advertising effectiveness*: companies that design their campaigns around both elements are highly likely to succeed in increasing sales. Not even the deepest pockets, however, can make up for a campaign that falls short on both dimensions.
- *The right mix of creativity and content fit varies by category*: as a general rule, creativity is even more effective for products with high emotional involvement, while content fit is effective at driving sales of low-ticket price, fast-moving consumer goods that have lower consumer involvement.
- *Advertisers should use the list of criteria for creativity and content fit, as presented above, for pre-testing*: this will help them identify the key factors in a given case. What works well in one country for a specific segment of the market may not necessarily be transferable to other contexts.

Test and learn prior to, during and after activation
to make sure you get your money's worth in terms of target group impact

Advertising is effective if it succeeds in changing the behaviour of the consumers it reaches. Different media can convey the same marketing message very differently. To evaluate the effectiveness of each vehicle using a common yardstick, the quality of the medium needs to be taken into account: in this context, quality is defined as the level of influence of a given marketing vehicle on consumer involvement, attitude and behaviour toward a brand, a product or a service.

Pre-testing is the process of analyzing, testing and refining the quality of a commercial before airing it, or of a print ad prior to its activation in newspapers and magazines. To make sure the actual activation budget gives them their money's worth, advertisers and their media agencies use pre-tests to check whether a given campaign will have the intended impact on its target group. Insights gathered from advertising tests can be used to refine the campaign in question, even while it is on air or in print. For example, it is not uncommon for TV advertisers to change the cut or voice-over of TVCs halfway through the commercial's run in order to optimize its impact on the target group.

Keith Weed, Unilever's Chief Marketing and Communications Officer, says: 'We now have a methodology in place that enables us both to benchmark all our ads against our own proven experience – with reasonable confidence that our large investment in developing and producing ads will indeed pay off – and to understand where an ad is failing and take appropriate remedial action'. (Source: Paul Farris, 'Managing the Copy-Testing Process', Darden Case No. UVA-M-0680, Working Paper Series.)

Best-practice testing processes typically include three steps (Exhibit 14.4).

- *Concept testing*: testing at an early stage of campaign development will provide valuable insights prior to production. Creative agencies usually present more than one idea, or creative route, for a commercial or a campaign. Thus, it is essential to understand which ideas work best in delivering the advertiser's message to consumers. To find out how consumers react to different routes, research agencies typically combine field surveys, interviews and focus groups with quantitative approaches. Modern concept testing relies increasingly on online survey methods; these methods frequently yield more accurate results at lower cost.
- *Pre-testing*: Prior to committing to a given campaign, marketing executives will seek to minimize the risk of airing an ineffectual campaign. Pre-testing allows them to test the entire campaign, including the creative work as well as the intended media selection, before giving final approval.

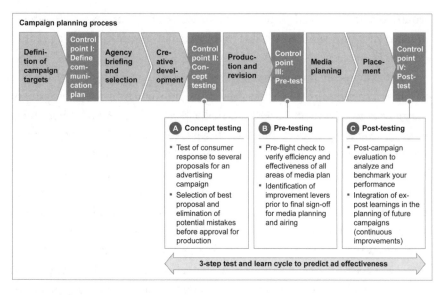

Exhibit 14.4 Three-step test and learn cycle to improve advertising impact.

- *Post-testing*: advertisers use post-testing to evaluate and benchmark the ac-complishment of an advertising campaign during or after airing. To build on past experience, it is critical to make sure the insights generated during post-testing are fed back into the development of future campaigns.

Media agencies and providers of copy tests offer a wide range of tools and methodologies that can help you predict and track the effectiveness of your advertising campaigns. The process laid out in Exhibit 14.4 can be used as a plausibility check to focus the discussions with the media agency, as well as a more general framework for thinking about the impact of the retailer's advertising efforts. But keep in mind that even the most meticulous tests can be misleading; their significance depends entirely on the quality of the indicators and benchmarks you use. Here are some of the key questions you should ask, especially in discussions with external providers of research.

- What is the objective of the campaign? Which are the right metrics and indicators to determine whether the objective is met?

- What are we testing for – is this a pre-activation check or a post-campaign analysis? What is the appropriate survey period?
- Do the techniques meet our requirements in terms of reliability and validity? How do we control for biasing effects?
- Which benchmarks should we use – our own past performance, market averages or specific (sub-)category benchmarks?
- Which resources (how much money, what period of time, etc.) should be devoted to testing?

Once the message is clear, optimize it across and within media *to ensure that it is delivered effectively to its target audience*

The evaluation and selection of different advertising channels and promotional vehicles is the pre-requisite for ensuring your marketing messages actually reach their target audience. To compare the efficiency of different vehicles in terms of their impact per EUR, marketers use approaches such as Reach–Cost–Quality (RCQ) or Marketing Mix Modelling (MMM) (see Chapters 9 and 10). In essence, the same logic can be applied within one type of media; for example, in order to select the most efficient TV network and time slot for a given TVC, or the most appropriate print title for a given ad. In the following, we provide guidelines on the relevant criteria and their application – although the actual media planning and buying is the prerogative of media agencies.

Despite a number of recent controversies over undisclosed discounts, the expertise and experience of media agencies is indispensable in light of the considerable complexity created by the proliferation of vehicles and channels. In fact, the selection of vehicles is only the first step. For TVCs, end-to-end media planning comprises the selection of networks, channels, formats, shows and daytimes, as well as the type, duration and frequency of actual commercials. Similarly, print planning includes the selection of publishers, formats, titles and relevant circulation, as well as types and sizes of ad.

To provide a sense of the trade-offs involved in these decisions, we will look a little more closely at the potential for refinement in print.

- *Efficiency*: magazines and newspapers differ significantly in terms of their reach among an advertiser's target group, but these differences are not always fully reflected in the selection of titles in a given media plan. Similarly, the cost for a one-page advertisement (per thousand persons reached) varies greatly due to publisher pricing and media agency discounts. The cost of communicating to the advertiser's target group can easily be determined for each print title by adjusting the cost per mille (CPM) for the share of the advertiser's target group found among the readership of the title in question.
- *Effectiveness*: the quality of print titles varies significantly, too. Due to differences in editorial content and readership profiles, some newspapers and magazines will fit well with the advertiser's brand and message while others won't. The long-term image impact of selected print media on the advertiser's brand should at least be rated in terms of the brand's key attributes.

Our experience with retailers across Europe shows that intra-media optimization is usually well rewarded. For example, an assessment of print media in Germany revealed substantial differences in terms of their cost efficiency and brand impact. The matrix shown in Exhibit 14.5 maps the print titles on both dimensions, in terms of their effectiveness (impact on brand image) and their efficiency (cost for reaching target group). In this purely illustrative example, the titles in the top right-hand quadrant are the most attractive ones because of their high effectiveness and high cost efficiency. (Obviously, this matrix is purely illustrative and cannot be generalized.) The assessment of either dimension depends on a marketers' target group and objectives. The effectiveness and efficiency ratings can be combined to evaluate the overall performance of each title and so create a ranking of print titles. Please note that the assessment given in the exhibit is specific to the disguised example it is based on, and may look completely different in another case.

But media optimization should not be limited to the choice of titles, networks or shows. It is also about getting the intensity right. In Europe, retailers spend more on marketing than do most companies in other sectors, but they struggle to demonstrate the effectiveness of their marketing activities. We believe that retailers can make substantial savings by fine-tuning the advertising intensity within specific types of media – without compromising their communication impact.

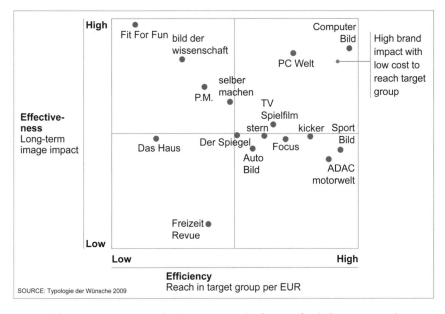

Exhibit 14.5 Assessment of effectiveness and efficiency for different print titles.

Many retailers set their media spend too high, others much too low. Of course, it is no trivial matter to strike the right balance: advertising effectiveness studies show that incremental gain in recall drops with increasing contact frequency – depending on the absolute frequency (the second contact is always much more valuable than the tenth) and the vehicle used (for example, the marginal utility of cinema advertising decays much faster than that of radio).

Advertising intensity is measured typically in gross rating points (GRPs). GRPs are calculated by multiplying the percentage of the target group reached by the average frequency in the target group. For example, a TV campaign that is aired three times and reaches 70 percent of the target audience achieves 3 × 70 percent = 210 GRPs. Both the minimum GRP requirements to achieve a competitive market presence and the best-in-class GRP can be determined at the industry level by analysis of comparable companies. Media agencies and independent media auditors can help cut through the increasingly complex media landscape and extract the relevant benchmarks by providing historical intensity levels and real-time changes in advertising activity.

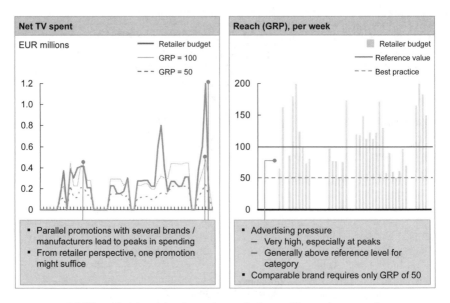

Exhibit 14.6 Advertising intensity analysis – an illustrative example.

The pricing of GRPs changes from week to week, varying in line with classic advertising peaks throughout the year. Once you know the cost per GRP and the optimal number of weekly GRPs needed to achieve the target reach and frequency, you can back-engineer the required advertising budget. Exhibit 14.6 provides an illustrative example of an advertising intensity analysis.

Pick your creative partners carefully, tailor the cooperation model to the needs of your brand and company – *don't be afraid to change horses*

Even the most sophisticated retailers depend on external support for many areas of their brand management and marketing strategy: the art, craft and science of marketing are all well served by specialists. While the science and craft is the domain of research institutes, analytical specialists, IT companies and production houses, the art of advertising depends on the inspiration and experience of creative agencies. But there is no one-size-fits-all solution, either in terms of choosing the right agency for the task, nor in terms of the appropriate cooperation model.

The list of Cannes Lion winners in Table 14.1 illustrates that both long-standing agency relationships and more flexible cooperation models can each lead to success. But which is the right strategy for your company?

Many advertisers, such as McDonald's, prefer to develop long-term relations with a single lead agency – in a true partnership that seeks to ensure consistency in their brand communication. But consistency isn't everything. To combine the benefits of global consistency with local relevance, Coca-Cola has pioneered a global advertising model that is based on the central development of a single creative idea, in some cases even by non-traditional challenger agencies, with subsequent orchestration by local agencies.

Clearly, not all long-term or single-source relationships are healthy. They also carry the danger of losing touch with current communication trends, shifts in media usage or changing consumer lifestyle. Quite a few advertisers experience a certain degree of inertia on their lead agency's part after a few years. And even when brand managers make a conscious decision not to change horses, they may not always get what they bargain for. Because of churn and frequent account team changes within many agencies, loyalty to the same agency over extended periods does not necessarily protect companies from inconsistencies or brain drain. In light of these facts, the benefits of the fresh thinking that challenger agencies provide can sometimes outweigh the advantages of long-term agency relationships.

More and more companies are moving from the traditional model of a single roster agency to a small group – or even a larger pool – of agencies. Since 2004, IKEA has worked with a network of partners, for example. It has modularized its creative service requirements and it now selects its agency partners depending on the media for which the creative concept is to be developed. While IKEA adheres to the concept of having a lead agency for a particular vehicle, e.g. in Germany this is Grabarz & Partner for classical advertising and Grimm Gallun Holtappels for internet marketing, it also works with other agencies on a project basis, e.g. DBB or Hjaltelin Stahl & Co. So far, this approach seems to be working for IKEA. Grabarz & Partner appears to have developed a deep understanding of the company's evolving brand promise that combines affordability with the idea of a holistic experience. (Source: Hajo Riesenbeck, Jesko Perrey, *Power Brands: Making and Managing Brand Success*, p. 307, Wiley, 2008.)

In yet another relationship model, certain companies continue to partner with a global roster agency but at the same time invite other agencies to pitch for specific projects, based on the budget, its strategic importance, special skill requirements or the type of communication objective. For example, the lead agency may be in charge of all brand campaigns, while selected product introductions, the launch of a new store format or new market entry may be handled by challenger agencies.

Forming more complex relationship patterns does have a downside – it requires more management input. In our experience, innovative models, such as challenger agency pools, selective pitches or modularized service procurement, require bigger efforts on the advertiser's part to ensure communication consistency and protect the heritage of their brands.

Interview: Dr Michael Trautmann

Retailers could become the advertising trend-setters of the future
Dr. Michael Trautmann is one of the founders and managing partners of the German advertising agency kempertrautmann. Launched in 2004, the agency has quickly gained reputation and served high-profile clients including Audi, Henkel, MediaSaturn, hagebaumarkt and Vaillant. In 2009, kempertrautmann was elected 'Global Newcomer Agency of the Year' as part of the New York Festivals.

Jesko Perrey spoke to Dr Trautmann about the current and future trends that will shape the use of classical media in the retail sector.

Q: Dr Trautmann, has the role of classical advertising vehicles changed in the retail industry in the last few years?

Michael Trautmann: Yes. The topic of image advertising hadn't played an important role in retail in the past. But is does today. While consumer goods manufacturers are cutting back on image advertising in favour of promotions and other tactical types of communication, the opposite is true for retailers. Compare campaigns like Edeka's 'We Love Groceries'. This campaign doesn't even mention specific products, prices or promotions. Rather, it focuses on attitudes, values and atmosphere. It is obvious that image advertising is gaining momentum across all retail categories and segments.

Q: In retail, price communication has always played a very important role. Do you think retailers should contemplate moving away from price communication in the long term?

Michael Trautmann: That is indeed very difficult. The trick is to avoid campaigns that focus solely on price. Anybody can offer cheap prices, and anybody can undercut cheap prices. It's like a drug; people want more and more of it. This downward spiral makes the discount argument extremely dangerous. To create and sustain value, retailers need to bring out other attributes of their brands as well. There are companies that do this very proficiently. Take Media Markt for instance. They have found a way to combine affordability with other benefits, such as wide product selection and superior service. Their VAT campaign is a fine example of how you can talk about prices without neglecting the broader brand values.

Q: There has been a lot of talk about digital marketing recently. Will the expected growth in online advertising crowd out classical advertising?

Michael Trautmann: I believe that classical advertising will continue to play an important role for retailers as long as online advertising fails to deliver comparable reach quickly. Retailers place their advertising to coincide exactly with the point in time when people are very willing to make a purchase. Usually, this means that you have to be able to reach people within three days. At the moment, this is only possible with classical media like TV, radio and daily newspapers. That's not going to change in the near to medium term.

Q: Do you think classical advertising will start feeling the pressure once online channels reach a broader base across all age groups?

Michael Trautmann: I can imagine that some traditional audience aggregators, such as major publishers or networks, will be able to transfer their reach from offline to online if they leverage the power of their brands. However, classical media will naturally lose out in the long term. But sooner or later, the distinction between classical and non-classical advertising will become irrelevant anyway. In the future, there will only be three principal types of vehicle: paid media, owned media and earned media. The question is whether paid media, including classical offline advertising as well as online banner ads, will become less important than social platforms like Facebook. That's not clear at the moment. Of course, the issues of privacy and data protection will play important parts in this context.

Q: If you were in charge of marketing at a major global retail group, where would you focus your attention?

Michael Trautmann: I believe that digital channels hold tremendous opportunity for retailers. At this year's Cannes Lion Awards, Best Buy was awarded the Grand Prix in the Titanium category for its *Twelpforce* campaign. *Twelp* stands for 'twittered technical help' and refers to free expert advice provided via Twitter. The *Twelpforce*, a team of some 2000 Best Buy experts, was set up to answer consumer questions on Twitter 24/7. The aim was to advise current and potential customers without pursuing direct sales targets. The *Twelpforce* also combed the Twitter network for technology-related questions and reached out to technology enthusiasts pro-actively. During the campaign, more than 22,000 tweets were answered, and Best Buy exceeded its revenue targets by as much as 40 percent. This example shows that the potential of social platforms doesn't stop at word-of-mouth marketing. It's really a new world, and it makes the CMO position at a retailer enormously exciting today.

Q: What can other industries learn from retail advertising?

Michael Trautmann: You can learn a lot from retailers, especially because they can measure and optimize their advertising effectiveness more easily than companies in most other industries. Because of their direct relationship with customers, retailers know exactly what works and what doesn't work. For example, we should ask ourselves why the retail industry still invests massively in above-the-line vehicles like TV, print and radio, and how they are using these vehicles to maximize return on marketing investment. In the past, retailers kept an eye on what manufacturers were up to. Today, the reverse might well be recommendable at times. If this development persists, leading retailers may well become the advertising trend-setters of the future.

Key takeaways – Classical media excellence

1 For many retailers, classical advertising remains a key element in their marketing mix, despite the importance of local media and digital vehicles.

2 Creativity matters, but it's not enough: content fit is equally important, especially in campaigns advertising low-involvement, fast-moving products.

3 Test and learn prior to, during and after activation to make sure you get your money's worth in terms of target group impact.

4 Once the message is clear, optimize it across and within media to ensure that it is delivered effectively to its target audience.

5 Pick your creative partners carefully, tailor the cooperation model to the needs of your brand and company – don't be afraid to change horses.

CHAPTER 15

DIGITAL MARKETING EXCELLENCE

Hanno Fichtner, Lars Köster, Mathias Kullmann

Even if you do not plan to sell your goods online anytime soon, you cannot afford to ignore the realm of digital marketing. The digital universe is evolving quickly and it holds tremendous opportunity for retailers. Self-empowered users go online to locate stores and research products prior to their offline purchases. They share their in-store and product experiences with millions of other users via social network sites and blogs. They reach out to companies to provide feedback and input, and they freely reveal their needs and preferences to everyone who cares to listen. Who would want to miss out on this wealth of information, interaction and influence? But online marketing requires different approaches, tools and capabilities to those of the offline world. Everything happens in real time, and word of mouth spreads at the tap of a finger. Reputation may be gained more quickly than in a traditional media environment, but it can be lost just as easily. And even if the vehicles are virtual, successful digital marketing is still all about the ROI of real dollars and cents.

In Chapter 11: 'The digital evolution of retail marketing', we outlined how the world of marketing is changing. In this chapter, we will show what it takes to succeed in this changing environment. Specifically, we will look at the most important digital marketing vehicles, and how to use them to generate customer insight, drive sales and build your brand. Because of the focus of this book on branding and marketing, e-commerce is mostly out of scope of this chapter, although we believe retailers will want to be prepared to encompass this channel as sales increasingly shift from offline to online.

Even if they have no e-commerce ambitions, retailers cannot ignore the importance of the digital arena *as a communication and interaction space*

In Western Europe, e-commerce is one of the few growth drivers in a stagnating retail environment. For example, the share of online sales in non-food retailing is forecast to grow at 12 percent annually until 2014, while offline sales are expected to be flat. Even if you don't have any e-tail ambitions, the internet is a treasure trove of marketing opportunities.

- *The growing usage and relevance of digital media*: media consumption is shifting towards digital media. While in the US, for instance, the daily media consumption of classical media such as TV, newspapers and radio has been declining by about 3 percent annually for a number of years past, digital media consumption has grown by up to 10 percent a year. Experts expect that by as early as 2011, some 50 percent of all retail sales will be influenced by digital media: almost all consumers use digital channels for pre-sales research, and a significant share actually makes their purchases online.
- *Digital channels are a shortcut to young audiences*: certain audiences are moving out of reach of traditional channels like TV, radio or print. For example, in Germany, the community platform StudiVZ has a higher reach in the target group aged 15 to 29 than any German TV station. (Source: VZ Group.) In general, McKinsey's iConsumer research shows that it is becoming more and more difficult to reach certain audiences through offline channels.
- *Digital natives are co-creators*: digital instruments offer new ways of product creation and development, e.g. through open innovation platforms, co-creation and online idea jams. Lego, Best Buy, Starbucks and Nespresso are just a few examples of well known brands that are using online platforms to engage consumers in their product innovation and creation process. Online co-creation is a low-cost complement to traditional product and business development processes; and as a welcome side effect, it strengthens consumers' commitment to the brand.

Despite its importance and allure, many retailers are hesitant to embrace the opportunities of the digital arena. In consequence, their new media marketing spend lags behind the important role digital channels play in consumers'

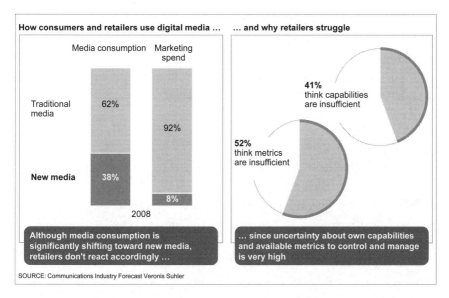

Exhibit 15.1 Media consumption is changing, but retailers hesitate to adapt their marketing mix.

consumption. Many retailers are unsure whether digital marketing is worth the effort, or how to even measure and monitor its impact. Others doubt their capability to succeed online (Exhibit 15.1). Our view is that the opportunities far outweigh the risks, provided retailers develop their digital footprint in a structured, yet pragmatic, way.

Develop a digital marketing strategy: *decide to what extent you wish to use it for insight generation, sales stimulation, or brand building*

The digital arena is a space of nearly limitless possibilities. More than any other channel or platform, it is all things to all people. But as a retailer, you have only one brand identity and one digital footprint. This makes it all the more important to clarify the objectives of digital marketing efforts. Even if most retailers have passed the early stage of 'we should have a website', there is still a lot of confusion around the rationale for their digital presence. Are you doing it:

- ... because everybody else is doing it?
- ... to promote your brand?
- ... to generate leads?
- ... to interact with consumers?
- ... to foster loyalty?

Digital diagnostics

Before you start developing your digital marketing strategy, you should have a clear picture of your current digital footprint. Until very recently, this was very difficult. While the digital arena is characterized by a proliferation of data, there are very few established, widely accepted and comprehensive indicators of digital marketing performance. To get an initial impression of the number and type of website performance metrics, retailers may wish to consult free services such as Socialmention.com or Google Insight. These services gather and aggregate indicators such as, for example, the number of visitors, reach or sentiment – to name but a few. But increasingly, more holistic tools covering a brand's entire digital presence are now becoming available.

One example of this is McKinsey & Company's Online Marketing Excellence tool (OMEX), developed in cooperation with Google in Germany (Exhibit 15.2). While most conventional tracking approaches are confined to individual metrics such as click rates or mentions in social media, OMEX is holistic in nature. It capture's a retailer's marketing performance across many digital touch points and all purchase funnel stages. OMEX combines some 20 key performance indicators, quantitative as well as qualitative ones. What is more, OMEX covers input factors, such as marketing spend, as well as rich output metrics, such as quality traffic or conversion rates compared to competitors.

However, there is no need to be overly scientific in analyzing your digital footprint. It is better to start with a pragmatic diagnostic approach that covers the most important touch points and objectives. Based on these initial

	KPIs		Retailer X	Competitor
		● Top 5 ◐ Top 6 - 25 ○ Top 26 - 50		
Awareness	○ Quality reach, percent		1.1	38.5
	◐ Quality traffic vs. total mktg spend, user/EUR		152/k	440/k
	◐ Quality traffic vs. online mktg spend, user/EUR		163/k	704/k
	● Brand search volume, percent		90	78
	○ Unpaid search visibility, percent		0.45	0.65
	○ Paid search visibility, percent		4.57	11.84
Consideration	○ Time per visit, minutes		6:54	9:36
	○ Page views per visitor		112	270
	◐ Google page rank		5/10	8/10
	◐ Online WOM index		3.4	29.1
Purchase	○ Online category market share[1], percent		5.2	24.7
	○ Conversion of quality traffic, percent, estimate		1.6	4.1
	◐ Revenue per purchase, EUR		148	261
	◐ ROPO feature index (max. 40)		26	31
Loyalty	◐ Monthly visits per visitor		4.2	4.5
	○ Sentiment, percent of positive minus negative posts		+16	+23
	◐ Likelihood tore-tweet/re-post, percent		39	50
	○ Affinity with competitors' sites[2]		28X	3X
	● Number of purchases per shopper		2.2	1.9

1 Relevant category: Apparel
2 The smaller the better

Exhibit 15.2 OMEX: Online Marketing Excellence Tool.

results, industry benchmarks and expert hypotheses, it will be much easier to identify individual touch points, customer segments or purchase funnel stages for further deep dives. Because of the high pace of digital media, speed is sometimes more important than being 100 percent accurate.

Conceptually, digital marketing can achieve three different objectives:

- *Generate customer insights*: digital natives are very generous when it comes to providing information on their identity, their needs and even their shopping behaviour. Within the boundaries of data protection acts and privacy regulation, this generosity offers rich opportunities for retailers to gather insights about current and potential customers. Internet users leave a digital trace when they search for information, make a purchase or discuss the merits of a given product or service with their friends and peers. Services like NM Incite, a joint venture by Nielsen and McKinsey & Company, can help you mine the world of blogs, message boards and social networks for relevant information (see Exhibits 15.3 and 15.4). NM Incite combs social media for a brand, a product or a company. Social media posts across millions of sources are screened systematically and converted into meaningful metrics that can be used as input for multiple business functions, including marketing, customer service and even product development. The gathering of online consumer insights is sometimes referred to as 'netnography'.

- *Drive sales*: more and more customers are researching online and purchasing offline (ROPO), or alternatively, going directly to their favourite e-tail site to see what is available. So even if you do not have an e-commerce channel as such, you can still use new media for the online stimulation of your offline sales. Take the example of Esprit, the apparel retailer. Their website not only features a store finder, detailing locations and opening hours, but also an online inventory tool. It lets consumers check in real-time whether a specific

Sample metrics	
Volume	Number of comments Number of individuals talking
Sentiment	Overall tone, polarity to product, issue, brand, feature
Topics	Features and words associated with brand or issue
Reach	Size of audience viewing CGM for brand or issue
Dispersion	Number and types of community where buzz exists
Influence	Ability of individual to create buzz
Impact	Connection to sales/Nielsen data
Advocacy	Are consumers advocating ?

"Turns out the contaminated wheat gluten that has sickened and killed so many cats and dogs recently has ended up in quite a few brand names. I finally found a complete list of the affected brands here. I feed my cats --- dry food, and fortunately the dry food was not on the list. The --- wet is, though. Don't assume that your brand is safe. Check the list!"

- *sfynes.blogspot.com*, 04/05/07

Exhibit 15.3 NM Incite methodology: Buzzword mapping.

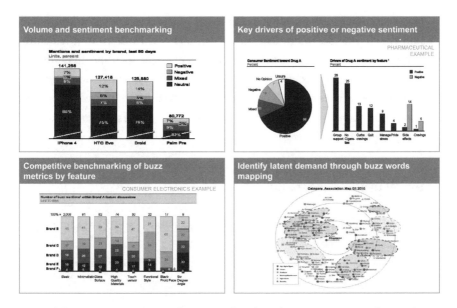

Exhibit 15.4 NM Incite sample output – benchmarking, sentiment analysis and association mapping.

garment, including details of its colour and size, is available in the store they have chosen, based on the postal code of their current location.

- *Build brand image and loyalty*: perhaps most importantly, the digital arena has become an environment in which brands are built and consumer involvement fortified. Take the example of IKEA's Facebook showroom: for the launch of their new outlet in Malmö, Sweden, IKEA uploaded pictures from the store's showrooms. Facebook members could tag themselves to specific items and thereby enter a prize draw to win that particular IKEA product. News of the tagging appeared on user's news feeds, creating a buzz across thousands of their friends' profiles – at almost no cost to IKEA. (Source: *Most Contagious Report*, 2009).

In addition, digital tools can help retailers simplify or streamline other customer-related processes, e.g. in areas such as call center management, in order to increase marketing efficiency and effectiveness. However, given the focus of this book, we will not go into the details of these process-related topics.

No matter whether your digital marketing aspiration is to get to know your customers, to generate online sales, stimulate offline sales or promote consumers' involvement with your brand and company, bear in mind that you are operating in a quickly evolving environment. It is much better to set concrete and quantified mid-term targets for digital marketing activities, rather than develop a 10-year plan to conquer the world of digital natives. Chances are that, even if you got there, the world would have moved on.

Digital insights generation

The generation of digital insights, especially customer sentiment mining, is no substitute for established offline methods such as ad hoc surveys and panel research. However, advanced netnography techniques provide unbiased answers on a real-time basis, including competitive benchmarking – and at very low cost. Digital customer insight generation is already an important complement of traditional market research techniques; we believe its importance will keep growing because of its flexibility and cost-efficiency. Increasingly, even traditional market research approaches leverage online interfaces to speed up participant feedback and to minimize costs.

To determine your digital communication mix,
weigh push versus pull investments and identify
'must have' vehicles

As discussed in Chapter 6: 'Budget sizing: the million dollar question' and Chapter 7: 'Budget prioritization', there are different ways of defining budgets, from pragmatic approaches like 'last year $+/- x$' and competitive benchmarking to more sophisticated approaches, such as those that derive the costs of reaching the target audience bottom-up. Whichever approach you pick, once the total budget for digital marketing is defined, you have to decide how to allocate it to the different digital vehicles, guided by your overall digital marketing strategy.

The most fundamental categorization of vehicles is pull media versus push media. While push media, such as search engine marketing (SEM), serve to satisfy existing demand, push media, like outbound emails or online advertising, are geared at generating new demand and building brands.

Every day, users run more than 100 billion internet searches, most of them on Google. Because of the trend to ROPO (research online, purchase offline) described above, search engine marketing is becoming increasingly important for retailers. Search engine marketing comprises both search engine advertising (SEA; paid search results like Google's Adwords) and search engine optimization (SEO; unpaid search results). While search engine marketing is a key element in any retailer's marketing mix, it is even more important for those who have an e-commerce channel. For example, imagine a retailer selling printer toner direct to consumers. Google allows us to find out how many internet users from the retailer's target region searched for printer toner in a given time frame – let us say 600,000 people. Further, let us assume that 5 percent of those who see the retailer's Google ad alongside their search result click on it to be re-directed to its website. If the average cost per click is EUR 0.75, it will cost approximately EUR 22,500 for the retailer to have its ad placed on Google every time a potential customer searches for printer toner. If it then factors in the average conversion rate and basket size of unique visitors, it will be able to calculate the ROI of its Adwords investment. Because of its high contact quality and direct business relevance, retailers should use SEM as long as it is economically viable. This is especially true if driving sales is the primary digital marketing objective. That is not to say, however, that SEM cannot also drive brand equity.

Digital marketing doesn't stop at redirecting shoppers who are already contemplating a purchase to your website. The digital arena is also a space in which awareness is created and brands are built. Once you have decided which part of your digital marketing budget to allocate to SEM, you are faced with a wide – and partly confusing – choice of push vehicles.

- *Display advertising* includes advertising on mobile devices and rich media (flash animations, video), the online equivalent to newspaper ads. Semantic, behavioural and local targeting is available at most publishing houses, enabling retailers to focus their spending on specific audiences. However, demand for display ads has not kept pace with the increasing usage of the internet, resulting in declining prices. In most cases, ads are booked on a cost per mille basis, but performance related clearance is on the rise (cost per click, cost per lead, cost per order).

- *Outbound email* is the online equivalent of direct mail. Newsletters are the most frequent form of email marketing. In many countries, such as Germany, email marketing requires the user's permission, limiting its use to customer loyalty management. Although 'spamming' has somewhat diminished the perceived value and credibility of email marketing, leading e-tailers like Amazon make ample use of outbound emails for push marketing purposes. Based on past purchases, customers receive emails with customized offerings, e.g. for discounted products in categories recently purchased or researched.

- *Affiliate marketing* is the online equivalent of sales co-promotions and partner programmes. The affiliate – which can be any website owner other than the retailer – displays the retailer's advertisements in exchange for a performance-based commission, usually per click-through. The technical implementation and maintenance of digital affiliate programmes is often supported by third-party providers. The rise of performance-based fees has boosted affiliate marketing in recent years.

- *Social media marketing* is the online equivalent of word-of-mouth. Social networks such as LinkedIn for business contacts or Facebook for private contacts are emerging all over the world. If Facebook were a country, it would already be the third largest in the world, outnumbered only by China and India: in July 2010, Facebook's founder Mark Zuckerberg announced that it had 500 million members. For retailers, social media not only offers advertising space, but also opportunities for getting in contact with customers, e.g. through fan pages.

Which of these vehicles are 'must haves', which are 'can haves' and which should be considered 'playgrounds for experimentation and learning' depends on your digital footprint, business objectives, marketing strategy, competitive environment and capabilities. However, a few rules of thumb apply irrespective of the specific characteristics of your business and company. As discussed above, we consider search engine marketing a 'must have' vehicle to capture share of the relevant traffic. Traditional display advertising should be used opportunisti-cally, especially in light of recent price decreases, to create awareness and build brand. All push activities that are paid for purely on a performance basis, such as affiliate marketing, are generally low-risk vehicles, but can require dispropor-tionate administrative effort unless handled by dedicated service providers.

Social media are the most recent and, arguably, the most over-rated addi-tion to the digital marketing mix. Different retailers haven chosen different social media marketing modes:

- Some merely listen in order to generate customer insights.
- Others react to online comments and complaints, leveraging social media as a new channel for customer service.
- A few companies have started to interact pro-actively with users to deepen their attachment to the brand.

Facebook is not the only social media touch point, of course. Others include the blogs and review sites. According to Nielsen, no less than 700 million people worldwide say they use blogs and reviews to make buying decisions. (Source: Nielsen Online Global Consumer Study, 2007.) They look to such sites as trusted sources of unbiased information, provided by 'someone like me'. This fact makes them tempting targets as vehicles for word-of-mouth campaigns, but such sites are highly sensitive to corporate interference. Many users consider paid endorsements the original sin of social media, and will go to great pains to denounce and castigate companies attempting to use social media for marketing purposes. The revelation of a single fake review can easily outweigh the positive effect of thousands of genuine recommendations.

In effect, retailers are afraid of losing control, knowing that a single negative post can spread almost instantaneously. But despite the risks, retailers have to acknowledge the growing role social media play in consumers' behaviour, as well as the insights they potentially afford. The very least needed is for retailers to 'listen actively' to social media discussions and analyze the implications for their business. Over time, they will develop a reliable sense of the dynamics of this latest addition to the marketing mix.

A marketing executive at Marks & Spencer in the UK says, 'We started with product reviews to bring conversations onto our website', but adds, 'it is hard to measure the value of this, but it is intuitively clear that there is a value. We are moving into a phase of constant listening.' According to Retail Week, Marks & Spencer has two full-time employees dedicated to social media, monitoring customer feedback and escalating pressing issues to departments such as customer service. (Source: Joanna Perry, 'Social media: Why M&S is listening to the word on the web', *Retail Week*, 20 November 2009.)

Rules of engagement

With the emergence of social media, online marketing has changed fundamentally: in the new landscape of blogs, online communities and social networks, brands find themselves in a constant and public dialogue with customers. In order to exploit the opportunities that arise from social media marketing, retailers have to understand and apply the rules of the new engagement. One of the most important success factors is to encourage active engagement with the audience – 'listening' to what customers say, and reacting to it in flexible, personal and original ways. Content is king, and constant updates are required to maintain the attention of the audience.

The example of social media illustrates how hard it can be to quantify, compare and optimize the relative value of different digital vehicles. In general, however, the criteria that govern the ROI optimization of offline media also apply to online media: what is their reach, what is the cost per reach, and what is the quality, or involvement level, of the different touch points and contacts? But there is one big difference between offline and online ROI optimization: digital media are all response based. If an online ad does not appear on someone's computer screen or mobile phone, it simply does not exist. This makes it easier to assess the effectiveness of digital vehicles, but it also increases the need for sophisticated tracking and measuring techniques. As much as possible, retailers should strive for an approach that links actual or expected sales impact to digital media investment. As demonstrated in the examples above, this is comparatively easy to achieve for search engine marketing or traditional display ads with quantified click-through rates, but it can be tricky, or even

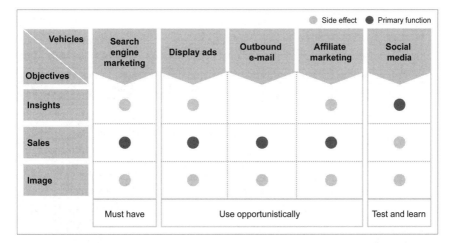

	Side effect ● Primary function

Objectives \ Vehicles	Search engine marketing	Display ads	Outbound e-mail	Affiliate marketing	Social media
Insights	◐	◐		◐	●
Sales	●	●	●	●	◐
Image	◐	◐	◐	◐	◐
	Must have	Use opportunistically			Test and learn

Exhibit 15.5 Relevance of digital marketing vehicles to different marketing objectives.

impossible, for newer and less linear vehicles like social media. Exhibit 15.5 provides a conceptual overview of how well the digital vehicles described above are suited to different marketing objectives.

Hands-on digital media optimization: Grocery example

A large European grocery retailer took a simple, but systematic, approach to developing a rough blueprint for their digital marketing mix, comprising three steps:

- quick, but fact-based, diagnostic
- prioritization of digital vehicles
- set-up of lean structures and processes.

During the diagnostic phase, the company benchmarked its performance on a comprehensive set of KPIs along the brand purchase funnel, using tools like OMEX and NM Incite to understand their current digital performance compared to their competitors. From this, they found how much traffic they were generating within their target group, how long people browsed on the company's website and how much 'buzz' they created in social media. The gaps to competitors were used as a fact base to prioritize the company's digital marketing objectives.

In a second step, the retailer assessed the fitness of various digital marketing instruments, such as banners, display ads and search engine marketing, to advance customers through the purchase funnel. Based on the combination of these results with the earlier benchmarking, the company adjusted its allocation of marketing funds to the different digital instruments.

As a result, the retailer came up with a set of 'must-have' digital instruments on which they have since focused their activities and investments. Secondly, they have defined a cluster of instruments for testing and learning. All other vehicles were classified as 'wait and see' instruments.

The process was concluded by the establishment of a simple, but comprehensive, digital marketing dashboard, displaying 25 KPIs, and the set up of a small, but dedicated digital marketing team.

Digital marketing is real-time marketing:
leverage outside expertise, but keep the set-up flexible and be willing to test and learn

New media requires new capabilities. Today, most online marketing activities are implemented by specialized agencies and service providers. Nevertheless, some capabilities are too important to be left in these hands. Retailers need to stay on top of objective setting and performance tracking for their digital marketing. If there are no clear guidelines about what you are trying to achieve and how to measure whether it is working or not, you will not be able to get the best value from third-party suppliers. For example, if you want to use display ads and affiliate marketing to drive brand awareness, you should specify the quantified objective before commissioning or even hiring a digital marketing agency. This objective might, for example, be to increase brand awareness by 10 percentage points among users aged 15 to 35 in a given country over a period of 3 months. Using average purchase funnel transfer rates, this kind of objective setting even allows you to calculate the estimated ROI of the online marketing agency's quote. You might have to partner with a specialized online research agency to make this approach work, unless your usual market research agency provides 360° solutions across all media.

The Digital Factory

In order to support companies in developing the necessary skills for successful digital marketing management, McKinsey & Company founded the Digital Factory. The Digital Factory company – an online wine shop – allows companies to experience digital marketing in a risk-free environment. It enables current and future e-marketers to gather hands-on experience in real-life digital marketing situations.

The marketing arsenal of the Digital Factory comprises all major online marketing vehicles like SEM, display advertising, affiliate marketing, email marketing, social media and homepage optimization. A typical briefing for a participant could read as follows: 'Your objective is to increase awareness by x percent and generate EUR y in new sales. You have a budget of EUR 5000. Spend your budget any way you like to reach your awareness and sales targets.'

The Digital Factory is a real enterprise, running real campaigns, generating real clicks, serving real customers, stimulating real sales, supported by real experts – and everything happens in real time.

Vendor management is a key element of digital marketing management. Because many trends rise and subside almost over night, digital marketing does not lend itself to rigid structures or long-term planning. A digital marketing team needs to have an appropriate mindset and flexibility; for those starting out, it can be useful to hire a few dedicated digital marketing specialists, ideally experienced practitioners from digital marketing agencies or seasoned web enterprises, such as Google, Amazon and their peers.

The good news is that, in many ways, digital marketing operations are a lot like traditional retail marketing: it is a game of learning by doing. For example, you test and refine a display ad much as you would a traditional promotion scheme. Initially, you display the ad to everyone who surfs your own website. After a few thousand impressions, you profile those customers who clicked on the ad, requested more information or made an online purchase. This analysis becomes the basis for defining the target group for the wider rollout of the ad to third-party websites and online marketing partners. Additional information from other sources such as online surveys and offline customer profiles can help to make the main campaign more effective and more efficient, driving marketing ROI.

In the offline world, marketers sit down to plan a campaign months or even years prior to its activation. In a series of iterations, they develop, test and refine it, finally producing it at tremendous expense, and putting it out in the market for a pre-defined period. Months later, they examine the advertising tracking data to assess the impact of the campaign. In the digital world, none of this applies: digital marketing is real-time marketing. So get started, stay flexible and let the traffic be your guide.

Key takeaways – Digital marketing excellence

1 Even if they have no e-commerce ambitions, retailers cannot ignore the importance of the digital arena as a communication and interaction space.
2 Develop a digital marketing strategy: decide to what extent you wish to use it for insight generation, sales stimulation or brand building.
3 To determine your digital communication mix, weigh push versus pull investments and identify 'must have' vehicles.
4 Digital marketing is real-time marketing: leverage outside expertise, but keep the set-up flexible and be willing to test and learn.

CHAPTER 16

Ben Armstrong, Lars Fiedler, Roland Harste, Jürgen Schröder

Like fine wines or vintage cars, customers become more valuable over time. But like other collector's items, they need special care as they mature. This is what customer lifecycle management, or CLM, is all about. CLM is the key that unlocks each customer's full value over the entire lifecycle from acquisition and development to retention – and, if need be, re-acquisition or re-activation.

CLM-based activities comprise a wide variety of marketing vehicles, mainly focused on the later stages of the purchase funnel, especially conversion, re-purchase and loyalty. CLM enables retailers to use the information they have in their customer base to optimize the allocation of their marketing funds, making it a direct driver of marketing ROI.

In this chapter, we will discuss the relevance of CLM for retailers and outline the dos and don'ts along the four steps of customer lifecycle management. Specifically, we will demonstrate that CLM is more than fancy maths applied to optimize direct marketing campaigns. As we see it, CLM is a holistic way of thinking about quantified customer lifetime value (CLV) that can be applied to inform decisions about almost all the elements of a retailer's marketing mix. To illustrate the power of CLM, we will present a wide range of case examples.

CLM helps drive effectiveness and efficiency in targeted marketing, *enabling retailers to extract the full value from their customer base*

Because of the scope and richness of customer information it generates, retail is in a better position to benefit from CLM than many other industries. Transaction data typically includes the number, type, price and category of products purchased, as well as the date, time and location of the purchase. One major US retailer, for instance, processes one million customer transactions every hour, feeding databases that exceed 2000 terabytes in size. This data flow does not stop at the checkout. Transaction information is enhanced by personalized data gathered from loyalty card programmes over long periods of time. Not only do the majority of top retailers run loyalty programmes, but the use of credit and debit cards now accounts for up to 50 percent of all transactions in some countries.

This abundance of information, in combination with today's affordable supercomputer power, enables even smaller retailers to slice and dice the data anyway they wish. In short, now is the time for retailers to set up CLM programmes in order to reap the benefits over the entire lifecycle of their customers in terms of new customer acquisition, customer development and customer retention (Exhibit 16.1).

Acquisition	Development	Retention
• **Monster**'s click-through optimization based on browsing behavior	• **Virgin Mobile**'s automated top-up SMS reminder	• **ebay**'s special offers and discounts based on churn prediction
• **Restoration Hardware**'s prospecting based on 3rd party data	• **Best Buy**'s loyalty redemption expiry warning	• **Lufthansa**'s distinctive superior service for top frequent flyer tier ("HON circle")
• **Neiman Marcus**' re-activation of "dormant" high-value customers	• **Amazon**'s customized recommendations	• **Bertelsmann**'s dynamic discounts based on customer tenure and value tier
	• **Harrah**'s differentiated offers based on expected customer value	

Exhibit 16.1 Best practice examples along the customer lifecycle.

- *Customer acquisition*: by quantifying the impact of specific promotions and other activities on conversion, retailers can allocate their marketing spend where it makes the biggest difference – e.g. by shifting funds from TV advertising to more targeted media. CLM can also help identify the most valuable targets for new customer acquisition and create a fact base to target potential customers in the places in which they spend their time, such as in online social networks. In short, it enables retailers to acquire new customers more quickly and efficiently, increasing the share of new customers who stay valuable in the longer term.

- *Customer development*: CLM supports retailers in their efforts to encourage customers to buy more often, to include more products in each purchase, to try new categories and to increase their commitment to the brand. For example, by modelling the 'next product to buy' (NPTB) propensity, retailers are able to identify the most promising categories or product groups for cross-promotions. CLM also provides the facts to improve a retailer's overall category strategy and product assortment.

- *Customer retention and win-back*: CLM enables retailers to devise early-tenure interventions if certain indicators point to an increased probability of churn. For example, if a customer's shopping trip frequency, basket size or number of purchase categories drops, the retailer can trigger targeted promotions or special offers, such as rewards for multiple trips, to minimize attrition rates. It also enables them to identify the customers who matter most and reward them with special loyalty tiers, exclusive offers or VIP events. Ultimately, it can also be used to pinpoint and win back high-value former customers.

But CLM is not only of help to retailers in increasing the effectiveness of their targeted marketing activities; it also helps to increase cost-efficiency. For example, CLM data can be used to pick the most cost-efficient communication channel for a given cross-selling campaign in a specific high-value segment, be it direct mail, email or phone outreach. More broadly, it can help retailers move from mass-marketing campaigns with low response rates to highly targeted and tailored campaigns with much higher response rates and lower costs. Says Mike Emery, a Clubcard operations manager at Tesco: 'Clubcard has helped us to grow the business ... We've been able to target offers far more effectively

– reducing the number of promotions but increasing the effectiveness of each. In total, we estimate a savings of around £300 million a year.'

CLM-based refinement and re-allocation recommendations have a big impact due to the size of the marketing budgets of many retailers. Investments in CLM have yielded significant economic results in a variety of situations and industries. Tesco and Amazon are widely known to make systematic and comprehensive use of CLM for loyalty management and targeted marketing. Both retailers have outperformed the market on all the important KPIs, such as market share, revenue, EBITDA and TRS (Exhibit 16.2). But it is not only the market leaders that are able to benefit from CLM; companies newly embarked on such a programme frequently report profit increases of the magnitude of 20 percent or more.

So the size of the prize is substantial. But what do retailers have to do to claim it? In the following, we will examine the principal elements of CLM-based campaign optimization (Exhibit 16.3):

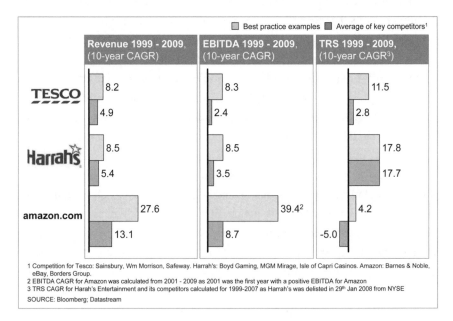

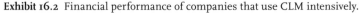

Exhibit 16.2 Financial performance of companies that use CLM intensively.

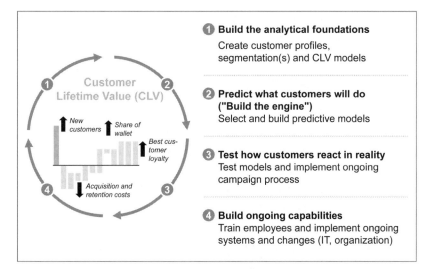

Exhibit 16.3 Campaign optimization process to drive CLV.

- Create the analytical foundations.
- Build predictive models for future campaigns.
- Conduct and refine targeted test campaigns.
- Put in place the structures and capabilities required for sustainable impact.

Successful CLM requires a deep understanding of your customer base: *identify relevant data and aggregate the information in meaningful ways!*

The first step to successful CLM is to create a clear and comprehensive picture of the customer base. In most cases, the issue is not the lack of information but its excessive abundance. In order to avoid drowning in data, we recommend starting with a few straightforward analyses:

- an overview of revenue percentiles
- the creation of value flow diagrams
- a segmentation matrix and
- customer lifetime value (CLV) models.

Simple and well known as some of these analyses might be, such analyses are often very instructive, both in their own right and as the basis for fact-based campaign optimization.

Customer percentiles can provide a good start for understanding the customer base. Using net present value (NPV), or revenues if cost information is unavailable for individual customers, the customer base is split into equally sized groups, e.g. five ('quintiles') or ten ('deciles'). A profile is then created for each percentile, including demographics and behavioural indicators, such as trip frequency, basket size, favourite brand or weekend purchase share. The result is a one-page overview of who the most valuable customers are and how they differ from lower-value customers.

Customer value flow analysis provides a sense of how well you are developing your customers over their lifecycle. The diagram shown in Exhibit 16.4 works like a magnifying glass, revealing, for instance, that even when revenues have changed very little, there can be substantial shifts in the customer base. Understanding which customers have traded down, or churned out, and which

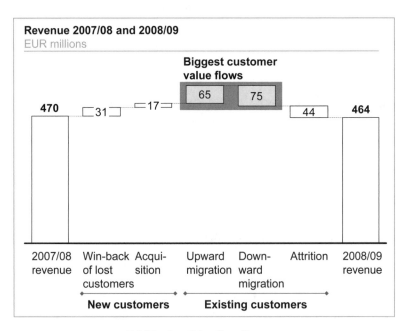

Exhibit 16.4 Value flow diagram.

customers have increased their average purchase, is critical to safeguarding the future economic health of the company.

A **segmentation matrix** aggregates information from multiple sources to inform target selection and targeted marketing. While Chapter 2: 'Segmentation' provides more background on its use as a strategic tool, segmentation in the CLM context is usually more hands-on. Typically, CLM segmentations are limited to a retailer's current customer base and leverage available data on past customer behaviour. For example, a retailer may use a CLM segmentation to run a dedicated campaign for buyers of high-end items who make frequent trips to the store (Exhibit 16.5).

The revenue-based percentile analysis, the customer value flow diagram and the segmentation matrix are all powerful tools that provide a good indication of the nature of the customer base. However, these are only snapshots of your clientele. To obtain a comprehensive and dynamic overview of the customers and their value, you need to model the **customer lifetime value** (CLV) of each individual customer. A robust CLV model should include all the revenue and cost generated in each customer relationship. Understanding the CLV of your customers – and its drivers – is the only reliable basis for value-creating targeted marketing.

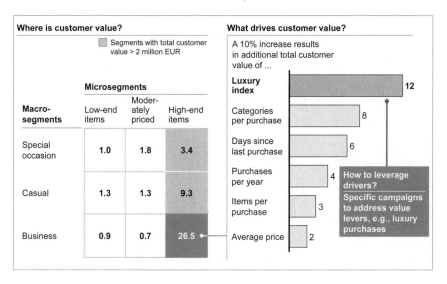

Exhibit 16.5 Customer segmentation and customer value drivers.

Leading companies calculate individual net present value at a very early stage of the customer relationship to determine whether it is worth their while to invest in the acquisition, development and retention of a given customer. The richer the basis of this CLV calculation, the more reliable will its output be. Retailers can use indicators, such as the acquisition channel and the initial response behaviour, to obtain an early sense of a customer's future value – and to differentiate their targeted marketing accordingly. For example, a visiting shopper from out of town – lured into the store only by a voucher offering a

Modelling customer lifetime value (CLV)

There is some debate over whether the customer lifetime value (CLV) calculation necessarily needs to reflect expected future value, or whether it should be based on past revenues alone ('CLV to date'). Any forecast of future value adds predictive power, but also adds a degree of uncertainty and methodological bias. Experience shows that the relevance of past value as a proxy of future value grows with tenure: the better you know your customer, the better you know their future value.

But some CLM activities simply don't work unless you have at least a rough estimate of a customer's future value. For example, early-tenure interventions, when the customer has no track record to speak of, have to be based on forecasts. Leading retailers use factors such as the basket size of a customer's first purchase, or their initial share of items from high-price brands as indicators of high future value. Other indicators can be used as warning signs: if trip frequency or basket size is decreasing it may be time to take pre-emptive action.

If, however, the customer has a long and stable history with the retailer, it is often safe to say that the future value will resemble past value. But take heed: in categories that are sensitive to life-stage changes or other similar changes, this rule does not apply. Even the most devoted parents will stop buying diapers once their youngest child is trained. Either way, newcomers to CLM will want to start with (average) past revenue as a basic approximation of customer value – in order to keep things simple.

large discount from the local paper that came free with their hotel breakfast – might not be the world's most valuable customer. In contrast, a new loyalty club member, signed up by a friend as part of a 'member gets member' programme, probably has a much higher lifetime value and is hence more worthy of the retailer's attention.

Up-front impact estimates allow for more targeted CLM activities: *use predictive modelling to assess probable customer reactions before piloting!*

CLV is the gold standard of value-based, targeted marketing. If you know who your most valuable customers are, you can focus your funds and resources on these customers. But to fine-tune your marketing mix, you also need to understand the expected impact of different activities on customer value. It is all well and good to know that 'Mr. Luxury', a highly involved shopper with a penchant for upscale items, is a high-value customer, worthy of your best cross-selling efforts. If he has a loyalty card, you might even know who he is, where he lives and how to reach him. But how do you succeed with this kind of customer? Is it by offering discounts on selected luxury items in outbound emails? Is it by announcing a VIP reward scheme in the customer club newsletter? Or is it by highlighting exclusive offers in personally addressed direct mail?

CLM-based predictive modelling answers these questions. Its objective is to predict the reaction of customers to different marketing activities and, frequently, predict their bottom-line impact. Certain modelling approaches use regression analysis to predict the CLV impact of specific marketing activities, but such models make high demands, both in terms of analytical capabilities and maintenance, chiefly because they require the many assumptions in the model to be revised and adjusted for each new modelling effort. Because of these challenges, most retailers predict customer *behaviour* rather than customer *value*. Campaign responsiveness modelling, for example, calculates the likelihood of particular events, such as a specific customer reaction to a potential campaign. A simplified output of this kind of model could read: 'If we send Mr. Luxury a personalized letter offering an exclusive preview of the new collection, there is a 55 percent chance that he will show up at the store (if you have the capability to measure store visits) and a 32 percent chance that he will make a purchase.'

Other types of probabilistic modelling go one level deeper and focus on customer product preferences to help retailers select items for targeted promotions. 'Next Product To Buy' modelling, or NPTB, is based on an association analysis of the products in customers' baskets that predicts what they will buy next (Exhibit 16.6). Once you know Mr. Luxury is probably looking for a shirt and tie to go with his new suit, you can use this information to make a targeted offer. But it also works vice versa: If you sit on a stack of last season's dress shirts earmarked for promotion, NPTB helps you to select the group of customers who are most likely to respond and make a purchase. The more data that is gathered from past campaigns and fed into the NPTB model, the higher its predictive reliability. Exhibit 16.7 shows a real-life example of a Best Buy campaign that leverages basic NPTB thinking to drive repeat purchases. For details, please see the article on 'Supermodeling', by Ben Armstrong and Ian Ross, in McKinsey & Company's *The Journal of Problem Solving*, 2009.

While NPTB draws its inferences primarily from the track records of customers' past purchases, product DNA modelling recognizes specific product

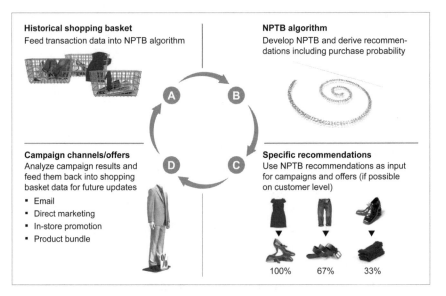

Exhibit 16.6 Next product to buy (NPTB) modelling.

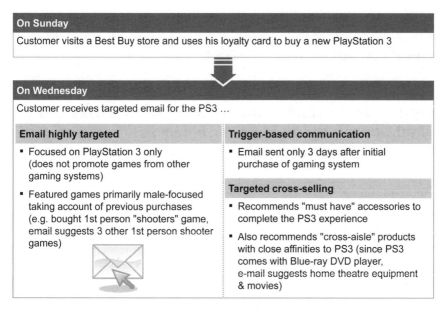

Exhibit 16.7 Real-life example of targeted email to drive repeat purchase.

characteristics as input factors. Product attributes such as price level, colour and shape collectively represent the product's 'DNA'. DNA modelling was pioneered by online providers, such as Netflix and Pandora, for matching movie and music recommendations to users' past favourites. The same kind of approach can be put to good use in retail. By matching the DNA of a given product with the customer's preferences derived from their purchasing history, retailers can identify the most attractive target group for the item in question. This approach is particularly valuable for recent additions to a retailer's assortment when there is no prior transaction history. Based on DNA analysis, the brand new, machine-washable wool overcoat might be just the thing for Mr. Luxury.

The practical relevance of probabilistic approaches, such as NPTB and DNA modelling can be further enhanced by adding a secondary dimension – that of time. The models that make use of this to predict the distribution of the additional purchases a customer will make over a given time period require a number of additional input factors, such as the time elapsed since the last purchase ('how recent') and the number of purchases made in a given period ('frequency'). A number of retailers combine responsiveness modelling and purchase distribution analysis to capture both the 'what' and the 'when' factors in their predictions of future customer behaviour.

Optimization starts with knowing what works and what doesn't work: *test different campaigns and keep track of campaign parameters as well as impact metrics!*

Once you know who your most valuable customers are and which types of campaign stand the highest chance of eliciting positive responses, it is time to put the CLM model to the test. Despite all efforts to fortify its conceptual backbone, retail marketing is still a question of testing and learning. This is particular true for outbound marketing campaigns. But the analytical foundations and predictive models described above make campaign pilots more valuable than ever. Target audiences can be pre-selected with high granularity and offers can be tailored to the needs of a given audience. Still, the pilot should follow the long-established foundations of systematic testing and learning.

- *Define the objectives clearly and specify relevant metrics*: the retailer will need to decide at the outset whether the pilot's objective is new customer acquisition, the development of the existing customer base, churn prevention or the re-acquisition of former high-value customers. Relevant metrics need to be specified to track the results. These could include, for example, the conversion rate for acquisitions, campaign response rate for cross-selling offers or repurchase rate for overall development of the customer base.
- *Log all parameters for future reference*: prior to an actual pilot, it is imperative to specify and log the key parameters for future reference, analysis and refinement. How has the target group been defined? Which communication channel is used? At which point in time does the campaign reach the customer? Which products and services are promoted? What is the incentive for the customer (e.g. the discount rate)? What promotion materials were used?
- *Use control groups to capture the value the campaign adds*: the target sample should be divided into a test group that receives the mailing, newsletter, text

SOURCE: Barnes & Noble, Inc.

Exhibit 16.8 Example of testing and learning through variations in test design.

message, email or other relevant materials, and a control group that does not. The test group may be split into sub-groups in order to test variations in the campaign, e.g. different discounts rates and types, such as 10 percent, 20 percent or 10 EUR flat. Exhibit 16.8 gives a real-life example.

- *Track and review the campaign's impact*: the predefined metrics (such as the conversion rate or response rate) and other more general impact indicators (such as revenues, profit or average basket size) should be tracked carefully. Once the pilot has concluded, its results should be reviewed by the CLM team in order to identify improvements to be introduced in future campaigns.

Retailers find that targeted CLM campaigns based on robust analytical foundations and predictive modelling yield much higher success rates at lower costs than generic offers made available to broad audiences. Ted Brewer, Vice President of Customer Information Management at Royal Bank of Canada, confirms this: 'Thanks to the [...] Customer Relationship Management solution, RBC has reported direct marketing campaign response rates as high as 40 percent, compared to the industry average of 2 to 4 percent'. (Source: 'RBC Royal Bank uses a Teradata Warehouse and Teradata Value Analyzer to realize its CRM strategy', Teradata 2004.)

Once the pilot is complete, the design of all stages of the campaign process, including its key parameters and impact metrics, should be stored in a standardized campaign library so that the insights derived from the campaign's development and testing are available for later use. Based on the insights from multiple cycles, retailers will be able to roll out proven campaign formats across multiple stores, regions and formats to capture scale advantages – and boost their marketing ROI.

Build sustainable CLM capabilities: *secure top talent, set up clear interfaces and processes, and take precautions regarding data availability and quality!*

Successful CLM implementation requires the combination of a clear strategy, well-structured CLM operations and robust analytics supported by a superior technical team. There are three main pre-requisites that need to be put in place to ensure these elements work together smoothly and effectively:

- the right people, endowed with a true CLM mindset
- an efficient CLM set-up, with clear processes and interfaces, both within and beyond the CLM team
- reliable CLM data, supported by a powerful IT infrastructure.

We will look briefly at each of these elements.

In terms of talent, you need a dedicated CLM manager with a strategic marketing mindset to develop a long-term CLM strategy, define the priorities for specific programmes and campaigns and assume overall responsibility. Secondly, the CLM team should also comprise at least one hands-on marketer who has the product or category management experience necessary for managing campaign execution. Thirdly, you need at least one business analyst with strong quantitative skills, ideally with previous experience of the relevant software, such as SQL, SAS, SPSS and advanced modelling techniques. Even if the bulk of the analyses is conducted by outside vendors – or by a dedicated corporate department – it is still important to have someone on the team who can manage and audit their work. Last but not least, CLM depends on a skilled and dedicated IT taskforce that is able to take care of the technical side of data gathering, data mining and output consolidation.

Managers of newly established CLM units will need to ensure that their team does not over indulge in advanced analytics and highly customized marketing activities. You can always get sophisticated once the basics are in place. A number of companies also find it useful to set up a cross-functional CLM steering committee to manage and monitor the CLM team.

But even the world's greatest team needs a game plan to score. Make sure roles and responsibilities of individual team members, the processes within the CLM team and its interfaces with other departments are clear and well documented. While the interface between the marketing department and the IT department may be the most important one for development, modelling and testing of CLM, the link to commercial operations is key for ensuring its ultimate impact. To this end, the executives in charge of CLM should make sure that its insights are made available to all the key players in their company's principal commercial processes. The finest insights on the world's most valuable target group, or the most promising high-impact campaign format, will have no impact if line managers in a retail organizations functional or regional departments don't know about them.

Once you have hired – or trained – the right people and set up the appropriate processes, the remaining challenge is data quality. Data is the raw material of CLM: without readily available, reliable data the CLM engine will not run. But where do you start? The list of potential sources is endless: POS transaction data; financials like revenue and cost on a daily, weekly, monthly or quarterly basis; loyalty card schemes; customer surveys; payment details; after sales service logs; general market research – and so on. Fortunately, the essentials required for basic CLM are simple and straightforward:

- *Customer data*: addresses; socio-demographics; store preferences; start dates of loyalty programme membership; 'permissions to contact' for promotions and other activities.
- *Transaction data*: dates of transactions; products purchased; prices of products purchased; stores; payment methods; returns (if any).
- *Marketing details*: selection of customers for specific campaigns; campaign dates; coupon redemptions.

Additional customer data on household income or household size can be gathered through surveys or by purchasing third party data; however, since these details regularly change over time, it can be challenging and costly to keep them up to date. To ensure the sustainability of CLM data, it is preferable to work with as fewer data sources as possible, so that the date can easily be updated and maintained.

Ideally, all data should be consolidated into a single, dedicated CLM database. If this proves to be impracticable, for whatever reason, robust data matching and verification procedures need to be put in place to ensure that the data is compatible and easily digestible by the CLM model. In either case, CLM makes heavy demands on IT infrastructure, computing power and the specialized software required to handle the data (e.g. SQL, SAS, IBM Design Studio), perform statistical analyses (e.g. SPSS or SAS Enterprise Miner) and manage campaign execution (e.g. Unica, SAS, Neolane).

Practical hints for increasing data availability and quality

- Start programmes to *capture e-mail addresses and cell phone numbers*; make sure you also get customers' permission to use these vehicles for advertising ('opt-in marketing').
- Pay special attention to the *quality and reliability of customer data*, and make sure it is up to date, so you can reach customers with direct marketing activities when you need to.
- To compensate for customers who do not use their loyalty card at all times, *employ alternative means to link a customer's identity* to a given transaction:
  - campaign response elements: e.g. personalized coupons
  - online data: e.g., login data, cookies or shipping addresses
  - payment details: e.g. account details from credit or debit card payments.
- At all times, make sure you know and observe local *privacy protection regulation*. Certain countries, for instance, prohibit the use of payment details for marketing purposes.

But never forget that tons of data and fancy maths alone won't get you anywhere. Rich customer data and advanced modelling techniques are part of the CLM toolkit, but to see real impact, you have to pay at least as much attention to organizational factors like information flow, decision patterns, incentives and mindset. Simply speaking, the concepts of the customer lifecycle and its stages, as well as of customer value and its drivers, have to become a living part of a retailer's organizational DNA.

CLM need not be limited to direct marketing
but can be applied to areas such as category management and format development

Conceptually, CLM is about understanding the distinct stages of a customer's lifecycle and the drivers of customer lifetime value. Operationally, it is about optimizing the drivers of customer value using all the available levers. Direct marketing is just one of these levers, although it is often the one where results are seen most quickly. There are other levers: these include assortment strategy, pricing and store operations. Let's take a look at a few real-life examples of CLM applications in areas beyond that of direct marketing.

- *Assortment and pricing in category management*: details on segment-specific customer preferences and product penetration can be used to inform assortment reviews and pricing. In these processes, the preferences of predefined high-value target segments should carry disproportional weight. Mr. Luxury, the prototypical top-target customer, has a weakness for specific brands and products in the high-price band of a given category; this suggests that the retailer should carry a relevant selection in this area. Similarly, price setting for a given SKU should reflect the price sensitivity and overall price perception implications for preselected target segments. See Exhibit 16.9 for a real-life example.
- *Promotions in category management*: CLM enables retailers to disaggregate the impact of promotions: increases in traffic, entries into new categories, premium switches, value switches, cannibalization, stocking-up, simple

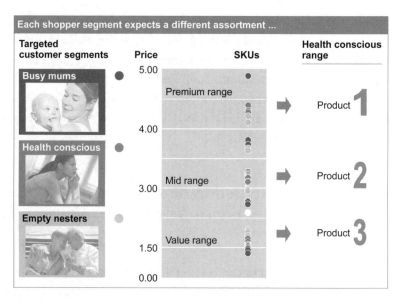

Exhibit 16.9 Example of CLM-based assortment and pricing in category management.

discounts. Based on this information, category managers can optimize promotions. See Exhibit 16.10 for an example of this.

- *Network and format development*: retailers can use CLM-based information on customer preferences to optimize their store network, fitting formats and layouts to the needs of local user pools and specific high-value customer segments. See Exhibit 16.11 for a disguised example.
- *Personalization of in-store offering*: retailers can leverage the CLM database to provide their commercial functions and stores with periodic, structured analyses of consumption trends and customer characteristics. Based on this information, managers can optimize the in-store experience at both the store cluster and the individual store level. If the majority of the user pool of a given store, for example, has a special preference for fresh fruit, the store can reflect this in its assortment.
- *Localization of the go-to-market approach*: a CLM database and campaign library that covers multiple regions or countries will also enable retailers to account for local differences in customer preferences. These might be in the assortment, for example: while grocery shoppers in downtown areas might show a preference for convenience products and prepared foods, a cluster

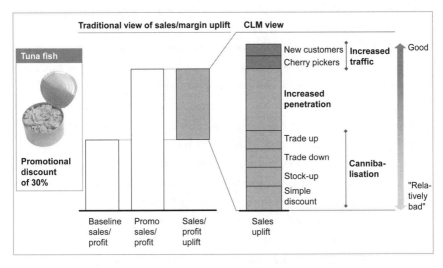

Exhibit 16.10 Example for category penetration optimization through promotions.

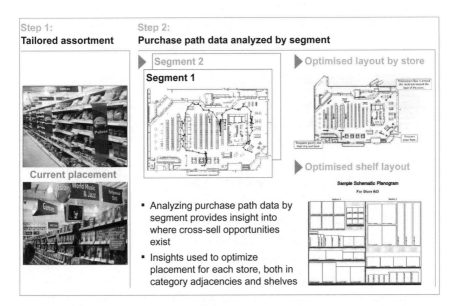

Exhibit 16.11 Example for CLM-based store and shelf layout optimization.

of suburban outlets could find that the high percentage of single mums in their user pool makes it advisable to stock a small selection of toys. Or take beauty retail, where 'functional skin care' means very different things in different contexts, depending on the continent: sunscreen in Australia, whitening cream in Asia and self-tanning lotion in Europe. Similarly, the success rates of different promotion types varies greatly by territory: while many US shoppers thrive on coupons, most European customers are much more responsive to in-store discounts or bundling offers. Localization can go as far as format strategy and store layout. While shoppers in one region or country will be attracted to branded 'store-in-store' concepts, shoppers elsewhere might expect to find all the items from the same category in the same section of the store, whatever the brand or the price band.

CLM is not a specific tool or approach, but a way of thinking. Its value is not limited to direct marketing; it can be brought to bear on many other key elements of a retailer's marketing mix to enable it to extract the full value from customers over their entire lifecycle. Thorsten Ganzlin of Adidas says: 'Without the transparent and real-time understanding of a customer's interactions [provided by CLM], sales per retailer would have dropped rapidly'. (Source: Wolfgang Martin Team, 'Strategic Bulletin: CRM 2005', Annecy, November 2004.)

Interview: Daniela Mündler, Board member for international marketing at Douglas: 'CLM takes us closer to customers'

Daniela Mündler is in charge of international marketing at Douglas, a leading European fragrance and beauty retailer.

Q: What role does CLM play in your marketing efforts?

Daniela Mündler: I think CLM is one of the most important levers available for active marketing. As offers, channels and target groups become increasingly fragmented, all marketing decisions and actions need to be based on real, individual customer behaviour.

Consider that 90 percent of the population regard our industry's products to be luxury items – in other words, not something people really need. Yet CLM provides us with a tool to develop relevant, attractive offers for every customer. This ability represents a real competitive advantage for us. Of course we can communicate with customers in a number of ways. But the best way to get closer to customers is to understand what their behaviour tells us.

Q: What is the key benefit CLM offers to Douglas?

Daniela Mündler: The focused view of our customers that CLM provides opens up many opportunities for us to improve. Of course, considerable potential exists in the areas of campaign design and cooperative efforts with manufacturers. Optimized campaigns help us to build long-term loyalty to the Douglas brand by providing each individual customer with tailored offers. In terms of working with manufacturers, we can not only target our efforts to support new product placements even more precisely, but we can develop innovative packages of offers as well. But CLM can also help us with decisions regarding assortment and pricing, the breadth of our offering, product development, store location and of course customer acquisition.

Q: What factors determine whether CLM is successfully implemented?

Daniela Mündler: Obviously, you need high-quality data, a corresponding IT infrastructure and highly skilled employees. But what matters most is a strategic perspective for the longer term. Only companies that are willing to make the customer the centre of their world will reap the full benefit of CLM. Customer relationships are like living organisms, constantly changing in a continuous process that demands ever better skills. The entire organization must accept this fact.

Q: What skills do employees need?

Daniela Mündler: The main prerequisite is very good analytical skills. This sounds obvious, but often proves to be a problem in practice: marketing functions, where CLM is generally located, tend to be full of people who think they can get by without numbers. This belief is a fallacy for any marketer, and in this case an especially dangerous one.

But analytical abilities alone are not enough. Openness, curiosity, creativity, a critical spirit and a strategic bent are needed too. CLM will never be a success story if employees cling to their routines. Rather, they must be able to accept that things are always in flux. To be successful, you must constantly review your systems to see if better solutions are possible.

Q: How will CLM develop in the future?

Daniela Mündler: I am convinced that marketing departments will increasingly need to ask whether they are investing their money efficiently. In the future, we will focus even more on how precisely marketing efforts reach their targeted audiences and how accurately their impact can be measured. I therefore see CLM as a key future tool for realizing tailored campaigns as cost-effectively as possible.

This is a good thing, because it will be possible to steer marketing activities much more effectively. But the flipside is that some CLM devotees have a tendency to want to steer everything, sometimes to such an extent that no leeway remains. When it comes to image campaigns, we also have to acknowledge that impact requires a certain amount of time to become apparent and cannot always be measured directly.

In any case, only very few retailers will be able to get by without CLM much longer. The days of mass target groups are definitely drawing to a close. Of course we would still like to see as many people as possible coming to our stores – but we can no longer afford to take a one-size-fits-all approach to get them there. CLM offers an excellent alternative.

Q: What experiences with CLM have surprised you the most?

Daniela Mündler: I was initially surprised that CLM can be applied at so many different levels. Later, I also realized how much can be mined from existing data and how much potential can be tapped in this way.

Having this extensive data led to another 'Eureka!' moment: watch out for supposedly logical explanations! In the past, I had a tendency to respond to particular findings by saying, 'of course, this or that is the reason for it.' But you can't do that with this volume of data. For example, a CLM analysis may reveal completely unexpected customer behaviour. When something like this happens, we have to see how we should deal with the analysis, what new findings we can extract and what old beliefs we need to throw out.

That was probably the biggest surprise for me. I have been in the fragrance business for many years now, and I was certain that I fully understood it. CLM taught me better. You can never assume that you know it all. This insight alone was immensely valuable.

Key takeaways – CLM

1 CLM helps drive effectiveness and efficiency in targeted marketing, enabling retailers to extract the full value from their customer base.
2 Successful CLM requires a deep understanding of your customer base: Identify relevant data and aggregate the information in meaningful ways!
3 Up-front impact estimates allow for more targeted CLM activities. Use predictive modelling to assess probable customer reactions before piloting!
4 Optimization starts with knowing what works and what doesn't work. Test different campaigns and keep track of campaign parameters as well as impact metrics!
5 Build sustainable CLM capabilities. Secure top talent, set up clear interfaces and processes, and take precautions regarding data availability and quality!
6 CLM need not be limited to direct marketing, but can be applied to areas such as category management and format development.

CHAPTER 17

SMART SOURCING

Steffi Entenmann, Björn-Uwe Mercker, Thomas Meyer, Nicolas Reinecke

Retail marketing executives often look at their peers in consumer goods with great envy: 'Why is it that manufacturers of beverages, snacks or household products pay only a single-digit commission on activation to their creative agencies, while the same agencies charge us 10 percent or more and keep asking for extra compensation as soon as we request a single change to a TV commercial or print ad?' Surely, advertising volume cannot be the only reason for this difference? It is not. Of course, consumer goods companies' huge global accounts make it easier for agencies and other service providers to offer them favourable conditions. But, to a large extent, marketing efficiency is a function of smart sourcing management. While most consumer goods giants have already implemented comprehensive marketing procurement programmes, many retailers are still in the early stages of efficiency optimization.

In this chapter, we show that smart sourcing is much more than simply a case of outmanoeuvring suppliers and providers in negotiations. Most importantly, it includes a critical review of internal demand and procurement process management at retail companies. To illustrate both some key levers and the impact of smart sourcing efforts, we have included an exemplary deep-dive examination of commercial print, an important line item in the marketing budget of many retailers.

Increasing marketing efficiency might be hard work, but it is well worth it: *smart sourcing yields sizeable savings without compromising quality*

Marketing spend *effectiveness* is familiar territory for many retailers. Topics like brand positioning, message definition, budget allocation and media selection feature prominently on their agenda (see Chapter 16: 'Boosting customer value through CLM'). By comparison, marketing *efficiency* – i.e. the improved purchasing of marketing-related services – is less well established. Yet improved efficiency enables retailers to capture substantial savings without compromising the quality of services rendered; alternatively, it can help them improve the service level without changing the budget. In short, marketing effectiveness is about doing the right things, while marketing efficiency is about making sure the right things are done at a fair price.

The scope of marketing efficiency programmes typically ranges from creative agency services to the production of physical materials such as leaflets. In general, they comprise three types of spend:

- *Above the line (ATL)*: classical advertising, including creative and media agency services.
- *Below the line (BTL)*: POS materials, catalogues, direct marketing, events and related agency services.
- *Other services*: market research, IT support, long-term contractual obligations (e.g. sponsorship).

It is clear even from this simplified overview that retailers will have to deal with a large number of different external partners in order to optimize their marketing efficiency. This is no simple matter, especially since service providers such as creative agencies and media agencies have undergone large-scale consolidation through M&A in recent years (Exhibit 17.1). As a result, marketing is one of the most consolidated professional service industries. As buyers of marketing services, retailers now face global conglomerates with considerable negotiating power.

The structural complexity and scale of the service provider landscape is not the only obstacle in the way of retailers' marketing efficiency efforts. There are

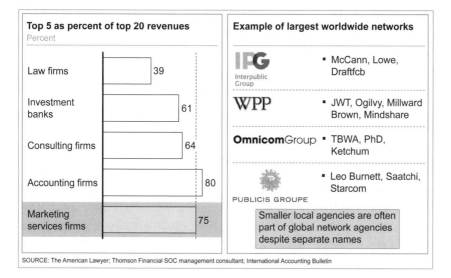

Exhibit 17.1 Marketing has become one of the most consolidated professional service industries worldwide.

Scope of marketing efficiency efforts

The positions covered by marketing efficiency programmes are sometimes referred to as non-working spend or indirect cost, defined as investments that are necessary enablers of marketing effectiveness but which do not actually reach end consumers. But both terms are misleading since media buying is often one of the biggest line items in the marketing budget and should, therefore, be part of any holistic marketing efficiency effort. Media buying includes all expenses incurred to secure customer contacts, e.g. TV airtime or print advertising space purchased through media agencies or directly from media owners such as TV networks and publishing houses. Comprehensive marketing efficiency efforts should, in fact, include all external marketing cost positions.

also serious internal challenges. Responsibility for marketing spend is often scattered across many functions, regions or business units. The budget is highly fragmented, especially in BTL, both in terms of territories and in terms of individual cost positions and items. Since most executives are reluctant to relinquish or even suspend their decision power, it can be very challenging to overcome traditional 'silo' thinking and establish a comprehensive efficiency mindset. This problem is further aggravated by the fact that marketing and purchasing functions often fight over budget clearance procedures. While major cost positions, such as lead agency contracts or media buying, are usually handled by both functions, or at least overseen by purchasing, smaller line items are often still under the marketing department's exclusive control. With marketing focused on effectiveness and purchasing focused on efficiency, target conflicts are bound to arise.

So is it worth the fight? Absolutely. The marketing budget often eats up a substantial share of a retailer's revenue. In many cases expenditure for external services is also growing quickly because of the tendency to outsource more and more marketing-related services. This is especially true for the 'hidden' part of the budget, i.e. for all positions that relate to enabling services, rather than to actual activation; while media buying is usually overseen by the purchasing department, as well as media audit firms, service fees are often subject to far less scrutiny. Additionally, media prices have declined during the recession, while agencies have been slower to adapt the level of their service fees. As a result, in many cases enabling budgets appear to be spinning out of control (see Exhibit 17.2 for a disguised example).

Companies that conduct comprehensive marketing efficiency efforts often capture savings of the magnitude of 5–30 percent of their marketing spend without compromising effectiveness. This impact goes straight to their bottom line. Look at Exhibit 17.3 for a disguised example of the savings opportunities across all major line items of the marketing budget.

Marketing efficiency is not only about saving money. By streamlining demand and consolidating their suppliers, retailers can also improve the consistency of their marketing mix. Says Toni Palmer, CMO of Kimberly-Clark, according to Advertising Age (April 2007): 'We [...] have a big opportunity around the efficiency of our marketing spend. As a company, we're not using our scale as effectively as we could, for example, with our service providers [...].

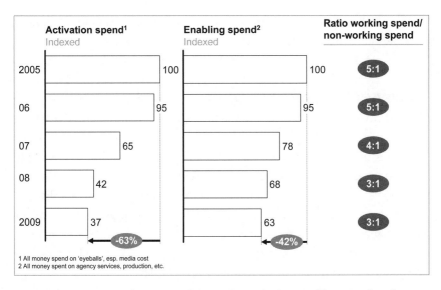

Exhibit 17.2 As the hidden part of the marketing budget, enabling spend is often managed less rigorously than activation spend.

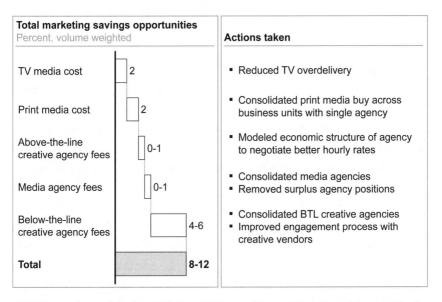

Exhibit 17.3 Comprehensive marketing efficiency efforts yield savings of the magnitude of 10 percent.

Increasing the consistency in strategy and creative implementation is another key factor for managing the spend.'

Efficiency levers *include rigorous supplier management, streamlined demand and procurement process optimization*

Marketing efficiency can be improved by pulling three types of lever: supply levers, demand levers and process levers. While most traditional cost reduction efforts cover only supplier management, our experience shows that the improvement potential is just as substantial, or even larger, in the areas of demand management and purchasing process optimization. For example, a global retail company found that 60 percent of its marketing efficiency improvement impact came from demand and process levers.

Supplier management

Supplier management is about paying less for what you buy, i.e. improving sourcing conditions without changing the character or quality of products purchased and services rendered. Examples include:

- *Bundling volume*: buying from fewer suppliers or service providers enables retailers to capture volume discounts. Relevant cost positions include creative agency services, production services, media agency services and media buying. Volumes can be bundled across legal entities, business units, departments, brands, regions and countries.
- *Switching to cheaper providers*: while switching creative agencies may be too sensitive from a strategic perspective, less critical items, such as POS materials, can often be purchased more cheaply from providers in low-cost countries (so-called LCC sourcing). A point to note is that it is important to have a physical presence in the low-cost provider's home country in order to be able to monitor quality.
- *Supply chain optimization*: this includes de-bundling, e.g. by separating print production from paper supply. Furthermore, it includes 'make or buy' decisions, as well as the tactical use of intermediaries. For example, when media

agencies pool the demand of multiple media buyers, they are often able to obtain higher discounts from media owners. In other cases, intermediaries, such as commodity brokers, can be helpful for coping with complex sourcing environments, such as fragmented suppliers in low-cost countries.

- *Rigorous negotiation*: with thorough preparation and full data transparency, retailers frequently succeed in reducing commission percentages, establishing performance-based fees or extending payment terms in their negotiations with suppliers.

Demand streamlining

Demand streamlining is about defining what you really need and getting rid of the waste. It comprises all activities that cut the volume or reduce the complexity of products and services purchased. Examples include:

- *Standardization/harmonization*: by standardizing or harmonizing the specifications of certain media products (e.g. the format of a catalogue), you can increase demand volume and decrease complexity. This usually results in lower design and production costs.
- *De-specification/design-to-value*: by reducing product or service specifications to what is really needed and valued by consumers, you can reduce costs significantly. For example, an addressed direct mailing in black and white may be just as effective as a full colour version at a much higher price.
- *Just-in-time configuration of materials*: for example, by pre-producing a standard media product (e.g. a TV commercial for all European markets) and then tailoring it to specific needs late in the value creation process (e.g. by adding a voiceover in the local language). This approach reduces costs and increases flexibility.

Procurement process optimization

Procurement process optimization is about increasing the internal transparency and discipline around the sourcing of materials and services from external providers. Examples include:

- *Advanced procurement processes*: the overall aim of smart sourcing is to standardize, streamline and automate procurement-related processes. This includes applying advanced sourcing techniques across the company, such as IT-enabled auctions or sophisticated online catalogues.
- *Inventory and logistics management*: in the case of physical marketing materials, inventory and logistics is a major driver of cost and working capital for many retailers. For example, by optimizing your network of print shops, you can often capture major transportation cost savings.
- *Demand planning, approval processes and order management*: streamlining the planning cycle and approval processes, reducing the number of decision makers and using off-peak production periods increases efficiency. In addition, you should also review your order management process. Simple measures, such as ensuring planning is carried out sufficiently early and that clear guidelines are put in place on minimum order quantities, can save a great deal of money.
- *Centralization/best-practice sharing*: the provision of central online catalogues, the centralized coordination of content and materials management, and the exchange of best practices all enable the whole company to leverage existing content, materials and expertise more effectively.
- *Cooperation of marketing and procurement functions*: the early involvement of the procurement function in product development and service selection helps reduce costs without sacrificing quality. It also shortens the time from concept to execution. Procurement can support marketing when making trade-off decisions (e.g. quality versus price) by providing the cost of individual 'product components', thereby establishing a more cost-conscious decision logic.
- *Cooperation of retailers and service providers*: streamlining the briefing, alignment and approval processes between retailers and their agencies and production houses almost always helps to cut costs and shorten the lead time from concept to execution; this is also known as a 'lean agency approach'.
- *Performance and compliance tracking*: in order to ensure the potential savings or improvements that have been identified are actually realized, retailers should define relevant KPIs, set up a tracking system and monitor the performance of external service providers. Similarly, executives in charge of smart sourcing should put in place procedures and incentives that

ensure internal functions and departments comply with the new sourcing guidelines.

The relevance of these levers varies across media and types of spend. See the exemplary deep-dive into commercial print below for further detail.

Efficiency optimization is a five-step process: *gather facts, create a long list of improvement ideas, select ideas for execution, negotiate and implement*

A typical smart sourcing process comprises five phases (Exhibit 17.4). Because of the complexity of marketing efficiency improvement, you should set up a dedicated team to run a pilot programme in selected formats, categories, countries and/or regions before rolling it out to the wider organisation. This two-stage approach will help generate results quickly, focus the effort on the biggest levers and enable the rollout to be based on insights gleaned from the pilot phase.

Phase	① Establishment of fact base and definition of approach	② Development of sourcing model incl. improvement ideas	③ Finalization, approval, and execution of ideas	④ Negotiation and supplier selection	⑤ Launch implementation and tracking
Key activities	• Data collection • Agree on focus categories (high impact, ease) • Agree on countries in scope • Define optimisation levers and support tools • Ensure buy-in of marketing and procurement functions	• Conduct market scans for all focus categories • Conduct interviews with countries to establish market-ing requirements • Conduct optimiza-tion workshops with all stakeholders • Conduct bench-marking analyses	• Prioritize ideas based on savings estimate and feasibility • Define supplier shortlist • Develop requests for proposals/ quotes • Complete bid sheet including qualitative information/ savings ideas	• Screen and vali-date quotes and shortlist suppliers for negotiations • Prepare nego-tiations • Conduct initial rounds of negotiation to select preferred supplier(s) • Negotiate final agreement	• Finalise contracts and place orders • Track lead times, quality, etc. and take counter measures if needed • Adapt roles/responsi-bilities where needed • Optimize processes (e.g., demand planning) and establish policies • Consolidate learnings and prepare global rollout
Deliverables	• Category and country scope • Spend breakdown • Levers to be pulled	• Market prioritisation • Supplier long-lists • Harmonisation/ despecification ideas	• Idea shortlist • Supplier shortlists • Scenarios/ specifications • Request for quotation	• Selected suppliers • Agreed conditions	• Contracts/frame agreements finalized • Performance tracking KPIs • Optimized structures, roles, and processes • Rollout plan and timing

Exhibit 17.4 Five-step sourcing optimization process.

We will now examine each of the five steps in more detail.

1. Establish a fact base and define the approach

At the outset of an efficiency improvement effort, you should put in place a strong cross-functional and cross-regional core team comprising marketing executives, media planners, procurement experts and experienced analysts. As a first step, the team should compile detailed data (ideally in an integrated database) on activation and enabling expenditure. This data will need to be retrieved or collected from internal sources such as the enterprise resource planning (ERP) system, marketing plans, procurement contracts and various types of internal performance tracking. Wherever possible, the sourcing team should leverage data already gathered for similar or related marketing ROI efforts. Almost always, however, data sources of external providers will also have to be tapped, e.g. agency data or external market research data.

All the data should be segmented according to preset criteria, such as the category, subcategory, supplier, internal purchasing organization, spend location and so on. It should span several years and comprise sourcing-specific information, e.g. specification descriptions of individual products or service types.

Once this fact base has been established, analyses and qualitative interviews should be conducted to identify the categories and regions or business units that will take part in the pilot effort. The selection criteria should include the potential impact, ease of implementation, absolute size of spend and strategic relevance of the category, region or business unit in question.

Finally, the broader internal marketing and procurement community, as well as the company's key suppliers and service providers, should be informed about the programme. Continuous communication throughout the process, both internally as well as externally, is essential to ensure the buy-in, commitment and cooperation of all involved.

2. Develop the sourcing model, including quality improvement and cost eduction ideas

In phase 2, the team compiles a long-list of improvement ideas. The overview of the levers listed above – i.e. supplier management, demand streamlining and procurement process optimization – can act as a guiding framework in this phase. Relevant sources for improvement ideas include the initial analyses carried out in the first phase, interviews, selective in-depth research in market supply and internal optimization workshops. The latter are a good way to leverage the wisdom of the entire organization, especially regarding the harmonization and de-specification of services or products. For instance, who is in a better position to assess the required paper and printing quality of POS posters than a store manager? These workshops are also a good format for involving marketing stakeholders outside the core team in the process in order to ensure their buy-in from the outset.

This phase will produce a long list of improvement ideas: these should include ideas by category as well as over-arching process improvement ideas. Additionally, the supply market scans should be consolidated into a long-list of potential suppliers and providers for each category. Finally, the team should define guidelines for the sourcing process, the so-called sourcing model, for each category. The sourcing model should comprise any decisions that need to be made about the sourcing process, such as whether to source directly from the manufacturer or from the distributor, the types of request for proposals and quotes, the negotiation process and an overview of the regional sourcing markets in focus. At the end of this phase, the team should have produced strong hypotheses about which of the existing contracts should be terminated.

3. Finalize, approve and execute the improvement ideas

In the third phase, the team will short-list the improvement ideas that deserve closer inspection. Each short-listed idea will eventually be backed by a solid savings estimate, an assessment of its feasibility, an overview of the additional analyses that will need to be conducted and identification of the person or sub-team that will be in charge of the idea's implementation. In parallel, the long-lists of suppliers and providers should be whittled down to short-lists.

Requests for proposals and/or quotes (RFPs, RFQs) should be developed and sent to the short-listed suppliers and providers. At this stage, a separate task-force should outline all the implementation requirements (e.g. organizational changes, roles and responsibilities, IT support). Because of the sensitive nature of this part of the effort, the taskforce should be kept as small as practicable. Additionally, it should be overseen by senior executives.

4. Prepare for negotiations, negotiate and select providers or suppliers

Once suppliers and providers have submitted their proposals and quotes, these will be analyzed and validated by the team. As soon as any questions that have arisen in this process are resolved, the suppliers and providers should be short-listed for negotiation. In the case of creative agency services, this is usually the point at which the pitch process begins. Because of the high strategic relevance and visibility of creative services, this part of the process often takes several months.

Negotiation role-plays

Even the most thorough negotiation preparation can go to waste if your negotiators are taken by surprise during the actual talks. In order to prepare for a variety of different scenarios in a risk-free environment, many companies conduct role-playing sessions prior to the actual negotiations. Based on these sessions, you can refine the negotiation strategy and the tactics of individual negotiation team members. If the team comprises a large number of people, the role-play dry-runs also serve a useful purpose in providing a safe environment in which to address and resolve any internal conflicts that might exist, thereby improving the alignment of the team during the actual negotiations. Last not least, role-plays can help alleviate some of the anxiety that even experienced executives are likely to feel prior to and during high-profile negotiations.

Thorough negotiation preparation should include the following array of activities: setting negotiation goals, aggregating all available supply market data, constructing supplier profiles, summarizing internal requirements, comparing in detail the price points and other conditions, analyzing the negotiating power and option spaces for each of the parties, determining the roles for each of the negotiation participants, and assessing the roles and characters of the negotiators on the supplier side. Based on these preparations, the team should define a negotiation strategy for each supplier and contract, including any potential tactical moves.

Once all the preparations have been completed, the negotiation teams will conduct the initial rounds of negotiations and then submit their outcomes for sign-off with the board or other relevant internal stakeholders. Once approved, the final agreements, conditions or frame contracts will be negotiated with suppliers and providers. At the same time, internal stakeholders should sign off on any major changes to relevant processes.

5. Launch the pilot, track its performance and prepare for roll-out

In the last phase of the efficiency improvement process, the team should finalize the contracts and – where appropriate – hand over the operational responsibility to dedicated personnel, ideally in the procurement department. Best-practice retailers set up functional or strategic units within their procurement departments to acknowledge the fundamental difference between basic materials sourcing and the procurement of elaborate products or services. The operational owner of a given type of service or product will place the orders and monitor pre-defined quality indicators. The team should also prepare guidelines for the implementation of process improvements, e.g. how to select suppliers.

Compliance with the new processes and guidelines is best enforced through a comprehensive governance model that includes control functions, a systematic tracking system and transparent enforcement mechanisms. As a final step, the team should consolidate the insights generated during the project or pilot for future rollout to other categories, countries, regions or business units.

Follow best practice in preparation, negotiation and implementation *to capture the full value of smart sourcing efforts*

How do you prepare for the unpredictable? Only advanced game theory would enable you to map out all the potential moves of internal stakeholders and external partners in the complex web of marketing services. However, over the course of conducting many smart sourcing projects in retail and in other industries, we have compiled a set of hands-on guidelines to help navigate this web. In the words of Louis Pasteur, 'chance only favours the prepared mind'.

- *Involve all relevant functions, regions and business units in the core team*: the team should consist of marketing, media and procurement experts. Clarify the roles and responsibilities at the outset to avoid last-minute discussions about who gets to participate in negotiations or sign-off procedures.
- *Communicate to all relevant marketing stakeholders*: in order to ensure buy-in from your entire marketing community, all the relevant senior marketing stakeholders, both central and local, should be informed about the objectives of the programme and process early on in the proceedings. Involve the marketing stakeholders in idea generation or optimization workshops, then keep in contact with them throughout the course of the project, providing them with updates and asking them for their input. In addition, the wider marketing community, including regional or local marketing staff, should receive regular progress updates.
- *Centralize steering, but ensure local involvement*: the more centralized the smart sourcing process, the higher the improvement potential. On the other hand, an increase in centralization usually brings about less local entrepreneurship and local buy-in. This is not only a political issue but also carries with it the danger that you could neglect local consumer needs. Nonetheless, at the very least, all the marketing managers (both central and local) need to commit to the final implementation plan. Without this commitment, they will be the first to bypass the global frame contract and hire their own favourite local agency.
- *Pick your battles*: at the lowest level of detail, a retailer's marketing budget can sometimes comprise more line items than there are SKUs in the store.

Global retail corporations face additional complexity in operating in multiple regions and countries that often have incompatible reporting standards and which use different marketing terminology. You are bound to fail if you try to optimize everything at once. The best approach is to conduct pilots in a select number of countries or categories in order to identify the biggest levers prior to wider roll-out. As a rule of thumb, it is often better to opt for implementing fewer categories and then to roll these out to all the relevant regions and/or business units before adding more. This ensures that there is full leverage in terms of volume while reducing the complexity of implementation.

- *Strive for win–win situations with providers and suppliers*: many interactions with providers and suppliers happen in a distributive bargaining context, but there is often also room to create win–win situations and performance partnerships. For example, if retailers and creative agencies jointly engage in the content development process, this will often produce a more cost-efficient campaign that meets marketing needs *and* wins creative awards.

Commercial print:
Deep dive into one major spend category

Optimizing commercial print sourcing, an important cost position in retail marketing, can yield cost savings of 10–30 percent.

The commercial print category comprises a wide array of formats and applications: catalogues, mailings, leaflets, brochures, calendars, greeting cards, cardboard displays and so on. Since local marketing is an important element in the marketing mix of many retailers, commercial print can be a major cost driver. But most retailers source print locally and have no standardized sourcing process in place. As a consequence of this, print spend is usually fragmented across hundreds or thousands of items, with each region or business unit having established different cooperation models with suppliers, different contract terms, item specifications and quality standards.

The print provider supply base in most countries is also very fragmented and in recent years many providers have struggled with low utilization rates and structural overcapacity. Commercial print has high fixed costs, making utilization a key profitability driver. In times of low utilization, printers are therefore keen to lock in volumes and so are willing to enter into longer-term contracts that will provide them with predictable demand. The least profitable vendors often are the small ones in terms of revenue. Capabilities differ significantly, depending on the segments served by a given vendor. Hence retailers need to be careful about which vendors they select for a specific marketing vehicle. Because of the considerable fragmentation of materials, formats, services and suppliers, those agencies or brokers that specialize in print services are in a position to act as valuable intermediaries in print buying.

Specific supply levers in commercial print

- Consolidating volume across brands, business units or countries into a limited number of vendors, e.g. by establishing national contracts for paper and freight.
- Sourcing printing services directly, e.g. by limiting the use of brokers to cases of high complexity.
- Unbundling select value-chain steps, e.g. print production could be separated from paper supply and pre-production services (creative, layout, logistics) could be separated from the print production proper.
- Applying more rigour in negotiations, e.g. by conducting reverse auctions to take advantage of the spot market prices for large projects.

In general, as part of the sourcing model, you need to determine whether you want providers pitch for every single product or service, or whether you prefer to enter longer-standing relationships with a small number of vendors. Working with just one vendor – even if this were feasible – is clearly not to be recommended, as it could result in a loss of price leverage and certainly increases the danger of serious damage to your business if there were to be any disruption of service on the vendor's part.

The dangers of unbundling

Despite the promise of better terms for products and services sourced individually, unbundling does not always make good sense and so needs to be evaluated on a case-by-case basis. For example, in times of rising costs for basic materials like paper, it might be advisable to bundle the purchase and have the vendor bear and hedge the risk. Furthermore, a large paper buyer, such as a major printer, is always likely to get more favourable terms due to their volume.

Specific demand levers in commercial print

Print products are traditionally considered to be highly creative. But often this is used as an excuse for avoiding any discussion about the necessary specifications of printed advertising. Retailers need to take a sober 'design-to-cost' approach and identify the drivers of 'perceived' quality on the consumer's part. Many characteristics of print products that are often deemed necessary are in fact over-specifications that can be the source of considerable savings. Examples include:

- Standardizing paper types and formats, using cheaper alternatives and reducing general specifications for paper (e.g. weight, composition, coating, finish/varnish).
- Simplifying the printing process itself. For lower print runs, the key issue is offset printing versus digital printing. While offset usually provides higher image quality, digital allows for cheaper low-volume printing.
- Reducing the number of colours used in printing and even the quality of the ink used.
- Reducing the complexity, in terms of the number, form and size of flaps and folds, and simplifying the binding (e.g. stapling versus saddle stitching versus gluing).
- Reducing the degree of customization or personalization and the number of additional extra features.

To identify opportunities such as these, you can conduct classical physical 'tear down' exercises or idea generation workshops, followed by a detailed target–cost analysis. To make sure harmonized or reduced specifications are actually adhered to, make sure to put in place clear and strict design guidelines.

Even before starting the harmonization and de-specification discussion, the retailer should challenge the purpose, circulation and management of its commercial print items. Is it really necessary to mail four catalogues a year? Does every customer need the full catalogue, or can you restrict this to A and B customers, sending a stripped-down ten-pager to C/D/E customers? Can you increase page density (i.e. show more items per page) and, hence, reduce the number of pages?

Another driver of cost savings can be to establish a central repository of creative materials and rights (e.g. photos, standard mailing layouts, etc.); these can be leveraged across the entire company.

The disguised example in Exhibit 17.5 shows the specification reduction for a mail-order catalogue; the savings impact was estimated at 15–20 percent of cost.

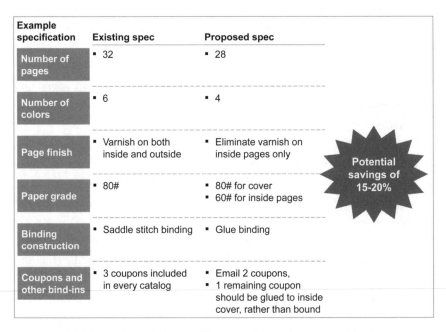

Example specification	Existing spec	Proposed spec
Number of pages	• 32	• 28
Number of colors	• 6	• 4
Page finish	• Varnish on both inside and outside	• Eliminate varnish on inside pages only
Paper grade	• 80#	• 80# for cover • 60# for inside pages
Binding construction	• Saddle stitch binding	• Glue binding
Coupons and other bind-ins	• 3 coupons included in every catalog	• Email 2 coupons, • 1 remaining coupon should be glued to inside cover, rather than bound

Potential savings of 15-20%

Exhibit 17.5 Example for specification reduction in commercial print.

Specific process levers in commercial print

One of the biggest levers on the process side of print is to streamline the coordination, review and approval procedures: pre-press management, electronic press checks, online audits, regular feedback regarding print quality and colour variance (to ensure consistency) and electronic file sharing. This will reduce complexity and lead times. A retailer's internal order process management also often holds significant improvement potential. Typical levers here include refined forecasting and order planning, the extension of acceptable lead times, ensuring that orders are placed on time, minimizing the number of rushed orders, reviewing the cost of warehousing and distribution costs and optimizing order quantities. Furthermore, retailers with high print spend should investigate the possibilities for minimizing transportation costs by picking their printing locations strategically. Finally, introducing semi-automatic pricing mechanisms, which calculate the price of the product from a base price, adding a variant-specific mark-up, can help avoid having to price each individual item separately and so limit the need for individual pricing to the rare occasions on which truly unique printing products are requested (Exhibit 17.6).

Situation	Key savings levers	Impact
▪ Global specialty retailer with $ 10 bn in annual sales and distribution of printed materials to more than 20 countries	▪ Leverage company-wide spend through unified request for proposal process	**Total annual spending,** $ mn
▪ Purchasing of printed materials already centralized	▪ De-bundle paper, printing, binding, and distribution, thereby eliminating printer markups	110 / 89 - 95 / -14 - 19%
▪ Initial target to achieve 3 - 7% savings; 15% over a three year period	▪ Bid out most predictable projects	Before After
▪ Relatively fragmented supplier landscape with >20 paper suppliers and >30 printer suppliers	▪ Use requests for proposals to identify potential specification changes that generate additional cost savings	▪ Huge savings from price reduction on printing (30 %), smaller price reduction on paper supply (5 %)
▪ Many different paper and print specifications	▪ Consolidate spend and lock in pricing for 1 - 3 years with a small base of 'preferred' paper suppliers and printers	▪ Additional 20 - 30 % savings identified, including specification changes of paper and printing and moving printing to low cost countries
		▪ Rigorous internal process to avoid over-specification and late changes

Exhibit 17.6 Commercial print sourcing at a global retailer.

Key takeaways – Smart sourcing

1 Increasing marketing efficiency might be hard work, but it is well worth it: smart sourcing yields sizeable savings without compromising quality.

2 Efficiency levers include rigorous supplier management, streamlined demand and procurement process optimization.

3 Efficiency optimization is a five-step process: gather facts, create a long list of improvement ideas, select ideas for execution, negotiate and implement.

4 Follow best practice in preparation, negotiation and implementation to capture the full value of smart sourcing efforts.

5 Real-life examples show that optimizing commercial print sourcing, an important cost positions in retail marketing, can yield savings of 10–30 percent.

Part III

Ten Perspectives on Retail Marketing

CHAPTER 18

Jesko Perrey, Dennis Spillecke

1 **Brands are value generators.** In an increasingly differentiated retail and media landscape, consumers use brands as signposts for their decision journey. As a result, brand image is a key factor in retail customer acquisition, development and retention efforts. This makes branding a top management topic that should not be delegated to marketing departments or agencies.

2 **Successful brand management requires a combination of art, science and craft.** A large part of this book focuses on the analytical foundations of retail marketing. But successful brands also depend on the art of creative minds and the craft of seasoned practitioners. It is through the interplay of the three elements that strong brands are created – and sustained.

3 **Retail branding is a three-front war.** Retailers face brand-related challenges at three levels: corporate umbrella branding, store (format) branding and product branding, especially regarding the ever changing mix of manufacturer brands and private labels. This calls for a systematic approach, but one that leaves room for flexibility in daily brand management decisions.

4 **Money doesn't change everything, after all.** A bigger budget is not necessarily a better budget. Strive for clarity in what you are trying to achieve in the marketplace, and make your budget level and allocation a function of these objectives.

5 **New media have triggered evolution, not a revolution.** The advent of digital media, mobile platforms, interactivity and social networks is changing

retail marketing – but not completely, and not overnight. Get ready for the digital adventure, but do not overreact.

6 **Hands-on local media will remain important.** Shopping is an everyday activity, and it requires customer contacts in everyday contexts. ATL image campaigns will complement rather than displace leaflets and local print ads.

7 **Make the most of your direct customer relationships.** Retailers have the unique privilege of direct relations with their customers. The potential for direct communication, tailored propositions and personalized offers is greater than in any other industry.

8 **You don't need direct reporting lines to influence local marketing.** Even if decision power resides locally, central marketing departments can still shape the overall strategy and support their subsidiaries or franchise owners with tools and guidelines that will help ensure consistency without curtailing localization.

9 **Don't allow yourself to be overwhelmed by data.** Retailers possess reams of data, but only a fraction of it is relevant to their marketing decisions. Let commercial strategy be the guide of your data mining, not vice versa.

10 **Keep core capabilities in-house and outsource execution.** While brand positioning and marketing strategy should be kept close to the retailer's heart, do not hesitate to outsource creative services, research or technical support. However, a robust vendor selection and management process is a must.

CONTRIBUTORS

Ben Armstrong

Associate Principal, San Francisco

Ben Armstrong is a member of the leadership team of the North American Marketing & Sales practice at McKinsey with over 14 years of professional consulting experience. He is the co-founder and manager of the Customer Solution Center, McKinsey's advanced analytics capability, which helps clients capture value from data. He primarily serves clients in consumer industries including retail, consumer goods and financial services. Ben Armstrong holds a BA from the University of Cardiff, an MSc from the University of Bradford and an MBA from the University of Georgia.

Francesco Banfi

Principal, Rome

Francesco Banfi is a member of the leadership team of the European Consumer Industries & Retail Practice at McKinsey. He leads the Retail Pricing Service Line in Europe and co-leads the Global Media Mix Modelling Initiative. He has mainly served clients in the retail and telecommunications sectors in Italy and France. Francesco Banfi holds a degree in Electronic Engineering from the Politecnico di Milano and an MBA from INSEAD.

Reinhold Barchet

Expert, Düsseldorf

Reinhold Barchet is a Practice Expert and a core member of the Consumer and Shopper Insights Group in the European Marketing & Sales Practice at McKinsey. He works with consumer goods and retail clients in Europe and Asia. His main fields of expertise include customer segmentation, brand performance and CLM modelling. Reinhold Barchet holds an MA in Mathematics and Economics from the University of Freiburg.

Dr Thomas Bauer
Associate Principal, Munich

Thomas Bauer is member of the European Consumer Industries & Retail Practice as well as the European Marketing & Sales Practice at McKinsey. He is also a core member of the Branding & Marketing ROI Service Line. He serves companies in consumer-facing industries mainly on marketing and sales excellence, online business building and performance transformation. Thomas Bauer holds an MA in Business Economics and a PhD in Strategic Management from the University of Witten/Herdecke, as well as an MBA from the University of Miami.

Gabriele Bavagnoli
Principal, Milan

Gabriele Bavagnoli is a member of the leadership team of the European Consumer Industries & Retail Practice as well as the European Marketing & Sales Practice at McKinsey. He has worked in Italy and in the UK mainly on marketing studies in the retail and consumer goods sectors. He co-leads the Commercial 2.0 initiative within the European Retail Practice. Gabriele Bavagnoli holds an MA in Management Engineering from the Politecnico di Milano and an MBA with honors from Columbia Business School of New York.

Rishi Bhandari
Senior Expert, Chicago

Rishi Bhandari is a Senior Expert in the North American Marketing & Sales Practice at McKinsey, and leads its efforts in Marketing Mix Modelling. Rishi has served clients over the past 14 years on marketing spend effectiveness across the consumer goods, retail, entertainment, and fashion and apparel sectors. Prior to joining McKinsey & Company, Rishi led analytic development and was a member of the management team at MMA, a marketing analytics boutique. Rishi holds degrees in Economics and Statistics from the University of Rochester and an MBA from the Kellogg School of Management at Northwestern University.

Adam Bird
Director, Munich
Adam Bird is the leader of the European Media and Entertainment Practice and Digital Marketing Service Line at McKinsey. He has 20 years experience in advising leading media, entertainment, leisure and consumer goods companies. He often speaks on media topics at conferences and has been cited in leading publications. Prior to McKinsey, Adam Bird was a Senior Partner with Booz Allen Hamilton and the Managing Director of their Global Consumer and Entertainment Practice. He holds a degree in Political Science and Economics from Wesleyan University.

Jean-Baptiste Coumau
Principal, Paris
Jean-Baptiste Coumau is a member of the leadership teams of the European Marketing & Sales and European Strategy Practices at McKinsey. He has covered a broad spectrum of innovation and marketing topics and has served companies in various industries - consumer goods, high tech, telecommunication, media, entertainment and retail. In particular, he has developed expertise in the fields of branding and innovation. Jean-Baptiste holds an MA in Taxation and Finance from the Institut d'Etudes Politiques in Paris.

Linda Dauriz
Engagement Manager, Cologne
Linda Dauriz is a core member of the European Consumer Industries & Retail Practice at McKinsey. She has worked for McKinsey both across Europe and in North America, where she spent a year in the New Jersey Office. She focuses on strategy, marketing and sales topics. She predominantly serves apparel manufacturers and retailers; she has had several opportunities to help her clients face the impact of the digital world on their business. Linda holds a Masters in Industrial Engineering and Management from the University of Karlsruhe.

Georges Desvaux
Director, Paris

Georges Desvaux is a member of the leadership team of the Global Marketing & Sales Practice, where he leads the Global Consumer & Shopper Insights Center of Competence. He contributes to and authors research on consumer and macroeconomic trends such as the "European Consumer in the crisis", the upcoming "The French Consumer in 2030" and the "Next $20 trillion in emerging markets". He advises clients on their growth strategy as well as on their marketing capabilities and organization. Georges holds a degree from Ecole Centrale of Paris and an M.S. in Mechanical Engineering from the Massachusetts Institute of Technology (MIT).

Steffi Entenmann
Engagement Manager, Düsseldorf

Steffi Entenmann is a core member of the European Marketing & Sales Practice at McKinsey. She serves clients across Europe on marketing spend optimization (effectiveness and efficiency) and marketing/sales transformation projects. Steffi holds a degree in Business Administration from the University of Cooperative Education in Stuttgart and an MBA from Bocconi School of Management and Melbourne Business School.

Dr Hanno Fichtner
Engagement Manager, Cologne

Hanno Fichtner is a core member of the European Consumer Industries & Retail Practice and the European Marketing & Sales Practice. He mainly serves retail clients in Germany and has developed expertise in the fields of marketing spend effectiveness and digital marketing. Hanno Fichtner holds a degree in Management from the University of Cologne and a PhD from the University of Bremen.

Dr Lars Fiedler
Engagement Manager, Hamburg

Lars Fiedler is a core member of the European Marketing & Sales Practice and the Global CLM Service Line at McKinsey. He primarily serves clients in the retail and consumer goods sectors on a variety of marketing topics.

Lars Fiedler holds a PhD in Marketing from the Leipzig Graduate School of Management.

Liv Forhaug
Principal, Stockholm
Liv Forhaug is a member of the leadership team of the European Consumer Industries & Retail Practice at McKinsey. She also leads the Scandinavian country hub for the Practice. She serves clients in the retail and consumer goods sectors. With a focus on Nordic and European grocery clients, she also has experience in DIY, sporting goods and home furnishings/textiles. Her client work focuses on strategy, marketing and sales related topics, and she is an expert on private label from both supplier and retailer perspectives. Liv holds an MSc from the Stockholm School of Economics and the Ecole des Hautes Etudes Commerciales (HEC) in Paris.

Nicolò Galante
Director, Paris
Nicolò Galante is a member of the leadership team of the European Consumer Industries & Retail Practice at McKinsey. He also leads the European Retail Marketing Knowledge Domain. In his career with McKinsey, he has served both producers and retailers of food and non-food products mainly in commercial transformation and turnaround projects. Typical recent engagements have focused on improving marketing effectiveness, unlocking brand value and improving ROI from store format renewal. Nicolò holds a degree in Nuclear Engineering from the Politecnico di Torino.

Jonathan Gordon
Principal, New York
Jonathan Gordon is a member of the leadership team in the North American Marketing & Sales and Consumer Goods Practices. He has served a number of clients across a wide range of consumer facing industries. He has built a strong expertise in packaged goods with deep experience in brand portfolio strategy, brand strategy, marketing organization and marketing ROI. Jonathan is a major contributor to McKinsey knowledge, having recently co-authored the McKinsey Quarterly article "Better Branding" and led an initiative on "Packaged

Goods Marketing Transformation". He is currently spearheading McKinsey's initiative on Marketing ROI. Jonathan holds a degree in Biochemistry from the University of Oxford.

Dr Roland Harste
Engagement Manager, Hamburg
Roland Harste is a member of the European Marketing & Sales Practice. He serves retailers and automotive companies on marketing and sales-related topics, mainly in projects on customer lifecycle management. Roland holds a degree in Engineering and Business Management from the Technical University Hamburg-Harburg. He also holds a PhD for his dissertation at the European Business School and INSEAD focusing on loyalty building in the professional service sector.

Ingeborg Molden Hegstad
Associate Principal, Oslo
Ingeborg Molden Hegstad is a core member of the European Consumer Industries & Retail Practice at McKinsey and of the Branding & Marketing ROI Service Line. She has served a range of clients on strategy, operations and marketing related topics both in food and non-food retail as well as other consumer facing industries. Ingeborg holds an MBA from the Norwegian School of Management, BI.

Dr Nicolai Johannsen
Expert, Hamburg
Nicolai Johannsen is a core member of the European Marketing & Sales Practice at McKinsey. His industry focus lies on the retail, consumer goods and tele-communication sectors. His main fields of expertise are brand management, marketing ROI and digital marketing. Nicolai holds a PhD from the University of Kiel for his studies on advertising effectiveness in online marketing.

Tobias Karmann
Senior Associate, Cologne
Tobias Karmann has gathered significant experience in the consumer goods and retail sectors, primarily focusing on marketing and consumer insights topics.

Recently he contributed to an initiative to develop retail marketing knowledge in the fields of retail branding and local marketing excellence. Tobias holds a CEMS Masters degree in international management from University College Dublin and an MBA from the University of Cologne.

Dr Lars Köster

Associate Principal, Hamburg

Lars Köster is both a member of the European Marketing & Sales Practice and the Retail Marketing Knowledge Domain at McKinsey. He serves retailers in the areas of branding, marketing ROI and e-commerce. Lars earned a PhD for his studies on brand management from the University of Münster and has an MA in Business Administration, majoring in marketing, retailing and information systems.

Dr Mathias Kullmann

Associate Principal, Düsseldorf

Mathias Kullmann is a core member of the European Marketing & Sales Practice and the European Consumer Industries & Retail Practice at McKinsey. He serves mainly retailers and consumer goods companies focusing on e-commerce, digital strategies and online marketing. He also has gained expertise in branding, marketing ROI and brand portfolio topics. Mathias holds an MA in Business Administration from the University of Münster and holds a PhD in Marketing from the University of Bremen.

Marco Mazzù

Principal, Rome

Marco Mazzù is a member of the leadership team of the European Consumer Industries & Retail Practice and the European Marketing & Sales Practice at McKinsey. He is also member of the leadership team of the Branding & Marketing ROI Service Line. He has worked in more than 15 countries mainly on marketing and sales studies in consumer-focused industries. Marco holds an MBA from INSEAD.

Björn-Uwe Mercker

Associate Principal, Munich

Björn-Uwe Mercker is part of the leadership team of the European Purchasing and Supply Management (PSM) practice at McKinsey. He has focused on operations engagements across different industries with a particular emphasis on purchasing and design to cost. Beside his client engagements, he is leading a research project on negotiation excellence as well as driving the development of next-generation PSM client capability building. Prior to joining McKinsey, he was employed for several years by a leading electronics company in the field of strategic purchasing and supply management. Björn-Uwe holds an MA in Industrial Engineering from the Technical University of Hamburg.

Dr Thomas Meyer

Senior Expert, London

Thomas Meyer is a member of the global Marketing & Sales Practice at McKinsey, specifically the ROI competence center. He serves clients across sectors on brand management and marketing spend optimization projects, and is the co-author of the German edition of McKinsey's book on branding "Mega-Macht Marke". Thomas received a PhD in International Management from the University of Braunschweig and holds a degree in Industrial Engineering and Management from the University of Hamburg.

Jan Middelhoff

Associate, Düsseldorf

Jan Middelhoff is a consultant in the Düsseldorf Office at McKinsey. He serves clients across Europe in the retail and consumer industries mainly in marketing and strategy projects. Jan holds a Master of Science, Diplôme de Grande Ecole and a degree in Business Administration from ESCP Europe.

Dr Boris Mittermüller

Engagement Manager, Cologne

Boris Mittermüller is a core member of the European Consumer Industries & Retail Practice and the Retail Marketing Knowledge Domain at McKinsey. He has gained significant marketing expertise in his work for large multi-channel retail groups and specialty retailers across Europe. Boris Mittermüller studied

Business Administration in Germany, the UK, France and Singapore. He holds an MA from ESCP Europe, an MBA from INSEAD and a PhD from RWTH Aachen University.

Alex Perez-Tenessa de Block
Principal, New Jersey
Alex Perez-Tenessa is a core member of the North American Retail Practice and co-leader of the Merchandising Service Line at McKinsey. He has served retailers and consumer goods companies in North America, Latin America, Europe and Asia on a broad range of merchandising and operations topics, including category strategy, assortment optimization and in-store marketing. Alex holds an MBA (Baker Scholar) from Harvard Business School and an MA from Ecole Supérieure des Sciences Economiques et Commerciales (Essec) in Paris.

Dr Jesko Perrey
Director, Düsseldorf
Jesko Perrey is global leader of the Branding & Marketing ROI Service Line and core member of the leadership team of the European Consumer Industries & Retail Practice at McKinsey. His focus is on brand management, marketing ROI and segmentation across different industries. Jesko is the author of many articles and essays in leading journals and compendiums, particularly on marketing-related subjects such as branding, marketing ROI and segmentation, and co-author of the book *Power Brands*. He holds an MBA and a PhD from the University of Münster.

Michele Porcu
Engagement Manager, Milan
Michele Porcu is a member of the European Consumer Industries & Retail Practice at McKinsey, with focus on retail marketing knowledge. He serves both manufacturers and retailers in Italy, mainly in commercial transformation. Michele holds a degree in Sub-Nuclear Physics and an MBA.

Dr Nicolas Reinecke
Principal, Hamburg

Nicolas Reinecke is the leader of the European Operations Practice, the Global Purchasing & Supply Management Practice as well as the Global Knowledge Leadership Team at McKinsey. In his 13 years of consulting experience he has led numerous engagements in Europe, North America and Asia on purchasing and savings improvements. He has broad experience in procurement transformations in several Fortune 500 companies across multiple industries. As a professor, he lectures at the European Business School and the Wharton University on topics including Global Sourcing, Global Production Networks, Lean Production and Product Development. Nicolas holds an MA and a PhD in mechanical engineering from the University of Hannover.

Toni Schmidt
Senior Associate, Munich

Toni Schmidt is a member of the European Consumer Industries & Retail Practice. His activities at McKinsey focus on retail clients, serving them mainly in the course of marketing and sales and corporate finance engagements. He holds a degree in Business Administration and an MA in Finance & Accounting from the University of St. Gallen.

Dr Jürgen Schröder
Director, Düsseldorf

Jürgen Schröder co-leads McKinsey's Marketing and Sales Practice in Europe and leads its Global CLM Service Line. Besides CLM, Jürgen focuses on marketing transformation and customer management work in both consumer and logistics industries. He holds an MA in Business and a PhD from the University of Bochum.

Carina Schumacher
Senior Associate, Hamburg

Carina Schumacher is a member of the European Marketing & Sales Practice at McKinsey. She mainly serves clients in the consumer goods and retail sector. Carina holds an MBA from the University of Iowa and a degree in Business Administration from the University of Frankfurt.

Dr Dennis Spillecke
Principal, Cologne
Dennis Spillecke is a core member of the leadership team of the European Consumer Industries & Retail Practice, as well as the European Marketing & Sales Practice at McKinsey. Dennis primarily focuses on marketing and sales topics at retail and packaged goods companies. In recent years, Dennis's work has focused primarily on the areas of digital marketing, marketing ROI and branding. Dennis holds a PhD from the Otto Beisheim School of Management (WHU) in Vallendar.

Björn Timelin
Associate Principal, London
Björn Timelin is a core member of the European Consumer Industries & Retail Practice at McKinsey. Björn serves both manufacturers and retailers, primarily on marketing and sales related topics, and co-leads McKinsey's Branding & Marketing ROI Service Line. Björn holds a BA from Durham University and an MPhil from Cambridge University.

Dr Kai Vollhardt
Senior Associate, Frankfurt
Kai Vollhardt is a member of the European Marketing & Sales Practice at McKinsey. He serves clients in the automotive, insurance and energy sectors, mainly on sales and branding engagements. Kai holds a degree in Business Administration as well as a PhD in Marketing from the University of Mainz, with his doctoral studies focusing on brand portfolio management.

Dr Anja Weissgerber
Knowledge Specialist, Berlin
Anja Weissgerber is a core member of the European Consumer Industries & Retail Practice. In her function as knowledge specialist, she focuses on marketing and multichannel/digital topics within retail. Anja holds an MA in Business Administration and a PhD, with her doctoral studies focusing on consumer behaviour research.

INDEX